D0914175

The Ethics of Computer Games

The Ethics of Computer Games

Miguel Sicart

The MIT Press
Cambridge, Massachusetts
London, England

11/2/09
WW
$26 —

MIT Press books may be purchased at special quantity discounts for business or sales promotional use. For information, please email special_sales@mitpress.mit.edu or write to Special Sales Department, The MIT Press, 55 Hayward Street, Cambridge, MA 02142.

This book was set in Stone Sans and Stone Serif by SNP Best-set Typesetter Ltd., Hong Kong and was printed and bound in the United States of America.

Library of Congress Cataloging-in-Publication Data
Sicart, Miguel, 1978–
The ethics of computer games / Miguel Sicart.
    p.   cm.
Includes bibliographical references and index.
ISBN 978-0-262-01265-2 (hardcover : alk. paper)
1. Video games—Moral and ethical aspects. 2. Video games—Philosophy. I. Title.
GV1469.34.C67S53   2009
175—dc22

                                                              2008039639

10 9 8 7 6 5 4 3 2 1

Contents

Acknowledgments

No book is written alone. Behind this book, there are countless hours of discussion, disagreements, guidance, and gameplay. I would first like to thank the IT University of Copenhagen for considering that writing a PhD on the ethics of computer games was a risk worth taking. I also have to thank Espen Aarseth and Charles Ess, my thesis advisors, for their feedback and comments.

I would also like to thank my colleagues at the Center for Computer Games Research at the ITU, and my students. They have all been a fundamental part of developing that initial PhD into this book.

I must thank following individuals for their contributions to my research: Ian Bogost, T.L. Taylor, Luciano Floridi, Mikkel Holm Sørensen, Gonzalo Frasca, Jonas Heide Smith, Jesper Juul, Susana Pajares Tosca, Lisbeth Klastrup, Simon Egenfeldt-Nielsen, Anker Helms-Jørgensen, Troels Degn Johansson, Olli Leino, Hanna Wirman, Douglas Wilson, Pablo Barreiro, Inma López Silva, Teresa Moure, Ángel Abuín, my colleagues from the information ethics Group in Oxford and Hertfordshire, and the people at the MIT Press.

Special thanks to Mikkel, Olli, Jesper, and Doug, with whom I relentlessly discussed ideas and early versions of this book.

Thanks to Ane, for keeping my feet on the ground, and my head in the clouds.

Finally, and foremost, thanks to my parents, for their support and encouragement, also when I was "just" playing computer games. This book is dedicated to them.

1   Introduction

I am not quite sure how it happened, but I felt guilty. No, no, I *was* guilty.

It started like so many other times: my weapons of choice, banal words, and action—*good* action. I was formidable, unstoppable, the master of my surroundings, a lethal instrument with one goal, vaguely heard while I was enjoying my newly acquired arsenal.

And then it all stopped.

That character, cannon fodder if only I had any bullets left, changed the meaning of my actions.

What if I am wrong? What if they lied to me? What if the goal is a lie?

Deus Ex[1] is a critically acclaimed first-person shooter/role-playing computer game in which players explore a dystopian world as a cybernetic supersoldier. The player's character, JC Denton, is presented as the ultimate combat tool of the United Nations Anti-Terrorist Coalition. At the beginning of the game, the mission presented to the player sounds simple: a shipment of a vaccine for a lethal plague is in the hands of the National Secessionists Forces (NSF), a terrorist group the United Nations is combating. The goal is to recover the shipment and gather information about the NSF. The player is given a choice of weaponry, from missile launchers to crossbows, and the game starts.

When I first played *Deus Ex*, I acted as a reckless assassin, eliminating all targets with a brutal use of force. Those terrorists I was fighting seemed ill-prepared, poorly armed, and not really confrontational, cannon fodder for a supersoldier. And then I ran out of ammunition. This meant I had to carefully navigate the environment to maximize my resources. This meant I could eavesdrop on some conversations. And what the terrorists were talking about contradicted the information I was given by my superiors. Who was right? What type of armed forces is the United Nations Anti-Terrorist Coalition? What does it mean to be a terrorist? What does it mean *to be called* a terrorist?

Deus Ex is a fascinating dystopian ethical game because from the first mission, the player doubts the goals and purposes of her assignment. Eavesdropping on NSF members' conversations reveals that not everything in this game should be understood as good versus evil. Ultimately, the player discovers that the United Nations Anti-Terrorist Coalition is a power-thirsty organization that contributes to the spread of the plague. The terrorists the player has been combating throughout the first half of the game may not be evil. As a matter of fact, the player's actions, commanded by the initial United Nations Anti-Terrorist Coalition, were in fact "evil." The plot twists, and a different understanding of the game narrative forces the player to reflect on her previous actions.

In many combat-based games, following the orders given to players means "doing the right thing." *Deus Ex* breaks that expectation, and forces players to reflect on the meaning of their actions. In *Deus Ex*, ethical thinking is as powerful a weapon as a handgun, and ethical responsibility the most adequate gameplay strategy.

The ideas behind this book arose while I was playing *Deus Ex*. I started thinking about this topic because, for the first time, a game made me consider the nature of my actions by means of game mechanics and game world design. *Deus Ex* starts as a rather generic science-fiction first-person-shooter, only to evolve into a strong narrative that gives players moral purpose. Furthermore, the goals and winning conditions were ethically questioned almost from the beginning, forcing players to think morally about the missions and their meaning. When playing *Deus Ex* I felt that a computer game was challenging me as a moral being, showing me new ways of understanding games as well as my presence and actions as a player.

Ever since, I have tried to understand what the ethics of computer games are, and how I could explain my experience of *Deus Ex*. My intention was to reveal what the conditions were for such an ethical game experience to take place, and how to understand them. This book is an academic exploration of ethical gameplay, ethical game design, and the presence of computer games in our moral universe. Most of it uses complex philosophical theory, and it requires from the reader a certain degree of openness to the rhetoric of ethics. But I have tried to write a text that can also be read by the non–philosophically oriented. There are chapters, especially in the first half of the book, which can be challenging. But there are also case studies, discussions of well-known ethical issues, and even game design reflections that should be of interest to those readers curious about the application of ethical theory to computer games.

With this book I have tried to explain an ethical experience. To do so, I had to understand computer games as a form of art and entertainment. I hope that by the end of this book, I communicate my understanding of the ethics of computer games and set up a fruitful dialogue between players, developers, and academics.

1.1   The Bull's-eye of Morality

Computer games have been a mass media target for a good part of the last two decades. Accusations that games are training devices for teenage serial killers with serious social issues made them a usual suspect in terms of creating moral panic. One common media argument claims that games lead to violent behavior and desensitization in the face of violence. This has even led certain groups to actively seek legislative restrictions on the distribution of violent computer games. Computer games are now what cinema and rock and roll once were: the bull's-eye of morality.

This moral panic is a symptom of a larger cultural issue. In our postindustrial societies we understand and promote computer games as a valuable medium for entertainment, creation, and socialization. Developed and developing societies, from China to the United States, are witnessing the economic and cultural benefits of computer games as a dominant cultural industry. Academia too now focuses on these games as objects of research, validating their importance in the configuration of our cultural landscape. Despite all this interest, we know little or nothing about the ethics of computer games. When considering such ethics, there are a number of important questions that arise: is it the ethics of the game, or the ethics of playing the game? Is there such a difference? Do game designers have moral responsibilities? If so, how and why? All these questions point to a broader field of the ethics of games, a field that has scarcely been explored.

This book is an exploration of the ethics of computer games. Ethics can be defined as a system or set of moral values, and the tools for analyzing these values. Morals can be defined as the right or wrong of actions or objects. The application of ethics is the rational, philosophical approach to the questions of good, evil, harm, duties, and values. This book is then an exploration of the moral nature of computer games and computer game players.

In this book I claim that computer games are ethical objects, that computer game players are ethical agents, and that the ethics of computer games should be seen as a complex network of responsibilities and moral duties. I explain why rules can have moral values that affect the ethical behavior of players. I also describe how players use ethical thinking to play computer games, and why incorporating these ethical players into the game design is crucial for the expressive use of computer games.

This book gives arguments for considering players creative, engaged, ethical agents. Players no longer are passive moral creatures, exposed to unethical content: computer game players reflect, relate, and create with an ethical mind. And the games they play are ethical systems. I will argue that *Manhunt*,[2] a game banned in several countries, is a rich ethical experience if played by mature players. On the other hand, a game like *Knights of the Old Republic*,[3] which allegedly allows players to take moral choices and play by them, is an example of unethical game design.

Computer games are complex cultural objects: they have rules guiding behavior, they create game worlds with values at play, and they relate to players who like to explore morals and actions forbidden in society. The ethics of computer games have to take into consideration all these variables. I will present a comprehensive perspective on why computer games can be ethical, and how players use their ethical values to critically engage with these games. Ultimately, this is a book about how players are ethical agents, and how we morally relate to computer games.

In this book, I propose a framework for understanding the ethics of computer games, a framework that will define these games both as designed objects and as player experiences. I am providing a theoretical approach from the fields of philosophy and game studies, a framework based on the formal understanding of computer games as moral objects and players as ethical subjects. The experience of a computer game is the experience of a moral object by an ethical subject. Thus the gaming experience is not only ethically relevant, but should also be analyzed by philosophy and game research. This framework also provides a tool for addressing relevant ethical issues that take place in the cultural context of computer games, from unethical content in computer games to the responsibility of game designers for the ethical issues raised by a game.

From an academic point of view, my research belongs to an emerging discipline that can be called computer game studies.[4] It also represents a philosophical inquiry into the moral nature of playing computer games. This book is a synergy between moral philosophy and computer game studies. It appeals to game scholars who want to use philosophy as a method for understanding computer games. This book also addresses philosophers, who can be interested in the challenges digital games pose to ethics and metaphysics. Finally, game developers can see in this text not only a cultural validation of their work, but also a serious approach to the ethical issues that games raise, and how to address them. Furthermore, parts of this book can be read as challenges for all of them: the challenge of using philosophy in games or games in philosophy, or the challenge of creating compelling ethical computer games.

Nevertheless, some clarification on this synergy is needed before I proceed. Philosophers who read this book may not be very happy with what they might see as a superficial approach to ethics and some ontological issues, such as the nature of games as objects or players as subjects. Game researchers, on the other hand, might find this book too philosophical, and perhaps too light on illustrative examples or deep discussions on notions like narrative and fiction. Finally, game designers, developers, and producers might think that the text is just academic gibberish, neither solving nor tackling the specific ethical problems they face when developing a game.

To all these possible critics I can only say they might be right. This is not a philosophy book, though I think there are some interesting issues that computer games raise, issues I will put in the language and perspective of ethical philosophy. I use philosophical methods that may seem formalistic and devoid of empirical value for some game researchers. Yet the philosophical method provides an alternative way of thinking about what players are, and about how games can be designed with ethical affordances and constraints. Philosophy does not close any doors, or try to impose its rhetoric: it attempts to widen our perspectives and broaden our capacities for discussion. As for reviews of some of the classic notions of game studies, I intentionally leave some discussions out of this book. The focus of this book is not to discuss the specifics of game ontology, but rather to apply what has been debated in game research to the development of a general theory for the understanding of the ethics of computer games. It is, then, an instrumental approach to terminology and its importance.

Finally, to game developers I would say that this is not a twelve-step program for solving ethical dilemmas when creating a game, and it is certainly not a do-it-yourself ethical course on computer games. But game designers, developers, and producers might be interested in understanding the complexity behind the products they develop. They should not just be told that they are morally accountable, but also understand why and how they are morally accountable. Confronting this responsibility is not an easy process, but it is one that, if undertaken, might provide new insights and creative challenges, thereby stimulating innovation that could erase stigmas and open perspectives.

This book has moral responsibility: it presents a foundation for the understanding of the ethics of computer games. Most of the theory comprising the first three chapters responds to that moral duty—the arguments have to be solid, and based on a theory that is explained so it can be discussed. This may make the first half of this book too dependent on the theoretical discourse. Yet that dependence is a requirement for the sound consolidation of a framework for the analysis of computer game ethics.

By the end of this book, the reader will have understood why we are ethical players, but also how we behave as we do in the virtual worlds of computer games. This book is a voyage to the ethics of rules, strategies, and game design. It is also a reflection on who we are when we play games. In the following chapters I will introduce the purpose and objectives of this book, as well as the methods that will inform each chapter and the overall reflection on the ethics of computer games. The choice of method, and especially the stress on ethical theory, makes necessary a chapter on the position of this research in the overall picture of the computer ethics field.

1.2   Purpose and Objectives

This book has one purpose: to understand the ethics of computer games. I will focus on giving an appropriate answer to this issue, providing a framework for the research, analysis, and application of ethics in computer games. Most of the research work informing my arguments consists of reflection on my experience of computer games from my knowledge of and interest in ethics. Therefore, whenever the first person is used, the reader has to take into account that I am a southern European, raised and educated in a Catholic environment, yet not religious. This book has been written in a Scandinavian country, which I believe has had an effect on the importance I place on communities and the individual responsibility of computer game users. I am also a long-time computer and role-playing game enthusiast. I started playing computer games with 8-bit machines and tapes, and I remember fondly the days when I made my games by copying code from magazines. This is the "I" in this book.

Given that my main purpose is to understand the ethics of computer games, I will need to define what kind of ethical discourses we find in these games, in which ways or where we find those discourses, and which theories can be applied. This means that a number of more focused analytical steps need to be declared. To understand the ethics of computer games, the first objective is to define what computer games mean for ethical theory and, related to this, what games are as moral objects. Without legitimizing the ontological relevance of games for ethics, my research would be meaningless. I also need to define the players' ethics, and how they relate to the ethics of computer games, describing which types of ethical theories can be applied to agency in ludic digital systems. Since my ambition is to open the field of ethics and computer games and apply the results of this research, I will suggest applications of the theory for analyzing ethical issues related to computer game culture, theory, and development.

Of course, like any other academic research, this book inserts itself in a tradition within which the success of the ideas can be measured. And this tradition is also a theoretical one: in the next pages I will present the work of other theorists of the ethics of computer games, and how my own research relates to them. This book should be read in the tradition of these precedents.

1.3 Precedents

No research is totally original. As academics, we are part of a tradition, and it is our duty to acknowledge that tradition and contribute to it. Even though research on the ethics of computer games from a philosophical perspective does not have many precedents, I would like to introduce here what I consider to be part of the tradition to which my work belongs, as well as some other texts having an affinity with my own approach.

This book takes a cross-disciplinary approach. Even though there is an analytical prevalence of philosophy, and the results of the research have to be understood as a work of applied computer ethics, there are a number of precedents from other disciplines that have to be taken into consideration. The works I present (and briefly review) have a certain affinity with my own arguments, yet there are significant theoretical and conceptual disagreements.

The first relevant precedent for the central claims of this book is Eugene F. Provenzo's *Video Kids: Making Sense of Nintendo*.[5] In this work, Provenzo describes the then-dominant Nintendo-produced computer games and their effects as cultural devices, focusing on issues related to simulated violence and the portrayal of gender in the Nintendo culture. Provenzo's work takes computer games seriously, granting them the status of objects that have an effect on the configuration of values and discourses in contemporary societies, specifically in the United States.

Video Kids is focused on children as game console users and how this use may affect their cultural and moral development. Provenzo always analyzes games with respect, yet with moral caution. He played the games he writes about, and his comments are often accompanied by samples from interviews with children. He presents a number of questions of extreme interest: what are computer games as cultural objects? What happens when we play computer games? How do video games affect our moral universe? Provenzo's framework for answering these questions is quite varied, ranging from psychology to cultural studies and Don Ihde's postphenomenology,[6] giving a solid foundation for his conclusions.

There are some aspects of Provenzo's work that differentiate it from my own, though. The author focuses on one exclusive company, justifying it by citing Nintendo's market dominance in the late 1980s and early 1990s video game. This research choice gives a partial perspective on the culture of computer games. It could be argued that *Video Kids* is a criticism of Nintendo and the culture that it created via its sponsored media. But computer games' culture is defined by a number of companies, institutions, and stakeholders. It is neither possible nor correct to make large assumptions about computer games and their presence in contemporary culture based on the exclusive analysis of one company.

Provenzo has an implicit discourse of child players as beings with creative capacities that also include their moral universe, and he presents the same caveats against computer games as I will present in this book: computer games can be ethically questionable when they do not allow players to create their own ethical game values, which should be also taken into consideration in the game experience.[7] This is an insightful perspective, analogous to some of the criticisms of computer games for which I will argue.

Nevertheless, Provenzo's work lacks some nuances: he seems to be a technological determinist, arguing that games do not give players the possibility of control and modification, therefore players subordinate to those instructions and obey mindlessly. That is a perspective on players, even on child players, that deprives them of their moral capacities. Perhaps games do not let players directly modify the conditions of play, but players, in their phenomenological experience of the game, have the capacity not to subordinate to the game, not to be totally determined by its rules. Players tend to be creative and reflective, even with games that do not afford them control over the rules.

Provenzo describes computer game players as uncritical creatures who give away their human capacity for reasoning and for moral thinking just because the game itself presents a limited amount of choices. I will counterargue that we become players not only by learning to play games, but also by developing a sense of computer game ethics and values that gives us the tools to ethically experience games. Even in the case of children, there is a presence of moral reasoning when playing games—a presence that has to be cultivated and encouraged by computer game culture. Provenzo sees players as isolated beings, whereas I will argue that a fundamental part of the process of developing our moral understanding of games is belonging to a gaming community, experiencing the presence of and interacting with other ethical beings who play computer games.

Provenzo's work, with his stress on the importance of game rules and the relevance of designers and developers in the final ethical configuration of computer games, is a valid precedent, but my understanding of players and their ethical being is radically different, and that justifies the divergent conclusions of his work and this book.

Another reference work within the field of ethics and computer games is Sherry Turkle's *The Second Self: Computers and the Human Spirit*.[8] Here Turkle explores the presence of computers as a part of our social and psychological lives, paying attention to the influence of computer games in the constitution of that "second self" that comes into being when in contact with digital technologies.

Turkle's work is essentially psychological research on the impact of computing in the rhetoric of the self. Therefore, her findings are definitively dissimilar to mine: the methodological divergence between philosophy and psychology is, in this case, too big. Nevertheless, there is a fundamental reason why Turkle's work can be considered as a precedent: the very notion of a second self. In chapter 3, "Players as Moral Beings," I will argue that the player is a sub-subject, a relatively autonomous self who comes into being when experiencing a computer game. Turkle argues that the contact and interaction with machines creates a similar second self in which our way of thinking and relating to the world is different than in a nonmachine culture.

In her chapter specifically dedicated to computer games, Turkle argues for an approach to the culture of rules and simulation, of which computer games are an excellent example. Computer games are largely liberated from mechanical constraints, and thus their expressive capacities are unparalleled. But, in an argumentative line similar to Provenzo's, Turkle points out that all those capacities do is limit players (children again—not adult players) in their own self-building and expressive capacities.[9] What computer games do, according to Turkle, is re-center our self,[10] but that is a second self in contact with the game experience. She also points out the presence of empowered users,[11] which means that players are not mindless zombies who just follow and obey rules.

Nevertheless, there are significant differences between Turkle's take on the second self and my own philosophical definition of players. While I agree that the presence of computer games creates a second subject, my take on that subjectivity is more complex. In this book I argue that the player-as-subject is an ethical being capable of morally reasoning about the ludic experience she is immersed in, because the player is herself an ethical subject. In Turkle's work there is, I believe, a certain confusion between the second self and the process of focusing on the act of playing, which undermines the possible ethical implications of considering the being of a second self.

The core of this divergence can be found in the phrasing of "second self." "Second" implies subordination, precedence, a "first." In Turkle's work the presence of that first is somewhat unclear, yet it does undermine the second self's ethical autonomy. I will argue that being a player means creating a subject with ethical capacities who establishes phenomenological and hermeneutical relations with the subject outside the game, with the game experience, and with the culture of players and games. It is not a self parallel to the out-of-the-game self, but a mode of being that takes place in the game.

These two precedents are not directly related to the topic of ethics and computer games. As I have stated previously, there is not much work done on this topic, and most of the examples are short academic papers or articles oriented to larger audiences outside academia. Nevertheless, they have to be taken into account, and put in the perspective of my own arguments. The following is a sample of the most interesting, complete papers related to the topic of this book. There is more work on the ethics of games, but it often is focused either on specific games or on the application of ethical theories to games, disregarding the particular ontological properties of computer games that are crucial for my own theoretical framework.

Perhaps the most quoted article on the ethics of computer games is Ren Reynolds's "Playing a 'Good' Game: A Philosophical Approach to Understanding the Morality of Games,"[12] in which the author applies three different ethical theories, consequentialism, deontology, and virtue ethics, to the analysis of *Grand Theft Auto III* (DMA Design/RockStar North 2001). Reynolds's article suggests a method for understanding if a game is good or evil, concluding that virtue ethics is the appropriate framework for the understanding of the morality of games: "I believe virtue theory is the most relevant theory for an analysis of 21st century computer games".[13]

While there are some similarities between this book and Reynolds's approach—for instance, when it comes to considering that the content of the games does not exclusively determine the morality of games, or arguing that virtue ethics can provide interesting approaches to this topic—there are strong dissimilarities. Essentially, Reynolds's article, which was intended for a nonacademic audience, does not define what a game is, nor who the player is or why players have virtues. Using *Grand Theft Auto III* as an example limits the perspective of the article: with that focus, it is only possible to determine the ethics of *Grand Theft Auto III* for the player Ren Reynolds—a necessary and interesting task, but limited in scope.

Reynolds's work was a primer, intended to call the attention of game developers. Yet it shows some limitations that need to be taken into account. First of all, in this type of research the game as a system with rules needs to be considered as a simulation of a world where players engage in activities while guided and rewarded by that same system; we also have to think about players as ethical agents who reflect upon their own values and the values they want to develop in their experience of a game, as the philosophy of sport tradition[14] has already argued for. Only within this perspective is it possible to say if a game is good or bad, and even that statement has to be nuanced: what does "bad" mean? Is it the game played or its design that is "bad"? To whom is the game harmful? All these questions are absent from Reynolds's approach, and as such his results, while valuable and insightful, have to be regarded as an introductory approach to the question of ethics in computer games.

There are other precedents that show a different value. Matt McCormick's "Is It Wrong to Play Violent Video Games?"[15] presents the issue of the moral concern that violent computer games raise, applying to that issue utilitarianism, deontology, and virtue ethics, and concluding that virtue ethics is the theory that gives deeper insights to the understanding of moral problems raised by computer games.

McCormick does not write about any specific game, but more in general about video games. This can be considered a problem, for not all computer games are alike, and the divergence between genres and types can have ethical implications. Furthermore, by not focusing on games but on the players, McCormick does not give any importance to the fact that games are designed to guide modes of interaction, rewarding some of them. As I will demonstrate in chapter 2, when defining the ethics of video games it is crucial to take into account that games are designed objects.

Nevertheless, McCormick's account is a nuanced and thorough analysis of the possible ethical implications of playing violent computer games. His article starts by applying utilitarianism to the act of playing these games, trying to answer the title's question. To his surprise, the results are not conclusive,[16] which leads him to the application of Kant's deontology to the same question. And again, the fact that "playing a game, whether on the computer or on the rugby field, is not the same as real life"[17] discards the possible Kantian criticism to playing computer games, because "if we are too sensitive about the detrimental effects of games on a person's inclination to do her duty, we will be forced to condemn a wide range of activities along with violent video games."[18]

Finally, McCormick finds in virtue ethics the ethical theory that can prove why playing violent computer games is wrong. Of course, at this moment in the article it seems clear that McCormick wants to consider playing violent games unethical, and his argumentation may be flawed by his determination. It is true that computer games raise moral awareness, but that does not necessarily mean that the moral concerns are right. That is the fundamental flaw in McCormick's argumentation.

Virtue ethics, the author argues, would define playing computer games as an unethical activity because "by participating in simulations of excessive, indulgent and wrongful acts, we are cultivating the wrong sort of character."[19] It is a strong virtue ethics argument, and Aristotelians make a clear point here. But it leaves out the possibility of considering the player a moral agent who has specific, game-related virtues attached to a ludic subject. In chapter 3 I will counterargue this position by presenting an alternative conception of players in which the users of games see their ethical autonomy increased by also increasing their ethical responsibility. Players have specific game virtues, and a specific, game-related character, within which, for instance, sportsmanship and other virtues have their meaning.

McCormick's account is well argued and nuanced. He does take into consideration the fact that what we do in computer games as players are simulated actions, and includes a closing remark connecting the ethical issues that computer games raise with the larger computer ethics perspective. His article is a valuable precedent for this book, even though the conclusions I will reach partially contradict McCormick's insights.

The December 2005 issue of the International Review of Information Ethics[20] was dedicated to the ethics of "e-games." In that issue two articles present the relations between games and ethics in a productive way: Mia Consalvo's "Rule Sets, Cheating, and Magic Circles: Studying Games and Ethics," and Gordana Dodig-Crnkovic and Thomas Larsson's "Game Ethics—Homo Ludens as a Computer Game Designer and Consumer."

While Consalvo's article presents a layered understanding of the ethics of computer games,[21] rather similar to some of my conclusions in chapter 5, it is Gordana Dodig-Crnkovic and Thomas Larsson's work my research is closer to. These authors acknowledge that "the ways we play vary with civilizations . . . they are influenced by our cultural environment,"[22] which is similar to the argument I build around the idea of players being part of cultures in and out of the game, cultures that play a role in the ethical configuration of the play experience. Furthermore, these authors also realize that we need to define the ontology of games before we can consider their ethics, a claim I will echo in my analysis of what computer games are.

Dodig-Crnkovic and Larsson's article focuses on the ethical responsibilities of game designers, and how they "often rely on free-speech legislation to defend their right not to take into account ethical considerations."[23] It is a strong and brave criticism, and the authors succeed in building a strong case from a philosophical perspective, but not also easily applicable by game developers and educators, a step that should have been taken, the absence of which nevertheless does not harm an insightful article on the ethics of computer games.

These articles show what I believe will be a trend in computer ethics: the interest in computer games and how philosophers and game researchers can define their ethical relevance. This book is a part of that larger trend that answers not only to the field of game studies, but also to the research area of computer ethics. It is necessary then to put my own work in the perspective of computer ethics theory.

1.4 The Computer Ethics Paradigm

For some readers it may be surprising that I write about the ethics of computer games, instead of the ethics of games. It might be seen as an arbitrary delimitation of the field of study, and it could raise the question of the extent of this research: are the ethics of computer games the same as the ethics of games? Or, in other words, using the framework I am proposing here, is it possible to understand the ethics of professional sports, children's games, or card games?

The answer is both yes and no. In this book I am focusing on the ethics of computer games and, even though there are some parallels between the ethics of digital and nondigital games, there are some specific ontological properties of computer games that raise unique ethical challenges. As may be obvious, the most important difference is the presence of computing power and the ways in which that power affects the game design and its experience by the players. There are strong analogies between digital and nondigital games, so it could be possible, though outside this book's scope, to apply some of the conceptualizations of this work to professional sports or nondigital games.

But given these similarities and possible areas of connection, I believe it is necessary to explain what the fundamental differences between computer games and nondigital games are, as relevant to the study of computer game ethics. This difference can be summarized by one fact: computer games are games played "using computer power, involving a video display."[24] Computer power brings forth new possibilities and demands that are significant for the ethical construction of the experience of the game.

Computer games are designed experiences in virtual environments with rules and properties that, in general, cannot be adapted or corrected by their users. When playing a casual game of basketball with friends, some of us change the rules to make the game more or less physically demanding, or to become what we believe is an offense-oriented, beautiful game. For instance, we could decide that the team that scores a basket keeps the ball, instead of the turnaround that we find in basketball's official rules.

When I play a casual game of basketball on my console, with my friends, we cannot do that. The computer system upholds the scoring and turnaround rules, so it is not possible for us to change them and make it a more pleasant, casual game. We can, obviously, change our play styles, because players determine how games are played, but the game world and its hardwired systems of rules are impossible to modify. Much like professional, refereed sports, computer games do not allow for players to change the rules while playing.[25]

The other element differentiating computer games from nondigital games is their simulation capacities. The game world of a video game is usually dependent on the simulation of other systems, be these the laws of physics, like the ball dynamics in *Pro Evolution Soccer 4*,[26] the colossi of *Shadow of the Colossus*,[27] or the musical instruments of *Daigassou! Band Brothers*.[28] Game worlds in computer games are simulated environments, with some fictional elements.[29] In classic, nondigital games, there tends to be no simulation (though there are nondigital games that are simulations, like *Monopoly*). Computer games, conversely, almost always present simulated environments (though again, there are digital games that are not simulations, like poker games).

To understand the ethics of computer games, we have to take into account that computer games present simulated environments designed to be interacted with in specific ways by players who agree to those constraints and who, in most cases, cannot do anything to change the rules or the possible interactions with the system. Both the simulation and the rules are upheld by the computer and affect the player's interactions, behaviors, and subjectivity. Therefore, the presence and importance of computer power and simulation capacities are relevant for understanding the ethics of digital games, and thus it seems obvious to relate this research to the field of computer ethics.

Computer ethics is the field studying the ethical implications that the use of Internet communication technologies and computational technologies create, determining if those ethical issues are new problems or just reiterations of old problems. As in any nascent field of research, the discussions between these two positions are long and detailed. It is not my intention, though, to argue for or against either of these. The vision of computer ethics that I am going to present here is related to the specific needs of this book.

The first issue for us to consider is the nature of the ethical issues that arise with computer games: should we consider those issues as new or as old ethical dilemmas? Is there a radical novelty in the ethical questions posed by computer games? To define what kind of ethical questions computer games pose I will use Deborah Johnson's threefold distinction: "The ethical issues can be organized in at least three different ways: according to the type of technology; according to the sector in which technology is used; and according to ethical concepts of themes."[30]

For computer games, this means that the ethical issues are related to the use of computer technology to create a virtual world and enforce a set of rules; to the fact that not all users of these games are mature enough to be exposed to certain content; and to the issues that computer games raise in the perspective of, for instance, virtue ethics: does the act of playing games reinforce moral desensitization? Only those problems related to the technology are unique to computer games. All the other questions have been present in history, in other forms of expression. Computer games pose old and new questions.

In terms of the general epistemological field of computer ethics, my theoretical framework is very close to the paradigm proposed by Philip Brey's[31] disclosive computer ethics: "Mainstream computer ethics focuses on the morality of practices, particularly on the use of computer technology. What is often marginalized in the discussion . . . is the moral role of the technology that is being used. That is, the design features of computer systems and software. . . . Technological artifacts may themselves become the object of moral scrutiny, independently from, and prior to, particular ways of using them."[32] Similarly, it is in the game as designed simulation system where the ethics of computer games can be partially tracked. The way games are designed, and how that design encourages players to make certain choices, is relevant for the understanding of the ethics of computer games.

But the main argument of this book, the one that I believe marks a turn from the conventional discourse relating to computer games and ethics, is my dedication to putting the player in the center. As designed objects, computer games create practices that could be considered unethical. Yet these practices are voluntarily undertaken by a moral agent who not only has the capacity, but also the duty to develop herself as an ethical being by means of practicing her own player-centric ethical thinking while preserving the pleasures and balances of the game experience. The player is a moral user capable of reflecting ethically about her presence in the game, and aware of how that experience configures her values both inside the game world and in relation to the world outside the game.

My arguments placing computer game players as the central element of any analysis of computer game ethics justify my choice of virtue ethics and information ethics as the philosophical theories informing my analytical framework. Both virtue and information ethics take into consideration both what constitutes an ethical situation, and what is an ethical agent. While deontology or utilitarianism provide a picture of the subject as ethical agent, virtue and information ethics, both constructivist theories, allow for an integration of the subject in an ongoing process of ethical reflection. In other words, these ethical theories allow the analysis of players and their relations with game systems. I will explain in detail the application of these two theories in chapter 4.

This is a book on computer ethics, since it uses some of the most relevant findings of this field and applies them to digital games. I have tried to write a text that, while applying a number of different disciplines to the explanation of the ethics of computer games, could be understood as a part of computer ethics—more specifically, as a part of the trends in computer ethics that designate users of designed environments as responsible moral agents who are capable and ought to protect and enhance the well-being of the environments where their interactions take place. This is, in summary, this book's contribution and allegiance to the field of computer ethics.

1.5 Structure of the Book

I have divided the book into eight chapters, but there is a conceptual division that should be noted. Chapters 2 to 4 are the core theoretical parts: there are examples, but mostly presented as short illustrations of conceptual problems and their solutions. In these chapters I present the theory behind this book's understanding of the ethics of computer games. Since there is much at stake with this topic, I wanted to provide a detailed framework justifying each one of my arguments. It is in those chapters that the theory on the ethics of computer games is explained, argued for, and presented.

Chapter 2 focuses on the ontology of games as designed objects, using design theory and game research as the main theoretical backgrounds. In that chapter I explore the relations between game rules and fictional worlds. I will argue that the ethics of computer games as objects have to be localized in the game system, and that the fictional world—the audiovisual element— while important, is secondary to the ethics of a computer game.

Chapter 3 explains the player as a moral being. In this chapter I will argue that players understand the ethical constraints and affordances of the game design and the game fiction, but they are ultimately empowered ethical beings who reflect morally about their actions in the game. The core idea in this chapter is that players are not moral zombies, but productive agents who understand the values of a game.

Chapter 4 presents the framework for the analysis of computer game ethics. This framework applies two different and consolidated ethical frameworks, information ethics and virtue ethics, to the findings of the two previous chapters. The central questions are: how do we play these ethical systems, and how do we tackle the ethical issues they raise? Chapter 4 concludes with a general theory for the understanding of computer game ethics.

In chapters 5 to 7, I apply the theory to different issues: I present three case studies, illustrating not only how to apply the theory, but also what its influence is in the analysis of single-player, multiplayer, and massively multiplayer online games. Chapter 6 focuses on more general questions, such as the issues raised by unethical content in computer games, and such content's possible effects on players. Chapter 7 applies the general theory computer game ethics to the craft of designing games, coming up with a synthesis of design theory and ethics that could be used both as an analytical tool and potentially as a source for reflection and inspiration in the creation of ethical gameplay.

This book may have, by nature, very different readers. The fact that it is an academic book, and that it reasons using the arguments of methods of philosophy, can make it seem difficult to read on occasion. It probably is. Nevertheless, different audiences will find different chapters interesting: those readers who are philosophically inclined will find the first half of the book relevant, while those who want a more concrete application of theory may find the second half more appealing. The ethics of computer games is a large, complicated topic, and I have tried to make it understandable and entertaining without sacrificing the rigor required to provide a complete answer to a critical question.

This book has the goal of providing a comprehensive overview of the ethics of computer games, a field scarcely researched but deserving of more attention due to the increasing ethical questions that computer games, as an emergent cultural form of expression and entertainment, pose to developed societies. It is, by no means, a complete work—there are areas that require more discussion, and games, in their unstoppable evolution, will likely render parts of the text old. Nevertheless, I intend this text as a first step, as the starting point of a dialogue in which designers, academics, and players share positions and discuss the moral importance of games in our culture.

2 Computer Games as Designed Ethical Systems

Let us start with a moral assassin. It all starts in a beach. I have been washed ashore. I cannot remember who I am, or how I got here. I have some shredded memories, nothing that makes sense. I am helped by a lifeguard. I follow her to a cabin. Then hell breaks lose: somebody tries to kill me. But I am better: I can use any weapon with deadly precision. I am an assassin, and my memory is returning.

My next step is to recover more pieces of my identity. I go to a bank. In the vault, ghosts from the past numb my senses. A bomb explodes, an alarm goes off, the police come. I have to get out of here. As I walk up the stairs, a policeman shoots at me. I shoot back. He dies. I read: "Game Over."

This is a brief summary of the first levels of the first-person shooter *XIII*.[1] This game puts the player in control of an amnesic assassin. The player is presented with fragments of a story that she will have to complete by following the game's linear narrative. One of the goals of the game is to reconstruct the story of the main character. Players are only presented with the fact that this character is a skilled assassin. There is no sense, at the beginning of the game, of this character's values.

Yet when players reach the the bank, they are commanded not to shoot the police. In fact, if they do so, the game will stop and force them to replay. Of course, this is a contradiction with the narrative of the game: if we are amnesic assassins, why is it that we cannot shoot the police? Why does that (unethical) action interrupt our gameplay?

Most computer games are systems of rules that encourage players to work toward goals in a virtual environment. And many computer games address players by means of a story. There are, then, two fundamental elements to these computer games: systems and worlds. These two elements have to

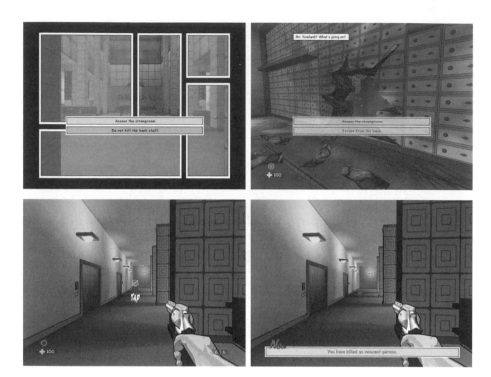

Figure 2.1
XIII: Game Rules as Ethical Design Affordances

be coherent, creating entertaining gameplay while crafting a game world. The ethics of games as designed objects can be found in the relations between these two elements.

Let's return to *XIII*: the fictional element of the game is telling the player that her character is a ruthless, skilled killer. On the other hand, the rules are forcing the player to behave in a specific way: police officers and innocents cannot be killed. There is a game rule that creates the values we play by, in clear contradiction to the game fiction. The design of rules, then, can create values we *have* to play by.

In this chapter I will explore the relations between games as systems of rules, and the worlds and fictions they create. I will argue that the representational aspect of a computer game—its visual and narrative elements—is of secondary importance when analyzing the ethics of computer games. Games force behaviors by rules: the meaning of those behaviors, as communicated through the game world to the player, constitutes the ethics of computer games as designed objects.

But what are computer games as designed objects? Despite what it may seem, this is not a trivial question. There is a relatively large body of theoretical work that tries to address this ontological problem from different perspectives.[2] This game research tradition explains from a variety of perspectives what the specificities of computer games as cultural objects are, and how they relate to nondigital games and other forms of expression. The purpose of this chapter is to provide a definition of what computer games are and how they operate, as relevant for the understanding of their ethics as objects. This definition will illustrate how and why these games can be a challenge to our ethical capacities and to our cultural environment.

In this chapter I will be writing about concepts like game rules, game systems, game mechanics, and game design. These concepts will illustrate the decision to understand games as designed systems, a key element in the description of their ethics both as objects and as experiences. My goal is to strike a balanced definition of games that both appeals to game theorists and game designers while providing a sufficient basis for claiming that computer games are moral artifacts. To achieve that balance, I will first review critically the computer game theory approach to the ontology of games, providing a framework for defining game ontology that will then be fine-tuned by applying the perspective of game designers. The result will be a formal understanding of computer games as systems that can have embedded ethical values, an essential element in the analytical framework I am introducing.

There is a caveat that needs to be made: this chapter focuses on theoretical abstractions of what computer games are. This means that players are defined as the necessary input providers for a game to be played. I will be writing about an implied player who always follows the rules in order to achieve the goals of the game. Since the focus of this chapter is on games as systems, this approach should not pose any problem. It is reasonable and enriching to have this implied player in mind, for it tells us much about how games are designed, understood, and how they have historically evolved.

This chapter will define computer games as systems of rules and mechanics guiding player behavior toward the achievement of goals by means of specific actions and behaviors. I will argue that the systemic core of computer games, their rules, is of fundamental importance in understanding the ethics of games. If we want to describe the ethics of a computer game, we should first analyze its rules: what the player is forced and/or encouraged to do. Only when we have described the rules of the game can we analyze the game world, the narrative, and other audiovisual elements in relation to the core values and behaviors proposed by the game system. In other words, a computer game's morals rest in its design.

Playing games is interacting with systems that have been created with the intention of encouraging their users to perform a number of actions to reach some predefined goals in pleasurable or engaging ways. As ethical beings, we have to be interested in what those actions and goals are. Thus, we need to understand why and how computer games are designed systems for interaction, and how that design can affect our moral fabric as ethical players.

2.1 Game Research and the Ontology of Games

As I have already mentioned, the question of the ontology of games has a somewhat recent but very influential tradition. The foundational work on nondigital games of Johan Huizinga,[3] Roger Caillois,[4] and Brian Sutton-Smith[5] brought games to the attention of a wide variety of researchers from different fields, and their formal concepts describing games are still present in many of the key texts of computer game studies. The cultural and economic importance of computer games, achieved in the closing decades of the twentieth century, contributed to the blooming of digital games as an academic research topic of its own, becoming a legitimate area of research in the field of game studies.

In this academic tradition, the ontological research of what games are is a common topic. Since this book is focused exclusively on digital games, despite the occasional reference to nondigital games, my ontological approach will be limited to defining the nature of computer games from an ethical perspective. Similarly, I will take into consideration only the research done on the ontology of digital games, leaving aside the broader perspective on traditional, nondigital games.

Computer game studies describes the properties that make computer games interesting cultural objects. The focus is not only the fictional layer of games, understood as its visual and narrative contents, but also, and more crucially for this chapter, the use of interactive simulation in creating their ludic experiences. This discipline argues that computer games are not just some new kind of game, but a cultural object of intrinsic value with essentially original characteristics that calls for specific analytical approaches.

What is, then, a computer game? In one of the foundational texts of the field, Jesper Juul's *Half-Real*, a game is defined as "a rule-based system with a variable and quantifiable outcome, where different outcomes are assigned different values, the player exerts effort in order to influence the outcome, the player feels attached to the outcome, and the consequences of the activity are optional and negotiable."[6] And video games would then be "games played using computer power," where the computer upholds the rules of the game and the game is played using a video display."[7]

Juul defines games as objects that have a level of systemic rules, and it seems to consign to a secondary level of importance the computer game's fictional level, at least when it comes to understanding what games are. This definition covers the game as a system of rules with which agents interact, paying attention to the emotional attachment of players to games. Rules will be, in Juul's approach, the "real" element of games, connected to the fictional element, the game world. This distinction means that games can be analyzed as systems, as fictional worlds, as both, and as the ways they interrelate, implying at least four dominant modalities of understanding games. These modalities, as I will argue throughout this book, are crucial for understanding the ethics of computer games.

In the case of *XIII*, this distinction describes the way the developers approached the ethical behaviors they wanted to create: while the fictional world is focusing on the character development of a killer, the game rules force players to act in a specific way. The fictional world may describe the main character as ruthless, but players have to play as ethical beings that respect the innocents, or the game will end. The actual gameplay, the actions taken by players, is forced to be ethical by the game rules.

But before unravelling the connection between rules and virtual worlds, it is necessary to argue for the specificity of computer games from a cultural, historical perspective. What makes computer games different than classic games?

Obviously, the answer is computers. Salen and Zimmerman provide four reasons why digital games are different than analog games:[8] first of all, a computer provides games with "immediate but narrow interactivity,"[9] meaning the game system reacts immediately to player stimuli. For example, rhythm action games like *Dance Dance Revolution*[10] provide a rather narrow interaction space for players, but the game system reacts immediately to their input, thus creating gameplay based on the same principles as dance: measured reaction to rhythmic input. Incidentally, this type of game shows how narrow the interactivity can be: it does not matter how players *play* a rhythm game, if they master the dance floor with the whole range of·possible bodily expressions, or if they are just barely able to follow instructions without any sense of rhythm whatsoever: what the game requires is a specific input. It does not care about how that input is actually provided, or about the aesthetics and kinesthetic elements of dance.

Second, computer games excel in the storage and manipulation of the data required to run that same computer game. For example, a game like the massively multiplayer online role-playing game (MMORPG) *World of Warcraft*[11] is a number of files that add up to 1.5 gigabytes of data, comprising a whole world of graphics and textures, plus all the other elements that make it work, from the memory management software to the client-server protocols allowing multiplayer gaming. A computer stores and manipulates that information with almost no effort, allowing the player to experience a world of vast proportions in an almost seamless fashion.

Third, the computer is capable of manipulating that data at a high speed and often without hampering the user experience, allowing for some interesting evolution of game genres in digital media. For instance, a very popular game engine[12] is the Wizards of the Coast's D20 system, which uses, in its analog version, the roll of a 20-faced die against some statistical tables in order to evaluate success, failure, and the different degrees of each. While playing a game like *Knights of the Old Republic* it is difficult to perceive that in the background the game engine is doing calculations based on a digital simulation of that engine, yet that is the way combat is resolved.

Finally, computers are very good networking machines, a feature that translates into games that can be simultaneously experienced by thousands of players, creating new types of gameplay that could not be imagined prior to the use of networked computing technology—online games, online communities, and digital distribution channels are examples of the scale and importance of computers in turning the games they run into interesting, innovative cultural objects.

Nevertheless, there is one element that clearly distinguishes computer games from analog games and that has a strong influence in the understanding of computer games as ethical objects: when games use computers to uphold the rules, it is not possible to discuss the rules during play. Except in professional settings, nondigital game rules are often the subject of discussion among the players, resulting in unconventional rules being applied only at the moment of playing.[13] It could be said that rules in analog games are seen as negotiable institutional conditions: all the players have to agree about the rules by which the game is going to be played. Computer games *impose* the rules: they are not subject to discussion. Computer game rules are insurmountable laws the player has to acknowledge and surrender to in order to enjoy the game. The possibility of bending the rules jumps outside the formal aspect of the game and belongs exclusively to the social level. Players of a multiplayer game can discuss which rules they will implement, how they will interpret the outcome of the game, or the specific gameplay. But they all have to submit to the hardwired set of rules, which are beyond interpretation or discussion.

For instance, with regard to the classic game *Warcraft: Orcs & Humans*,[14] game designers Andrew Rollings and Ernest Adams noted that "the Orc player producing warlock units would almost always win."[15] There is an imbalance in the game due to a combination of game rules and unit parameters that provides an unfair advantage to one player over the other. And because it is a computer game, and those rules are inaccessible and impossible to manipulate by players, there is no way of solving this design problem. Players can talk and agree about rules for *how to play* the game, but that does not contradict the fact that they cannot modify these rules.

Another ethically interesting outcome of the use of computers for playing games is the "black box syndrome,"[16] which describes how digital technology applied to computer games obscures the actual presence of a system of rules that determines the victory conditions and the inner workings of the system. By not showing how the games' rules are enforced, digital games tend to strengthen the supremacy of the rules system in the experience of the game.

Nonetheless, there are examples of players overriding the obscurity of the box to see, and exploit, the workings of the system. For example, it is not strange to read dedicated players of *World of Warcraft* discussing in the official forums the differences in skill attributes that provide advantages in combinations of actions and objects. These advantages are in the 1 to 2 percent range, which is nevertheless quite significant when engaging in player-versus-player gameplay. These players are consciously aware of the complexity of the algorithmic calculations that determine their possibilities for success in that online world—other players just experience the game without requiring a deep understanding of the mathematical models that construct the game experience.

Besides their implementation of digital technologies, computer games are reasonably similar to traditional games. It is precisely the use of these technologies that brings forth some of the interesting ontological properties of computer games as formal systems: the black box syndrome, and the difficulty for players to modify rules in the best interest of a specific group in a specific situation. Computer games are just one more of the Western world's cultural objects whose ethical implications and nature have been affected by digital technologies. What has been affected is the formal nature of the game, its systemic core.

This systemic core has to be understood as the rules of the game, which have an extraordinary importance when describing the ethics of computer games. Since rules are the operational parameters that encapsulate and guide both player behavior and the nature of the virtual world, it is of crucial importance to understand the ontology of rules. What then do we mean by rules?

In Salen and Zimermann's approach, rules are "the inner, formal structure of games."[17] The properties of rules are their unambiguous, explicit nature; their commonality to all the players of the game; and the fact that they are fixed and binding. Rules have also operational values: they limit what players can do, and they also reward certain actions; they create the winning conditions and the limits and boundaries of the games. The rules of a game create the possibility of the game by being easily shareable statements that limit and reward players' actions.

Salen and Zimmerman define three kinds of rules: constitutive (abstract, mathematical rules), operational (behavior rules for players—directly experienced by them), and implicit (rules of etiquette and sportsmanship).[18]

For example, the constitutive rules of the oriental board game *Go* would be the mathematical logic and combinations that allow gameplay; the operational rules of *Go* would be those printed in the game's box; the implicit rules would be thhose created during the game experience between a master and a student, which would allow the latter to learn the game by, for instance, correcting her mistakes. In computer games, the rules contained in the code are the constitutive and the operational, while the implicit usually derive from the player repertoire and the player communities, which I will explain in more detail when I focus on the ethical player.

Game researcher Espen Aarseth defines the systemic layer of digital games as "game-structure;" that is, "the rules of the game, including the simulation rules."[19] According to Aarseth, a game is a process that has a structure formed by sets of rules and that can only take place when there are players experiencing it. The reference to the rules of the simulation is rather interesting. As it turns out, most contemporary computer games use the processing power of the machines they run on not only to uphold and enforce the rules (among other things such as facilitating player communication), but also to create a simulation of environments and/or physics. While not every game is a simulation, and therefore need not have simulation rules, It is of particular interest to note the assumption that if a game is a simulation, then those simulation rules are a part of the game structure just like the game's rules are.

An example in which the rules of the game and the rules of the simulation operate alongside each other can be taken from *Half-Life 2*.[20] In this game, the rules that determine the simulated world are at least as important as the rules of the game. For instance, there is a moment early in the game in which the player is cornered in what seems to be an industrial pool. The only way of getting out is to flood the pool so the nearby wood crates will float high enough that the exit can be reached. Players have to understand the rules of the simulation in order to solve some of the puzzles and explore the game within its rules.

Additionally, it is worth mentioning that the rules of the simulation are often limited by the rules of the game. For example, I have several times tried to shoot the nonplayer characters that try to help me in my quest in *Half-Life 2*. But it is not possible: every time I point the gun at them, my avatar immediately lowers the weapon and does not respond to the firing

Figure 2.2
Half-Life 2: Don't Shoot Your Allies!

command. There is a game rule—no friendly fire allowed—that supersedes a simulation rule. And these types of overrulings, as I will argue later, are key elements for the understanding of computer games as ethical objects.

Up to this stage, I have focused on games and rules from a formal perspective, thus describing them merely as objects. Nevertheless, games are ontologically both objects and experiences; they are objects designed to be experienced, and they only exist fully in that process. Computer games can be described from a formal, procedural perspective, but the complete understanding of games and their capabilities is only possible when described as experiences. Those experiences have a formal, material sense that conditions the possible ways the users perform those experiences. In game research terms, games have an *ergodic* nature.

Ergodics, a term coined by Aarseth,[21] is a fundamental concept in the history of computer game research. Ergodics is the property of a system that evaluates the interaction according to some rules, most of them known by the user, and that determines a success state that the player strives to achieve. In the case of games, that process is playing. Ergodics is a structural property of an object: there are certain layers in the object that *contain* the ergodicity of the object.

What do these layers consist of? Succinctly phrased, these layers comprise the rules for the interaction with the game and the criteria for the success and/or failure while experiencing it. This statement implies that: 1) ergodic objects always have rules, and they tend to create systems with winning criteria; and 2) those rules are hardwired in the material level of the object. These rules are discrete and nonambiguous because they enable the system to discriminate between successful and unsuccessful users. As the system we are analyzing is a state machine,[22] the instructions it runs have to be formal, discrete, and unambiguous.[23]

In the case of a game like *Deus Ex*, the game evaluates the player's interactions with the nonplayer characters and reacts in consequence. There are three possible endings for that game, and a large but limited number of distinct outcomes for different situations. *Deus Ex* is a game that takes the ergodic component that is present in every game and makes it a key element in how the game is played. By acknowledging that games are played by interacting with an ergodic structure that reacts to the input of the player as agent, *Deus Ex* proposed a branched structure in which the choices the player made would affect the outcome of the game. And those choices were of a moral nature: shall I kill the enemy, or avoid it?

Computer games, though, are not exclusively an algorithmic system of rules with which players interact, and as such these moral dilemmas have to be seen in the larger perspective of a game played in a game world. In fact, what players usually reckon as interesting in a game is precisely the world where they can play. That world is also a part of the ontology of the game, and its feedback mechanisms with the systemic layer of the game offer interesting insights for the ethical analysis of computer games.

Let's start with a general assumption: the rules of a game tailor their world according to the challenges and goals of that game. This implies that

Figure 2.3
Deus Ex: Ethical Gameplay Choices

a computer game need not simulate the complexity of the world: it is enough to create a simulated world where play is interesting. Nevertheless, because rules configure the interaction possibilities in the game world, it is not possible to understand a game by only looking at its virtual world or aesthetic layers, as the world is largely determined by the rules of the game. This implies that the formal structure of the game, understood as its rules and mechanics, is to some extent accountable for the end result of the fictional world. This also means that level design and world design are also determinant when it comes to constituting the ethical values of a game, and therefore they may be considered as ethically relevant.

For example, a game like *Burnout 3: Takedown*[24] presents the players with a closed circuit in which car races take place—nothing new here. These circuits are not only designed to be dangerous, but also to be the only possible circuit in what seems to be a big city, an example of the notion of incomplete worlds that Juul applies to games.[25] In addition, these tracks have been designed to facilitate crashes between players, as there is a game rule that gives points and an extra speed boost to those players who make other cars crash without crashing themselves. The formal structure of the game—that is, the need for closed circuits where the rules of the game can be easily implemented—has determined the way the fictional racing world of *Burnout 3* can be experienced. And it has also determined that, in the competitive world of this game, making other players' cars crash is a desirable action, thus defining some actions as desirable or interesting to perform.

The virtual environments of games, then, are affected by the rules the players live by, as well as by the simulation rules that shape that world. In *Grand Theft Auto: San Andreas*,[26] some areas of the game world are locked at the beginning of the game, with the clear intent of guiding the player through a predefined gameplay progression. Nevertheless, if the player wants to explore those areas, she will be able to do so, since this game allows players to toy with the environment and game props in ways that are not predefined. So, for example, a player can climb the walls to the airport, steal a plane, and fly to those parts of the game world. But there is a game rule that states that before accessing those areas, the player has to complete a number of missions. This rule is enforced by a computer-controlled fighter jet that hunts down the player if she flies to those temporarily forbidden zones. The fictional world is limited by a game rule, showing the intertwining of rules and fictional worlds. Rules create the game; the fictional world contains it.

The importance of this linking of the virtual world to the simulation rules is that the virtual environment where the game happens or takes place is constrained, limited, and conditioned by the rules of the simulation. That is, the simulation rules determine what is possible and what is not—without needing to explain why—in the virtual environment where the game takes place. This ontology can be explained by using Juul's concept of computer games as *half-real*: their reality is provided by the rules, but the fictional element is also of relevance in the configuration of the game's actuality, in its experience.[27]

If the rules of the game have the ontological status of reality due to their objective existence, then there must be something else in computer games that is not real. According to Juul, that element is the fictional world. The fictional world is the instantiated world in which the game takes place, and that is created by means of several props, such as graphics, sounds, texts, cut-scenes, and all the other paraludic objects (the box, the advertisements) that shape what a game is.[28]

The worlds a game creates are fictional; that is, incomplete and possible worlds where the gameplay takes place. By incomplete, Juul means that fictional worlds created by games do not provide all the information about those worlds.[29] Some games use such incompleteness as a creative asset: *Shadow of the Colossus* is set in a world about which the player knows very little, and that lack of information becomes ethically relevant, since, as I will argue later, it empowers players to act like ethical agents within a game world governed by ethically designed rules.

Rules might create ethical discourses that are then implemented in the game world. But the fictional world, despite its incomplete nature, might also create some ethical instances that are not related to the rules, but to the cultural experience of the game. For instance, the player community around the first-person shooter *Counter-Strike: Source*[30] only accepts camping, understood as the act of staying still in a privileged space in order to ambush the opponents, in certain maps, even though there are no built-in game rules forbidding, limiting, or controlling that behavior. The world is also interpreted and experienced by the player, who can afford ethical discourses into the game that are not predicted or controlled by the rules of the game. For example, take harassing newbies in *World of Warcraft*:

while there are no rules against that behavior, players tend to view the practice as undesirable, and thus try not do it, or they publicly complain about those players who do it.

Game worlds are where gameplay occurs. A game world, in the case of computer games, is either the simulation of the material conditions of a game, like in the case of computer-simulated board games, or a simulation of another world. That simulation presents both simulation rules and game rules: in fact, virtual environments are constrained by the game rules, since all the elements that are not fundamental to the game are a mere setting for the actions of the game.[31] There can be simulated objects that have no game relevance, but interaction with those objects is usually guided by the simulation rules: for example, the wood crates in *Half-Life 2* are breakable and float, but except in some physics puzzles, they have no direct role in the gameplay (understood in this case as the optimal actions taken to achieve the winning condition).

A game world is of lesser complexity than the real world. But the complexity of these worlds cannot be stated in comparison with the real world, because they are fabricated worlds largely constrained by the boundaries of the game and simulation rules. As players, we compare the virtual environment with the real world because physical reality is a reference point that makes the learning process easier. We intuitively know that falling from a certain height is bad, and so we behave accordingly in virtual environments, unless there are some clues in them that explicitly break this assumption, or if we know from our previous experience in similar games that falling is not dangerous. This comparison implies that there are actually connections made between the real world and the game world in the mind of the player. These connections are related not only to the game world as a system (the physics simulation, the level design), but also to the player as an embodied being. This will be crucial when explaining the ways a moral player interacts with a game.

For understanding the ethics of computer games, it is necessary to keep in mind that these game worlds are, in Juul's terms, "optional worlds"[32]— worlds with a fictional layer that can be called off by the players for different purposes. One study of *Quake III*[33] hard-core players[34] shows that the more expert a *Quake* player is, the less the graphics matter, as the player tunes out all superfluous visual information, getting faster and better machine performances in order to master multiplayer conflict. It could be said that rules overtake the importance of the detailed *Quake* world, and that the players in the study focused only on the visualization of a formal system of rules. The players were only interested in the informational aspects of the computer game: playing a video game might be primarily understood as interacting with a formal system of rules hosted and refereed by a computer.

The game world, on the other hand, can also modify gameplay. That is, the rules are localized in a space that can also dictate behaviors. The game world has a certain pull over the way the game is experienced because it is the representation of the rules as well as their container. The game world is the immediately accessible system of rules information for the player. Rules are experienced *through* the game world in the process called gameplay. In the case of *Burnout 3*, the design of the game world guides and encourages players to crash into other vehicles, and specific parts of this world, like tunnels or bridges, are particularly effective since they give more points to the aggressor.

Once we have understood the importance of game worlds, it is time to briefly turn to the concept of gameplay. I will define gameplay for digital games as the phenomenological experience of interacting with a computer game, restrained by the formal structure of the game and its technological layout. The phenomenological experience of the game is what Salen and Zimmerman define as "interaction:" to interact with a system is to create meaning. The interaction we find in games is "explicit interactivity; or participation with designed choices and procedures."[35] Games are objects designed to be interacted with by accepting some rules that can/will grant a ludic experience. This design needs to bring ethical values to that experience, values that will be accepted and analyzed by the players in order to successfully experience the game.

To recap, game research has argued that a computer game is both a formal system and a ludic experience. It is possible to describe a game as a formal system that will then generate an experience when played. Given these conditions, what are the most relevant characteristics of a computer game, from an ethical perspective?

Game systems are designed systems, rules and procedures that create a ludic experience. Understanding the ethical implications of playing a computer game and how computer games can actually be moral objects requires an ethical analysis of the formal structure of the game.

Rules, defined as formal systems that arbitrarily constrain possibilities in a game, can create ethical values that are afterward enacted, interpreted, and judged by the players.[36] The rules forming the ontological structure of the game are not only the obvious rules of the game (what is right and wrong, how to win), but also the rules of the simulation: what the world is capable of, and how the player can manipulate it and inhabit it. This ontology of games calls for an expansion of our moral universe to take into account the simulated environment where a game takes place, because it is not about how we inhabit a world, but how that world allows us to inhabit it.

Rules can have embedded values determining how the world is constituted, like in the case of *Half-Life 2* not allowing players to shoot nonplayer characters who are supposed to be allied with them. Therefore, rules are relevant for the understanding of the ethics of computer games. If games as ethical objects were only their rules, then the values imprinted and interpreted from those rules would be the ethical values of the game. But players interpret the rules and they create rules. Though playing a game is an experience patterned by a formal and fixed set of unambiguous rules, it is also an experience of evaluating the game and creating implicit rules. Computer games seem to obscure and impose the rules due to their digital nature, but players are still empowered when playing a game, and the game experience is always under the sign of those rules that are not written, but that tell us how to play the game.

This concept of empowered players explains why in any massively multiplayer online role-playing game, users who participate in "ninja-looting" tend become social pariahs.[37] When a player, individually and without permission, loots the monsters killed by a larger group of characters, her avatar's name is publicly exposed so that other players will not party with her. Players understand that even though ninja-looting is allowed by the constitutive and operational rules of the game, it is ethically problematic and so they have to create rules governing that behavior within the world.

This does not rule out the analysis of the game as an object. A closer look into the ethics of the formal system of the game can yield only a partial knowledge of what the game as an ethical experience might be. But understanding what kind of values are embedded in the formal system can illustrate how games are experienced from a moral standpoint. The formal system of rules is determined by its ergodic nature. Those rules are formal, nonambiguous parameters that include the criteria for success or failure within the game experience, and these criteria are also of an ethical nature.

When considering games as designed systems from an ethical point of view, it is possible to conclude that those systems might have been designed with certain embedded values. Rules are restrictions that encourage behaviors and reward actions. If we want to understand the ethical nature of computer games, we need to pay attention to the ways their rules and their worlds are presented to the player. It is not only a matter of what the fictional world looks like—it is also, and more importantly, a matter of what kind of choices and constraints the players are presented with, and what these mean.

Ethically interesting games are those in which the existence of the rules predicts a game world in which ethical values can be deduced from the actual gameplay. If *XIII* fails to be an interesting ethical experience it is because there is an inherent contradiction between the game world and the system's ethics. As players, we are deprived of the ethical reflection that the fiction promised us. This process can be ultimately defined as unethical game design.

In summary, game research can be used to define a game object as a system designed to be interacted with in order to achieve an experience that is entertaining and absorbing. It is thus crucial to pay attention to the work done by game designers. Their reflection on their own practices will enlighten the theoretical approach taken by game research, and can be used to strengthen the notion that games, as designed systems, can have embedded values encapsulated in their rules and game worlds, where they are experienced by players who can morally relate to those design affordances and constraints. Besides, since game designers are responsible for the creation of computer games, it is also worth presenting an initial reflection on their responsibility regarding the ethical nature of computer games, and what types of morally driven decisions they take when creating a computer game.

2.2 Game Design and the Craft of Making Systems

Game design is a crossover discipline of many other fields, from software engineering to psychology to mathematics. We could broadly define game design as the discipline that focuses on the creation of successful ludic experiences with the use of different arts and technologies. For understanding the ethics of computer games as designed objects, then, it is crucial to understand how game designers think about their practice, and what techniques and thoughts inform the process of creating rules and game worlds.

I will now focus on two crucial questions: what have game designers written about the nature of games as designed systems, and what are the ethical responsibilities of game designers as creators of game rules and worlds with embedded ethical values?

Game designers create an object and try to map and predict the ways its users will experience it. In this sense, game designers are somewhat behavioral engineers: they craft objects that will afford behaviors in their users. But games can transmit more than just behaviors: the rhetoric possibilities of games, from *Monopoly* to *Counter-Strike*, are an almost untapped source of political, social, and cultural commentary. Though games have traditionally been identified with the very fuzzy concept of fun, games like *September 12th*[38] exemplify the powerful tools that games provide for engaging players in critical thinking. Thus it also puts game designers in the role of cultural opinion makers, of creators with a large role and responsibility in the shaping of our culture.

Game designers face the problem of creating meaningful gameplay through formal systems that generate the virtual worlds in which gameplay takes place. For designers, a game is the outcome of a creative process, an object that will be judged and evaluated by players. Most game designers have approached the ontological question of games trying to find the key to developing successful games. The computer games industry demands success, and designers have tried to distill what makes a game successful by answering these essential questions: what is a computer game, and what is computer game design?

Greg Costikyan and Chris Crawford, two well-known designers interested in the theoretical aspects of their craft, have provided definitions that prove interesting for arguments on the ethics of computer games. Crawford defines games as "conflicts in which the players directly interact in such a way as to foil each other's goals,"[39] while Costikyan argues that games are "a form of art in which participants, termed players, make decisions in order to manage resources through game tokens in the pursuit of a goal."[40]

Games are, then, an activity for players where goals are important. Even though designers tend to praise what appear to be goal-less games such as *The Sims*[41] or pen-and-paper role-playing games (RPGs),[42] most of the theory on game design[43] insists on the presence of goals (or success criteria) in their definitions: games tend to have goals, and if they do not, players will most likely provide them. In Crawford's definition, the presentation of the goals and the different strategies for succeeding are limited to stating that games consist of conflicts that need to be resolved by the players, using their creativity. These conflicts, in general, set players in opposition to one another, meaning either that single-player games are an anomaly, or that the game system in itself is a player, an opponent in the field. Costikyan solves this problem by not constraining the conflict to players, but presenting the conflict in a more abstract way. In any case, games have goals in the shape of challenges that have to be solved by players.

These two definitions include as well a crucial element for the understanding of the ethics of games: the responsibility of the players. Players are present in every game, but their presence is oriented toward their decision-making activities within the game experience. They decide which weapons to use in *Counter-Strike. Source*, or how to hit the controllers at the right time in *Dance Dance Revolution*, whether dancing or just sticking to the most effective strategy for achieving points. In clearer terms, a player's role in the game is to make choices. Games present a delimited set of choices to players, who have to find strategies, mostly optimal but in cases also aesthetic, to achieve these goals.

Following this same line of thought, game designer Raph Koster has compiled a list of the characteristics of games that summarizes the previous definitions:

- [Games] present us with models of real things—often highly abstracted.
- They are generally quantified or even *quantized* models.
- They primarily teach us things that we can absorb into the unconscious as opposed to things designed to be tackled by the conscious, logical mind.
- They mostly teach us things that are fairly primitive behaviors, but they don't *have* to.[44]

Koster suggests that games are systems that are quantified or quantized—similar to what the concept of ergodics implied, games have the rules for success built into their systems. If ergodics meant that computer games are systems with built-in rules for their manipulation and the evaluation of input, Koster's approach considers games as systems that use algorithms and computer code to model a reality, thus converting the act of playing into the process of interacting with that model in ways predefined by the tools used precisely to simulate the real thing as a model.

These systems simulate reality, albeit a highly abstracted one. The fiction of games has its roots in a model of the real world that is present in the ergodic core of the game; in other words, there is a relationship between the game fiction and the rules that are determined by the game's ergodic system. In the game *Manhunt*, for example, the fictional world in which the game is set simulates the grim industrial landscapes of a modern city, but that city is not totally open for exploration, so in fact the game world as experienced by the player is rather narrow. Furthermore, the model of those industrial landscapes is configured to enhance the game's gameplay: there are plenty of hiding spaces, shadows, and, in some situations, predefined optimal routes through which the player can actually sneak up on enemies and slaughter them. Conditioned by the design of its space, there is no other possible way for a player to inhabit the world of *Manhunt* than that which is sanctioned by the model—in this case the game world constrained by the game rules. To play *Manhunt*, to inhabit that world, is to play in a limited universe where the only means of interaction is savage murder. And, as I will argue later on, this makes *Manhunt* one of the most interesting games as an ethical experience.

Returning to the work of game designers, there seems to be an agreement on considering games as systems modeled with built-in success criteria, experienced by players who have to overcome a series of challenges by manipulating the system in order to achieve certain goals. A game designer takes an ideal model of players into consideration when creating a rule system, which has to ensure a successful experience and generate an engaging world where the player is voluntarily forced to follow the steps the designer plots.[45] A game designer is both an architect and an engineer, someone who lays the foundations of an experience, but who gets her hands dirty with the building itself by designing the rules and the success criteria. A game designer creates artifacts that are experienced by players in search of a particular emotional, rational, or moral outcome.

As Langdon Winner[46] has argued, artifacts can have political affordances. I am using the concept of affordances in the same line as Norman: "the term affordances refers to the perceived and actual properties of the thing, primarily those fundamental properties that determine just how the thing could possibly be used."[47] These "perceived and actual properties of the thing" actually have ethical properties too, for the design of an object's use is ultimately decisive in how we experience that object. Games can have ethical affordances because they are designed *and experienced* by moral agents immersed in specific cultural situations and times.[48] The game designer is responsible for most of the values that are embedded in the system and that play a significant role during the game experience, in a similar way as industrial engineers are responsible for the proper functioning of the objects they create.[49]

This does not mean that designers are exclusively responsible for the entire value system of a game. As a matter of fact, their ethical responsibility is rather limited: a designer is responsible for the object, but the players and their communities are ultimately responsible for the experience. What ethical values a designer hardwires in a system are only relevant when seeing the game as an object—when it comes to the act of playing, and being a player, those values are only relevant if they directly affect the experience. For instance, the developers of a game like *Counter-Strike: Source* are not responsible for the levels and content that players may create using the software development kits distributed by the developers. In the case of the *Counter-Strike* modification *Velvet Strike*,[50] a group of players decided to implement the game's spray function to flood this first-person shooter with antiwar and pacifist graffiti, in a subversion of the game's dominant discourses. The choice of implementing ethical discourses in the game was open to players, and the Velvet Strike team did use it to subvert the main discourse of the game.

Game designers and game researchers agree that ultimately, games are systems. That is, from a formal perspective, and ignoring the *act* of playing, games are a set of unambiguous rules projected to the player and designed to create a user experience. The role of a designer goes beyond implementing the rules: a designer has to create the rules and the settings and the props for the activity of playing, predicting also the strategies and techniques players might want to use to achieve the given goals. Game designers have to create gameplay.

Figure 2.4
September 12th: Winning is Not Playing

Sid Meier defined gameplay as "a series of interesting choices,"[51] a popular notion in the game design literature. Even Rollings and Adams built their formal definition of gameplay on Meier's classification: "one or more caus-ally linked series of challenges in a simulated environment."[52] Choices are the core of game design. The designer's task is to create a space of possibil-ity, plotting a number of decisions the player has to take, from which her strategies originate. A designer presents these choices to the player, usually with clues as to which choices are actually better than others for achieving the game's goal. But these choices are only created and presented by the designer, and thus they exist exclusively in the game as object. It is up to the players to understand these choices as relevant, and make them. Players are responsible for the choices made, and designers are responsible for the ways these choices operate within the game system.

Designers seem to have, then, responsibility over the way their systems are experienced by players. For example, the graphic adventure *Grim Fan-dango*[53] presents the player with the challenge of navigating through a story that can be solved in only one way, following one linear path. On the other hand, the more recent *Fahrenheit*[54] presents the player with the same genre conventions, but a branched game architecture based on reaction to player's choices makes players think about the consequences of their decisions. In *Grim Fandango*, the game designers are ethically responsible for how they limit the players' choices: there is one fixed path, but players should not get stuck, for example. In *Fahrenheit*, designers are responsible for the choices given to the player, and how those configure the experience of the game.

In computer games, the player must believe she is free when she is actually not; she must also believe in the inevitability of the choices she is presented with. What game designers do is manipulate this dialectic, presenting the choices they offer as the only possible solutions for the player to take into consideration. Games are systems in which we are voluntarily immersed with the clear goal of being manipulated—we believe in the freedom the game designers give us in order to achieve the successful ludic experience.

A computer game like *September 12th* plays with these conventions in a way that illuminates the understanding of the ethics of game design. In this game, the player controls what seems to be a sniper crosshair that can scroll through a simulated Middle Eastern village where civilians and terrorists move freely. The player will try to shoot, most likely at a terrorist. Then there is a conscious break of the game rhetoric: it is not a sniper rifle but a missile launcher that the player is using. When the missiles hit the village, terrorists and civilians die. For each civilian dead, a group of other civilians will gather, mourn, and then transform into terrorists. The game has no end. By removing the winning condition and manipulating the ergodics of the simulation (the action that could lead to a conclusion of the game is actually punished by multiplying the enemies), *September 12th* makes a powerful ethical statement: the only way of surviving this game is not playing it . . . but not playing it means letting those simulated terrorists "live." The Brechtian[55] destruction of the convention and the illusion implies a strong ethical discourse, a discourse that limits the choices given to the player via a conscious manipulation of the game ergodics and the fact that games tend to have winning conditions, and need to be played to win. In *September 12th* there is no victory, and the most valid strategy is not playing.

Game designers have reflected on the ethics of the objects they produce, paying attention to these moral issues as they are related to the media attention that computer games have attracted. Some game designers have even elaborated on how to apply ethics to the intended experience of the game. Chris Crawford points out the main reason why ethics is an interesting parameter to consider when designing a computer game: "the fascinating paradox of play is that it provides the player with dangerous experiences that are absolutely safe."[56] Furthermore, "the sense of underlying safety amid horrific dangers is an irresistible allure in a movie . . . games should do the same."[57] Play is engaging in an experience based on the controlled subordination of the player to a game's system of rules and the virtual world it provides—that is, engaging in a world that is not *real*. This lack of reality is perceived both as the great advantage of games and its great danger. Much of the research done on the effect of computer games on their users[58] shows a related concern: the "unethical" actions that take place in a game, because they are not real, desensitize the users to the real consequences of those same actions. I will formulate a critique of these analyses from an ethical theory perspective in chapter 6.

What Crawford calls for seems to be what Juul defines as the emotional attachment to the outcome:[59] we enjoy mastering a game, and we might get sad or disappointed when we lose. The experience of the game is so real that it affects our well-being. That experience is mediated, encapsulated in a fictional environment—the game world. The choices we take, our actions, all take place in the world of the game. They are *real* actions that take place and affect a ludic environment, a virtual world where interaction is limited by game rules. A game gives us the possibility of engaging without risk in ethical decision making in which we would otherwise never engage. From this point of view, the choices the designer creates in the game do not suppose any kind of moral risk for the player, as they are only relevant in the game world.

In multiplayer games like *Counter-Strike*, players usually die. Furthermore, the less skilled the player is, the more she dies. And even though there is a penalty for dying—waiting until the game round is over before being able to play again—death is quite safe, since it only means a temporary inability to interact with the system. The player's choices and actions in a game are real, because they have influence in the interaction with the state machine. The actions are real as well, but they take place and have consequences in a virtual environment and on their users, placing the player in an optimal space for exploring the possibilities of the system.

Rollings and Adams discuss ethics and the ethical role of the designer from a wider perspective. Without contradicting Crawford's reflections on the assumed safety of the risks in computer games, these authors do place a certain moral responsibility on the designer: "as designers, we are the gods of the game's world, and we define its morality."[60] Game designers should consider how the possible means of winning the game are presented to the player, and the nature of those choices, as they set the moral tone of the game. By stating this, Rollings and Adams are effectively extending the moral responsibility for the design of the game as an object to the developers. Their perspective empowers them, at the cost of, at least rhetorically, placing players in the role of ethical puppets with little judgment about the actions they are taking. They seem to deny the possibility of the player to actively participate and elaborate on the ethics of the game experience.

Rollings and Adams also try to define and categorize what they call "moral challenges"—that is, those choices the player has to make using her moral reason.[61] In their praise of *The Sims* they argue that this game is interesting because it leaves the player the freedom to self-evaluate the moral reasons for her choices. The problem is that Rollings and Adams create only one category of decisions that can be made in a game and that could be labeled as ethical, and those are the decisions that imply meta-ethical thinking by the player. While there are certainly those kinds of games in which the choices given to the player are those of an ethical nature, the ethics of games cannot be reduced to a single set of morally engaged challenges. The ethics of computer games do not necessarily depend on the nature of the choices presented to the player, but in the whole set of design and gameplay practices games encourage.

Raph Koster's work offers insights on the nature of the formal system of the game, which can be used to understand the ethical role of designers, and overcomes these criticisms in an elegant way. In Koster's model, fiction plays a secondary, yet quite important role: "Players see through the fiction to the underlying mechanics, but that does not mean the fiction is unimportant."[62] Koster states that the fiction is an important part of the game, but if we need to consider them as artistic objects, then "the art of the game is the whole,"[63] and that is so because what constitutes games is a core of game mechanics and what Koster calls a "dressing," a fictional world.[64] Koster's perspective is that of integration. It is not enough to look at the fiction; we also need to look at how the game's formal system is designed, and how that affects the game as a whole.

Nevertheless, Koster's approach is somewhat lacking because it implies that ethics are a semantic quality[65] of the game, while they have much more to do with the ontological nature of the game, as well as with the phenomenological experience of games. A game is not exclusively an object to which we can assign certain semantic values, even if we can do so to its formal system. A game is the experience of a system by a player or players in search of achieving goals that are coded in the game. Any game presents design affordances and constraints, some of which can be of an ethical nature. The designers are responsible for those affordances and constraints, since their task is to create interesting interaction modes in virtual environments that challenge players.

A game is a device created with the intention of providing a user or users with a series of challenges and the tools to conquer those challenges, limiting them by a set of rules hardcoded in the design. This design has to be invisible: the player has to be offered the feeling of freedom, but the designer must make clear which paths and choices are offered to the player. Computers are used to exert force on the player by their rigid implementation of the rules of the game and the limitations, constraints, and affordances of the game design.

Game designers are ethically responsible for the ways they have created the formal system of rules; that is, according to the behaviors they want to encourage in players. The rules of games are strong and constraining, formal models that force users to behave in certain ways by rewarding or punishing them. Designers are responsible for those player behaviors their game design encourages as a formal system.

Game developers define the products they create as objects that create experiences by limiting players' behavior, and by encouraging behavioral strategies that are immediately rewarded by the system itself.

In this sense, designers aspire to guide their users with an invisible hand through the limited possibilities of the world they present to them. The task of the developer, then, is to create behaviors in players by means of constraining and encouraging their actions. This task is, almost by definition, an ethical task, and as such game developers have to both be aware of and bear the responsibility for the ethics of computer games as designed objects.

I have presented the basic arguments for understanding games as designed objects, using concepts from computer game research and from computer game design theory. I have argued that computer games can be understood, from a formal perspective, as systems of rules designed to create a game world with which players will interact in interesting ways. Those interactions will be regulated by the game rules, which allow or disallow actions in the game world, and reward or punish accordingly. Game worlds are fictional, while game rules are real— and the uniqueness of games as designed objects is that they are ergodic: they include as part of their ontology their rules for use and success criteria.

So what are games as designed objects? Computer games are systems of rules that create and are experienced through game worlds in which the rules, a syntactic element, are often coupled with a fictional, semantic layer, in order to communicate with the player the ways in which she should successfully interact with the system. These rules are also coupled with a system of rewards and punishment for actions that guide the player experience. A computer game is also the space of possibility for player interaction created by those rules in that game world.

All these elements are essential components of games as designed systems created for ludic interaction. I will now explain in more detail how can we understand the ethics of computer games as designed systems, both in relation to what was presented in this chapter, and the larger theoretical approach of this book. Understanding games as ethical objects will also be of crucial importance when prescribing what good game design is and how it can be achieved. For now, though, it is enough to understand that games are designed systems for interaction that create a game world ready to be experienced by a player. The rules we play by in those worlds confirm the interesting aspects of computer games as ethical objects.

2.3 The Ethics of Computer Games as Designed Objects

So far I have defined computer games as objects, focusing on how they are systems of rules and means for interaction that create a game world, which players will experience in ways predetermined or preconceived by game designers. I will now present the conditions for understanding games as moral objects and what limits we might draw when considering the ethics of computer games. I will also analyze the main argument for considering games as moral objects: that they can have ethical values hardwired in their design, which condition and affect the player's experience.

The first question to ask is: can all games be considered ethically relevant? In other words, do all computer games, by nature, create ethical issues that need to be explained, addressing their formal properties as a designed object? If the answer is "no," a logical question follows: which games can be considered interesting moral objects, and why? I have already argued that for understanding the ethics of computer games it is necessary to pay attention both to the game world and to the game as an object, to the system of rules and mechanics. My approach has been inclusive: not only is the game world subject to ethical analysis, but also to the set of rules as a pattern for behaviors. As a matter of fact, we need to analyze games as systems in order to define the ethics of games as objects.

I have suggested that we have to extend the moral responsibility of computer games from the fiction to the rules, from taking into account exclusively the game world to including the game system and its design. Of course, this implies that computer games such as *Tetris*[66] or *Space Invaders*[67] are ethical objects, because they have rules. But the rules of *Tetris* or the rules of *Space Invaders* do not afford any kind of ethical values that have to be enacted, interpreted, or experienced when playing the games. Thus, these games are not interesting from an ethical perspective.

Comparing these games with a title that clearly calls for moral reasoning, like *Carmageddon*,[68] shows the conceptual difference between these two types of experiences. *Carmageddon* places players in a world where the meaningful, rewarded action is to run a car race, but with a twist: running over pedestrians will grant extra time and help achieve a higher score. The rules of the game *afford* certain behaviors that are culturally considered unethical. Similarly, *Grand Theft Auto: San Andreas* is a game about carjacking, crimes, and violence, in which having virtual sex with prostitutes is rewarded with extra health.

What makes both *Carmaggeddon* and *Grand Theft Auto* ethically interesting is that the rules afford player behavior that is violent, and player behavior that is not violent. In *Grand Theft Auto: San Andreas*, the player can only totally complete the game by performing vehicle stunts that are rewarded with points and completion percentages, among other harmless collection activities. And it is possible, though quite difficult, to play *Carmageddon* without actually running over any pedestrians. Therefore, both games can be understood as games that might have unethical affordances, but that are not necessarily unethical—it depends on the player's perspective and experience.

I will define an ethically relevant game object as a game in which the rules force the player to face ethical dilemmas, or in which the rules themselves raise ethical issues. An ethical game as object presents a game world that is ethically influenced by the rules in the way it is presented to the players. In other words, to understand the ethics of computer games as designed objects, we need to analyze first the rule system, then how those rules are actually experienced by the player and mediated within the game world.

Let's take a nondigital example: a game like boxing can be ethically questionable because the only way of playing it according to the rules is by hitting another human being. The rules are there to make the game possible, for it would otherwise be sheer violence. Yet those rules encourage controlled violence toward another person with the goal of knocking them down. It would be possible to argue that boxing is a game that raises ethical questions due to its rules.

On the other hand, a game like *Grand Theft Auto: San Andreas* raises ethical questions because of its game world and how we can play in it. Not, as it would seem at first, because of the representation of violence and urban decadence, but because of the ways the game as a system allows for player interaction within the game world. It is true that players are encouraged to interact with the world of *Grand Theft Auto: San Andreas* by means of what we would consider simulated unethical acts, but as a matter of fact, crime is penalized in the world of *Grand Theft Auto*. Committing a crime in the streets of San Andreas might raise the awareness of the police, and if the player is caught, then she will lose some money and all of the weapons she was carrying, which is a considerable gameplay penalty. Thus the rules of the game modify the player's interaction with the world, because if the player wants to survive, she has to take into account the police punishment. It is not a game about gratuitous violence, for each crime has a punishment.

How can we then analyze games as moral objects? The ethics of games are related to the ways players experience them, so it could be counterargued that considering games as moral objects is futile—the players will ultimately make the experience moral. This counterargument does not explain why some games are more prone to the construction of complex ethical discourses than others, and why abstract games[69] tend not to create ethical discourses (though remember that player communities can always create ethical discourses out of any game experience). There is something in games that cues the ludic experience, and makes it successful. That something is contained in the intertwining of the rules and the game world, in the space of possibility. As the space of possibility is partially defined prior to the game experience, and it is the outcome of the design process, this is where the ethics of computer games as objects has to be found.

Let's return to *XIII*: the game rules do not allow shooting the police, and thus there is a constraint in the player behavior, a constraint that clearly enforces an ethical discourse. To put it in the terms I have been using, *XIII*'s space of possibility is delimited by a set of ethical values afforded in the rules, which constrain the player's experience of the game world. Therefore, it is not correct to say that the *XIII* game world contains ethical values; neither is it correct to say that the rules of *XIII* are the embodiment of that specific ethical discourse. *XIII* is a moral object because it creates a space of ludic possibility that is determined by a set of ethical values.

As I have already stated, not all games are moral objects. Abstract games, which include a vast number of different genres and gameplay types, often cannot be considered moral objects because understanding their rules or their game world or both, from an ethical perspective, is an exercise of interpretation of the game world. Janet Murray read *Tetris* as a social allegory.[70] But it is a metaphorical interpretation: it is possible to play *Tetris* without understanding it as a moral object; furthermore, the possible "ethic" of *Tetris* does not affect gameplay, nor does it come from gameplay. Therefore, while it could be valid in some contexts to understand *Tetris* as an ethical object, the game is not ethical from a rules perspective. And even so, understanding *Tetris* as an ethical object is not productive in terms of explaining the ethics of computer games, or what ethical ludic experiences may be, since this understanding is, as I have said, a metaphorical reading of the game world.

This is not to say that it is impossible to have an abstract ethical game. The way the game system is designed, and its implications for the participation of different agents in the game experience, can bring an ethical dimension to an abstract game. Since game systems can be designed with embedded ethics, it is possible to think about abstract ethical games, though these are not common, and will most likely be confined to multiplayer games. So far I have not found interesting examples of ethical abstract games, but there are some examples that point at this possibility. Thinking about the online game *Cursor * 10* and its core mechanic,[71] based on cooperating with oneself in different iterations of time, the idea of a game in which players are faced iteratively with the consequences of their previous actions could possibly be an approach to abstract ethical games. In fact, it could be argued that *Cursor * 10* can be played as an ethical game, given the sudden detachment from the former self that the game encourages. Nevertheless, that would be another application of a metaphorical analysis of games as ethical experiences. So for now, it suffices to say that although it is not unthinkable that abstract games can be ethical objects, there are no convincing games of this kind yet.

With this in mind, I argue that the games that can be considered moral objects are those in which ethical discourses and values can be found embedded in the practices suggested by the rules and that take place in the space of possibility. If the space of possibility of a computer game can be analyzed using the tools of ethics, and if that analysis is corroborated by actual gameplay, then we can say that a specific computer game is a moral object.

Let's take two examples: the game *Manhunt* presents a set of rules that encourages violent acts, and the fictional world is geared toward

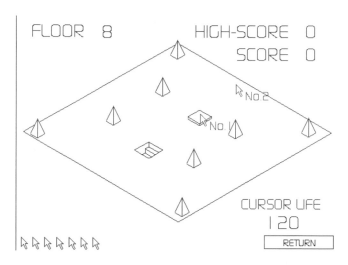

Figure 2.5
*Cursor * 10:* Single-player or multiplayer?

encouraging that gameplay. The game setting puts the player in control of
a morally despicable character who is forced, by some mysterious deus ex
machina, to commit unspeakable acts of cruelty in order to escape alive
from the making of a snuff movie. And, in the fictional world, the player
has no other choice: it is either kill, or be killed. *Manhunt* works ethically
as a mirror structure, for the game design, the rules, and the levels are
constructed to reflect this moral situation. There is only one way of
winning the game, and that is to comply with the instructions given in
the fictional world and commit these crimes. Both the levels and the rules
are designed to encourage those actions while making any other choices
impossible for the player. By creating a game world with a set of rules and
a level design that limits the player's choices, *Manhunt* creates an ethical
experience.

On the other hand, a game like *The Sims* can also be understood
as a moral object, but in a significantly different way. While *Manhunt*
creates a moral experience by constraining the players' actions accordingly
to the fictional world, *The Sims* offers a large degree of freedom to the
players—the rules only determine the context in which actions have
game meaning, and the game system reacts to them. But this freedom is
encapsulated precisely by the rules. While playing *The Sims* I decided

Figure 2.6
Manhunt: An Ethical Game about Murder and Gore

to create an avatar heavily inspired by the grunge rock musician Kurt Cobain. My avatar would have a large amount of money and a big house, but he would do nothing at all except lie on the sofa, play guitar, eat junk food, and drink alcohol. At some moment during this experience, my avatar refused to comply with my instructions. He started cleaning the house, adopted a healthier diet, and slept more. In the world of *The Sims*, the rules are there to enforce a certain ethical system behind the simulation, to the extent that the player is relieved of her interactive duties if the avatar's simulated existence cannot be accepted as a part of what the simulated environment ought to be, according to the rules and their ethical affordances.

Nonetheless, recognizing that the rules of a game can present ethical affordances is not enough to understand the ethics of computer games because this perspective does not take into account that players experience games. Yet it is crucial to acknowledge that the ethics of a game are partially determined by its system, by the game as object. This may also serve as a design paradigm for the development of games in which ethics play a coherent role in the gameplay, as I will argue later on. Games are not only objects, but also experiences triggered by that object. It is necessary to understand not only which games are ethically interesting, but also how we can understand their moral nature. Given the condition that ethically relevant games are those in which moral values are embedded in the space of possibility, it is necessary to understand how that space of possibility has an ontological existence, and how it relates to the phenomenological nature of games as experiences.

This perspective implies a latent distinction between games as objects and games as experiences[72] or, in Aristotelian terms, the *potentia* and the *actio* of games.[73] I will explain this difference more carefully: I can take the rulebook of any game, like chess, and read it. Holding that book in my hands, I can say: this is chess, and I am not making a mistake. On the other hand, I am neglecting not only the whole history of chess, but also many things that are a part of the game but that are not in that rule book: the physical presence or absence of the players, or the sudden glimpse of a flaw in the opponent's strategies. A game, we can agree, is not only its rules, its material aspect, but also its experience—the act of playing the game. A game is both its rules and the practical expression of those rules.

According to Aristotle's metaphysics, things present a potentiality, the capability of reaching a different and more complete state, which would be the actuality of that thing. The classic example is a boy being the potentiality of a man. In computer games, as in any other kind of game, this would mean that the rules of a game contain the potentiality of the game. But only when the game is played can we actually say something about the game as such. In a game like *Tetris*, the rule set (geometrical pieces fall down at an increasingly fast pace, and if the screen is filled with pieces, the game is over) presents the conditions for the game that the players have to accept in order to play. The rule set, on its own, contains the ways the game can be played, but only the presence of a player will activate those potentialities and make them become a game.

The potentiality of the game is then a designed formal system that predicts a certain experience by means of encouraging users to make some choices using predetermined game mechanics. We can analyze the rules of a game as ethical objects because they constitute the potentiality of a game. Nevertheless, we cannot say that it is the game's rule set or its design that sets its ethical values. A game is not the object we describe when we write about the rules and the game world, but the experience constructed by the interaction of a user with that world. In order to be able to understand the potentiality of a game, or a game as an object, we need to have experienced it first as a process. The understanding of games as objects provides an extraordinary insight into the formal aspects of the ethical capacities of games.

The distinction between potentiality and actuality provides an adequate framework for understanding games as objects without ignoring their procedural nature and the presence of players experiencing the game. I define the potentiality of a game as the material conditions of a system composed of rules intended to create a ludic experience. In other words, a game's potentiality is its formal system of rules and the game world it can create, without any agent experiencing them.

This game object has the potentiality to become something different yet related, and more complete: a game experience. The game experience is different from the game object because it presents a moral agent interacting with it, and it ceases being purely an object to become a procedural experience. And it is more complete because a game cannot be understood fully without being played. And so, a game as object can be understood as the potentiality of a more complete and different ontological entity, the game as experience.

We can use an analogy from architecture to explain this concept: blueprints predict to a large extent how the building will look and how it will be used. By looking at the blueprints, the skilled eye can imagine the building's possibilities, its constraints, and how those are projected into a concrete experience of architectural relevance. On the other hand, there are things that the blueprints do not predict. There are building uses that are not predetermined by the architect's blueprints, but that evolve from the use of the space. Similarly, there are uses of computer games that are not predicted by the formal system of rules, even though a skilled eye can predict to a certain extent, from the system of rules of the game, how it is going to be experienced by an ideal player.

Then again, the knowledge of games we can infer from their formal system is too limiting—the system of rules and the fictional world of the game say little or nothing about how the game is experienced, how the players will actually act, and what kind of behaviors will be enforced or will be considered unethical by the community. Even though games are objects, even though we can think and analyze the *potentiality* of the games, our inquiries must not stop there. We have to experience the games; we have to see them as *actuality* in order to understand what kind of ethical experiences they create.

Computer games can be moral objects because they fulfill a number of material conditions that predispose their users to experience a certain ethical reflection or behavior, because of their system of designed and engineered rules that create a world in and with which agents interact; a system designed to create a certain kind of experience determined by how the interaction is presented to the player and how the system reacts to the user's input.

Rules create affordances and constraints for interaction. The affordances of a designed object optimally show how the object should be used, and what its properties are. For instance, it is in the rules of *The Sims* and the therein-contained impossibility of playing a depressed character where we can find ethical affordances that determine the game values from a moral perspective—where we will find a first clue to understanding how the game was *intended* to be experienced. In the context of ethics, affordances have to be understood as those design elements that narrow any action the player can take. In the case of *Manhunt*, the level design in general presents a number of affordances cuing the player to experience the game in a certain way: it eases the practice of the most brutal murders, which yield a better survival probability, by strategically placing some architectonic spaces and objects where nonplayer characters' paths are. It could be said that levels are designed to facilitate these simulated brutal murders, the core of the ethical gameplay of *Manhunt*.

Computer games are designed with a set of affordances and constraints that can create or be determined by ethical values, thus making the game a designed moral object. These ethical affordances and constraints constitute the game as an object, the formal system of the game and the game world it creates. The formal system of a game is its rules, both the game rules and the simulation rules. The ways those rules control the player's interaction with the system and the response to that interaction can be ethically relevant.

But games as objects are not exclusively their formal systems of rules. In considering what is relevant when analyzing games as moral objects, it is fundamental to include the game world. For a computer game to be ethically relevant we need a simulated game world with which the player can feel a certain affinity. In other words, the representational layer of the simulation needs to be familiar. I am using "representational" to define the semantic layer of the simulation (what Juul would call the fictional world); that is, the signs that make it possible for the player to understand that world as coherent within the gameplay.[74]

For a game world to be ethically relevant, the representation and the actions afforded to the player raise ethical issues by means of their relation to the perceived real world. Let's take the infamous "prostitute hack" in *Grand Theft Auto: Vice City*[75] as an example. In this game, a player can have virtual sex with a prostitute, thereby gaining some extra health, and then kill her to recover the money. Here the simulation layers and the representational layers of the game raise the ethical issues: the morals of the rules as well as the morals of the representation. It is true that this is, from a formal point of view, an action allowed by the rules of the game, which gives the player a game-relevant advantage. Nevertheless, it is ethically questionable because of what it simulates and how it communicates that simulation via the representational layer.

A game could also relate to players in ways in which the ethical issues arise from the game situation, and not the rules or the system of the game. The game machine *Painstation*[76] is a total modification of the game *Pong* that has to be played using a specific cabinet. This cabinet is equipped with instruments that, if a player fails, will inflict a moderate amount of pain. *Painstation* is an example of how to embed ethical values in a game of abstract content. By physically punishing the players that commit mistakes, this game mod gives a moral dimension to its design. What raises ethical issues is not the rule system of the game, but the physical punishment that players suffer when failing one of the goals. In other words, it is not the rule system that raises ethical issues, but the particular implementation of the game cabinet.

Let's return to *XIII* and perform a brief ethical analysis of the game as a designed object: the game fiction presents to the player the character of an amnesic assassin. The player controls this character. There is a rule that states that if a police officer is killed by the player, the progression in the level will be stopped and the player will be forced to start from the beginning. Thus, on a first layer, there is ethical meaning in *XIII* as a designed game: a rule controls behavior on grounds of moral reasoning.

If we take into consideration the relations between the game world and the game system, the game shows a lack of coherence: if the player is an assassin, why can't she shoot policemen? Why is the game system evaluating the way the player experiences the game world? This contradiction shows how a rule can have ethical values. It exemplifies the prevailing of rules over game world representation in the ethical analysis of games. But the contradiction is suggesting that we need to take another step: if the police-shooting rule is ethical, yet it contradicts the game world fiction, how will players experience the game? In other words, is it enough to say that because a rule can be interpreted as an ethical statement, the game design is ethical?

I will answer these questions in more detail in the following chapters. For now, it suffices to say that an ethical game design can only be so if the values embedded in the design are coherently presented to the player. A player of *XIII* can feel that the police-shooting rule is actually depriving her of her moral reasoning, of her experience of the game world as an ethical agent. The design has values, but are those values creating an ethical experience? The answer is no, because players are deprived of their ethical thinking capacities. Morally embedded game design is a necessary but not sufficient condition for the understanding of the ethics of computer games.

In this chapter I have argued that the ethics of computer games as objects are the ethics of their design, including the rules and the game world. In order to understand and describe how a game can potentially raise ethical issues, or how it could enhance the experience of the game world by including ethical gameplay, we need to pay attention to its underlying rule structure and how it is projected into the game world. Given that computer games are designed objects, their ethics are present in the formal elements that constitute the game as an experience. Thus, game design can be considered as the task of creating an ethically relevant system. This also implies the possibility of creating games that are conscious about their own ethical ontology, their nature as moral objects.

A computer game is a designed system of rules that creates a game world. These rules and that game world can have embedded ethical values: the behaviors they create, and how those are communicated to players, constitute the ethics of computer game design. The creators of games are then ethically responsible for the design of the rules and world, while players are responsible for their experience of the game—the ways they interpret and enact the embedded ethical values of a computer game.

Ultimately, the ethics of computer games are the ethics of its system and how players experience that system. In the next chapter I will introduce an analysis of players as independent ethical beings capable of understanding and enjoying the experiences they go through when interacting with computer games from a moral perspective, which will complete this initial approach to the ethics of computer games.

3 Players as Moral Beings

Heraclitus wrote *"ethos anthropoi daimon"*—character is fate, or the design philosophy behind *Grand Theft Auto IV*.[1]

Niko Bellic just wants to begin anew, to leave behind the memories of war, the crimes, the ghosts of his past. Liberty City promises the American dream, a path to comfort and success, a clean slate from where the tired, the poor, and the huddled masses can prosper and fulfill their dreams. Niko Bellic arrives in Liberty City desiring nothing more than peace and prosperity, and the promised land with no past.

The reality, though, is quite different. Niko will soon be involved with shady characters, criminals at the brutal base of the mafia ranks. There are no jobs for Niko beyond those where who he was and what he did are significant assets. Niko is driven back to his past, to violence and crime as the only way—not to prosper, but to survive. In the world of *Grand Theft Auto*, there is no redemption, and character is fate.

Grand Theft Auto IV is an extremely compelling ethical game experience. Players control Niko Bellic, a Serbian war veteran in search of the American dream in Liberty City. Niko is presented as an affable, sarcastic, tough-but-tender man whose dreams are often in confrontation with reality. Players hear him complain about his past and about the dark side of violence and crime, and dream about how he would like to leave all that behind and move on. Niko just wants to be a better man.

Yet the game in which we play him is a gritty take on urban criminality, comparable with *Goodfellas* or *Mean Streets*: contemporary tales of violent men trapped in their own fates. Niko claims he wants to rebel against his past, but his character, as the game evolves, drives his fate: *Grand Theft Auto IV* is a violent, merciless dystopian tale about the American dream.

There are many aspects of *Grand Theft Auto IV* that are interesting from an ethical perspective, but I will single out one that reveals the importance of players in the ethical experience of a computer game. When playing *Grand Theft Auto IV*, we are presented with noninteractive dialogues in which the character expresses his dislike for the violent downward spiral of crimes he is trapped in since his arrival in Liberty City.

Grand Theft Auto IV is ethically relevant because of its sense of player responsibility. From the outset, we know that Niko despises the man he was and wants to begin anew. But as players, we are given the task of completing these criminal missions and fulfilling the fate of Niko Bellic. *Grand Theft Auto IV* is built around the fundamental tension between a character who does not want more violence, and a player who is commanded to play this violence. This is a tension that takes place between the fiction of the game and the actions afforded to players, its gameplay. There are other ways to play *Grand Theft Auto IV*, though. There are nonviolent, noncriminal missions that still allow for the enjoyment of the game world. But if we want to really play *Grand Theft Auto IV*, we need to become criminals. It is our responsibility to make that choice. Like any tragic hero, Niko Bellic is controlled by forces more powerful than himself: fate, gods, or players.

Grand Theft Auto IV is, among other things, a contemporary classical tragedy, a game experience built around ethos and daimon, values and destiny. *Grand Theft Auto IV* is a game about urban and cultural exploration but, more fundamentally, is an exploration of the meaning of being a player: what are the consequences of our actions? What are our values, as players and as human beings? All these questions will be answered in this chapter, in which I define the player as an ethical agent.

This is a key concept in the general argument of this book. I am advocating for a player that is morally aware and capable of reflecting upon the nature of her acts within the game world. This reflective capacity goes beyond the focus on goals and objectives, and effectively acts as a moral reasoning tool. As players we are moral beings, and our actions within a game are evaluated precisely from our nature as moral players. I will present in some detail the philosophical arguments behind these ideas, since it is a crucial cornerstone for the understanding of the ethics of computer games.

I have already reasoned that games are processes. In this same line, it is possible to understand the act of playing a computer game as an act of subjectivization, a process that creates a subject connected to the rules of the game.[2] Nevertheless, this player-subject is not confined to the borders of the game. The player is a reflective subjectivity who comes into the game with her own cultural history as player, together with her cultural and embodied presence. Becoming a player is the act of creating balance between fidelity to the game situation and the fact that the player as subject is only a subset of a cultural and moral being who voluntarily plays, bringing to the game a presence of culture and values that also affect the experience.

In this chapter I will explore this process of becoming a player. To this end I will again take up the concept of game as object, framing it within Michel Foucault's theories about power.[3] These structures create a being, a subjectivity that can be explained using the theory of Alain Badiou,[4] which has a certain tradition in the field of computer game research.[5] Barbara Becker's theories on the body-subject will lead a methodological turn toward a phenomenological and hermeneutical understanding of the player. This turn will set the player as subject into perspective, providing an approach for understanding the player as a moral being.[6] This will be the conclusion of this chapter: because the player is a subject that exists in a game situation, and because this subject operates by interpreting this situation both within the ethics and culture of her experience as player and as a human being, the player as subject can legitimately be considered a moral being. A computer game is then a moral object that is actualized by a moral agent.

If there is an argument I believe is crucial for the understanding of the ethics of computer games, it is the consideration of players as ethical beings. As players we reflect critically on what we do in a game world during a game experience, and it is this capacity that can turn the ethical concerns traditionally raised by computer games into interesting, meaningful tools for creative expression, a new means for cultural richness.

3.1 Becoming a Player

I turn on my PlayStation 2 console. I insert a game disc: *Rez*.[7] The game starts. I am immersed in a world of lights, colors, and sounds. I don't have instructions on what to do, or about this world. I start playing, hitting the buttons of the controller, and quickly I find out the rules and mechanics: *Rez* plays essentially like *Space Invaders*, only the experience is very different, based on the beats and rhythms I am creating by shooting down enemies and how those beats affect the evolving background music and the display of colors on-screen. I also know what I cannot do: there is a world surrounding my avatar that I cannot explore, and I cannot just stay immobile, staring. For me to enjoy this experience, I have to play according to those rules I have deduced, because then and only then does *Rez* give away its secrets, the pleasure of its ludic experience.

The situation I have just described happens in any linear computer game.[8] Playing a computer game is an act composed of multiple actions, some physical, some psychological, some cultural, some ethical, and some aesthetic. In the act of playing a game there are a series of operators that condition the kind of process or experience we are facing as players: it is not the same to play a massively multiplayer online role-playing game like *Everquest*[9] as it is to play a simulated massively multiplayer online role-playing game like the *.hack* series.[10]

If we want to understand the complexity of computer game ethics, we need to understand players as moral agents and how they relate their ethics to those of the game as object. To understand the ethics of video games, we need to consider the game as object, the game as experience, and the process linking both.

Let's return to both the material and the experiential aspects of the act of playing *Rez*: it begins with a physical manipulation of an object, the game disk. Once the game as object is initiated, it becomes an experience: by hitting the buttons I am actualizing *Rez* as the computer game it is, beyond its nature as object. I do so by discovering the rules—as a cultural being that has been playing games since a very early age, I have developed a repertoire that allows me to identify patterns of rules and apply them. Once I figured out the rules, I understood what my actions in the game were supposed to be and acted upon that knowledge. I did so because playing a game is acknowledging and obeying the rules. If I don't follow the rules, or if I never understood them, the game would not take place as a successful experience. Furthermore, the game is coded to punish me by not letting me play if I am not subdued by its rules. If I want to be a player, I have to understand the rules and play by them.[11]

In sports there are penalties against those who do not follow the rules, and in online computer games there are often bans for those who use software or hardware designed to obtain unfair advantages. Games are designed with tools to enforce the following of the rules, tools that are not only hardwired, but also to some extent lent to the players so that they can enforce their own set of values. An example of the tools for enforcing rule obedience would be the fact that if a player enters cheat codes in *Grand Theft Auto: Vice City*, she is warned that perhaps the save files will be corrupted, and her progress will not be recorded. On the other hand, a game like *A Tale in the Desert*[12] actually enforces the community policing that is commonplace in MMORPGs, creating a society in which players can be elected to rule over the world, enforcing policies and punishments. While these two examples represent extremes, they show the importance of the game design as an enforcer of rules, and also the importance of players when enforcing the codes of practice and behavior within a game, according to their previous gaming experience.

I am here referring to the set of knowledge that players have acquired by playing games, be they digital or not. This knowledge helps players build patterns when facing a new game, deciphering the rules and the modes of interaction and allowing us to learn to play new games with relative ease.[13] The repertoire also works on an ethical level: the more computer games we have played, the more we can identify, and in case of their absence, demand, those ethical constraints the design may pose.

The example of my personal experience with *Rez* is that of a successful game played by a player with a rather extensive repertoire. On the other hand, a player with less experience with computer games, when first playing a game like *Burnout 3*, will most likely hesitate to ram and smash other cars, even though that is the sanctioned-by-design way of achieving the goals. This happens because the *Burnout* series plays with the convention of car/racing games, in which crashing and destroying your avatar/car is generally punished. Because the conventions that we use to form our repertoire are reversed, the first experience of *Burnout* is rather surprising.

The repertoire shows that players are beings who come to a game experience with the cultural baggage of previous game experience. This implies that players with a certain experience will have a different subject configuration than newbies, which leads me to formulate the following hypothesis: players build their ethical subjectivity—their capacity to ethically interpret the content and experience of a game—only by being players, by virtue of experience. Playing, then, develops players' ethics through the development of their player repertoires and their virtues,[14] alone and as a part of a player community.

I have argued previously that games can be defined ontologically as ergodic systems of rules. A game is ergodic because it has built-in rewards and punishments for successfully experiencing it. These procedures are those game rules that can be applied to evaluating the players' experience. For example, the completion percentages in games like *Grand Theft Auto IV* or *Burnout 3*, which mark how much of the game the player has completed, are used to measure success in overcoming the games' challenges. Even the high scores in arcade games operate in a similar fashion: they are only given after the players have lost or completed the game, and serve as a numeric evaluation of how successful the game experience has been.

Within this perspective, it is plausible to say that when a player is immersed in this system, her behavior is shaped by the game system, its rules and mechanics. A player will act within the rules that govern the game world, which determine what is possible, impossible, and relevant or not within game experience. This is not to say that players always subordinate to or play by the rules: a cheater, for example, does not play by the rules, but can only be a cheater if she acknowledges the rules and explores their boundaries, as Suits has already pointed out.[15] Any kind of courtesy or sportsmanship that might lead to gameplay that lets the weakest players win (such as when playing games with small children) is seen as not strictly obeying the rules, but those rules are still necessary for the behavior to exist. Rules create behaviors.

These rules have to be freely accepted and agreed upon by the players.[16] It is only when these rules are accepted and acted upon by the player that the actuality of the game takes place. This transition operates by means of a power structure in the Foucaultian sense. There are three reasons why Foucault provides an interesting framework to describe the relations between players and the game: first, power and power structures in Foucault are devoid of any negative or positive conditioning, they merely exist. There is not any kind of value statement attached to the ontological being of games as power structures. Second, power structures are prerequisites for the subject. Likewise, I will argue that the game as an object is a prerequisite for the being of the player. Finally, the later works of Foucault on ethics are strongly influenced by classical Greek ethics, and thus it correlates with my predominantly Aristotelian approach.[17]

Foucault invokes power in ways that distance him from most philosophers and political scientists. For him, there is power in the societies we live in, but it is not possible to consider it in isolation. Power has ceased to exist in an absolute way: it only exists in relations, operations, or structures between agents: "there is no such entity as power, with or without capital letter; global, massive or diffused; concentrated or distributed. Power exists only as exercised on other, only when it is put into action, even though, of course, it is inscribed in a field of sparse available possibilities underpinned by permanent structures."[18] Power is manifested in the relations established among agents, but how does it manifest itself?

Power is a force of creation; it has generative attributes. Knowledge is created when agents are inserted in a power structure.[19] What power does when establishing the relations between agents is to produce something that was not there before, and it does so by delimiting, plotting, and relating the possibilities and the actions of these agents. Thus power need not be a negative element or a source of subjective or collective stress, as many conflict theorists might have argued.[20] Power in this decentralized way is the cause of the creation of certain knowledge between the agents involved in a specific power structure: "what makes power hold good, what makes it accepted, is simply the fact that it doesn't only weigh on us as a force that says no, but that it traverses and produces things, it induces pleasure, forms knowledge, produces discourse. It needs to be considered a productive network which runs through the whole social body."[21] Furthermore, to exist as a networked structure between agents, power has to be freely accepted, acknowledged, and recognized by those agents: "Thus, in order for power relations to come into play, there must be at least a certain degree of freedom on both sides."[22]

The productive being of power is twofold: power produces knowledge, and it also produces the subjects that make that power relation exist. By acknowledging the existence of a certain power relation between them, agents are constituted as subjects related to the knowledge they are creating: "the individual, with his identity and characteristics, is the product of a relation of power exercised over bodies, multiplicities, movements, desires, forces . . . the individual is an effect of power, and at the same time, or precisely to the extent to which it is that effect, it is the element of its articulation."[23] Power is a productive form of creating subjectivity. Those individuals who are freely involved in a power structure experience the productive nature of power by becoming subjects.

Given these premises, I will henceforth argue that computer games are power structures. Power creates subjects, and so games create players. The process of experiencing a game and becoming a player needs to take into account how the nature of the game contributes to the creation of that subjectivity. The game's ontological nature initially defines the ontological position of its subjects, the players. That is, the game as ethical object establishes the starting point for the process of subjectivization that takes place in the act of playing a game. A player is then at least partially affected in her moral being by the game she is experiencing.

If a computer game is a power structure, then the players are subjects of that structure. When I played *Rez*, I deduced the rules using my experience as a player of other games, and then I became a player of that game. If I tried not to follow the rules of the game and refused to, for example, shoot at the nonplayer characters, then the game would "punish" me with a "game over" screen. But if I follow the instructions, I enjoy the designed ludic pleasures of *Rez*. Only because I acknowledge that there is a game with clear rules, and only because I voluntarily accept to play by those rules, the game *Rez* comes into being and so do I as a player.

Games create subjectivities because they operate as power structures. Their ontology as objects starts a subjectivization process on their users that makes them become players of that game. This process, like any power structure, creates knowledge and values: the rules become knowledge, the player's repertoire. In this sense, the game provides a context and a set of principles that, when accepted by the player, create a subjectivity. The player is also aware of her state of being as a player. In order for the player to remain engaged in the game, successfully enjoying the freely accepted power relations, those relations need to be preserved, and for them to be preserved, the player needs to make the game situation prevail. The player is not only created by being attached to the game, she is also the keeper of its existence, since the absence of players means the absence of game. Thus it is possible to argue that players are responsible for the game's well-being. For instance, it is up to players of online worlds to create and enhance the social rules that govern the games. It is players who, to the extent the developers allow them, create behavior policies and control other players' behavior, leaving the developers the role of refereeing.[24] Active behavior by the player-subject is relevant because players are cultural beings that share a game culture in a game community.

There is another element that needs to be taken into consideration: for a power structure to exist, it has to be not only accepted, but also needs to be perceived as such. In the later works of Michel Foucault, his ethical theory took a drastic turn toward a more classical Greek approach, returning to a kind of communitarian ethics.[25] Acknowledging the importance of the community in the constitution of the game as a power structure implies extending the ethical responsibility for the game's well-being to that player community. Furthermore, it also implies that the player-subject should be ethically conscious of the nature of the power structure in which she is immersed. But what does it mean to be a player, or to become a player? To answer this question, I will use the works of French philosopher Alain Badiou, especially his work *Ethics: An Essay on the Understanding of Evil*,[26] where he links his theory of the becoming of the subject to ethics.[27]

But before delving into philosophy again, let's briefly return to computer games. *Sim City*[28] provides the user with a simulation of a city that the player has to create, expand, and develop over time. To do so, the player is presented with a set of simulation tools ranging from construction sets to policy makers, comprising the core of *Sim City*'s gameplay. Playing this simulation implies accepting the tools that we are given as system users. If we want to build a city that evolves successfully, given the parameters for success and failure built into the system, we need to accept those policies and apply them. *Sim City* is a North American computer game: its modeled economic systems and policies are those closer to the liberal market economy of the United States.[29] The example I will use is taxes: for the city to have inhabitants, taxes have to be rather low, below that of countries in Europe with different economic and cultural perceptions of the public good.

As a citizen, and as a cultural being, I am European, and I believe in a model of society that values the community in terms of its economic policies. Nevertheless, when playing *Sim City*, I do not hesitate to use policies with which in principle I do not agree. I do so because otherwise the game would be harder, perhaps impossible to play. When I engage in the act of playing *Sim City*, some of the cultural and political elements of my subjectivity are modified in order to achieve a successful experience of the game. Even some of the elements that are tied deeply to the values that I hold as a cultural being are set aside in seeking the ludic experience that *Sim City* promises.

But let's move beyond political ideas and serious games. The computer game *Vib-Ribbon*[30] uses its software to create challenges from the output of the game's music. When playing that game I am presented with a set of tasks, challenges, and rules regarding how I can play that music: *Vib-Ribbon* is a bizarre platform game where the levels and their challenges are generated based on the input of music loaded from a CD. As a player of *Vib-Ribbon*, I listen to the music in a rather different way: instead of understanding its formal beauty, I perceive it as a set of challenges that I need to fulfill in order to enjoy the ludic experience. The boundaries of the ludic experience are expanded, showing that the player is actually an embodied subjectivity beyond the graphical representation of the game world because, much like when playing a real instrument, players *play* the music, both in

Figure 3.1
Sim City: No Wealthfare State, Thanks!

the productive sense and in the ludic meaning of the word. *Vib-Ribbon* is an abstract game, almost a conceptual piece of art. To play it we need to consider only our rhythmical sense, which is a highly embodied sense: we play this game with our full body. Because we are embodied, we can understand that the rhythm of the music becomes a physical challenge in which we need to prevail if we want to succeed in the game; the music becomes rewarded actions that make sense and take place in our experience of the game. The game thus creates a subjectivity that embodies the values given to rhythmical mastery.

In this context, I argue that a player becomes a player-subject upon entering the game experience, when actualizing the potentiality of the game into a concrete experience. A player can then be defined as the subject that comes into being when playing a game. It is the mutual existence of the game and the player that makes the game's potentiality become actuality. The player is the subject/agent that, when experiencing a given game, comes into being; and similarly, it is only when there is an agent experiencing the game that we can consider it a process and not an object.

What are the conditions and characteristics of the player as a subject? In Badiou's philosophy, the subject comes into being when exposed to a process of truth, to an *événement*, (henceforth an "event").[31] An event is an act of absolute truth that shatters the established knowledge, a situation that calls for a compromise: "the event is nothing—just a sort of illumination—but the consequences of an event within a situation are always very different and it is true that there are major consequences, long sequences of truth, or brief sequences."[32] An event is also an experience of delimited boundaries with a series of imperatives that have to be assumed in order to become a subject. A game will be here considered operationally similar to an event: a delimited system with prerequisites that qualify their users to become subjects.

A game operates as an event that creates a subject, a subject that needs to be faithful to the event's constitution to come into being.[33] The constitution of the game as event is its ontology: the rules of the game and its game world. Faithful to those principles, the player as subject is created. Not being faithful to the rules implies not being faithful to the event, and therefore losing the ontological status of subject. When playing *Rez*, I have to be faithful to the game as experience if I want to enjoy the ludic process in which I am immersed. The subject created by *Rez* is a subject faithful to the harmonic interactive rhythms and colors triggered in the ludic act: it is in the fidelity to the game as an event where *Rez* becomes a successful synesthetic experience. Likewise, it is in the fidelity to the universe, economy, and highly competitive and associational society we are presented in *Eve Online*[34] where the player finds the pleasure of the ludic experience, where the player and the game come into full, actual being. *Eve Online* is a game for dedicated players: breaking that convention—not showing up or being less interested in all the trading or piracy rules and possibilities that the game offers—means a breakdown of the category of subject that arises from playing the game, which means the effective end of the player's subjectivity.

Games as events require commitment. We have all met players that did not take a game seriously and, by doing so, enraged other players. And cheaters are considered, in computer games, sports, and casual games, the worst kind of individuals one can meet.[35] This is because they do not commit to the rules of the game and the game experience. Being a player is an act of commitment to the rules, to the social community, and to the game experience.

A subject is, in Badiou, "the bearer . . . of a fidelity," a subject "in no way pre-exists the process . . . he is absolutely nonexistent in the situation 'before' the event."[36] The player does not exist before playing a game; that is, the player of *Vib-Ribbon* does not exist before playing *Vib-Ribbon* for the first time. But she certainly does during and after—carrying through the truth or knowledge from one process of subjectivization to the next, thus establishing the cultural tradition and the repertoire allowing players to deduce rules when exposed to a game for the first time. Nevertheless, this subjectivity presents a series of conditions and characteristics that are specific and critical for the understanding of the ethics of computer games. For example: even if we are not playing a game, we can participate in the player community as *players*, like in a fan convention or an online forum. Furthermore, our mood and our ideas can be altered by a game experience. We can be angry because we have lost in *Counter-Strike* and we are punished by having to witness the game in spectator mode—we are not *actively* playing, but we are still players.

The subject created in the act of playing becomes a part of the multisubjectivity of the agent that experienced the game. Thus, it is possible to relate to the game community without playing a game. Because a process of subjectivization is a strong ontological procedure, as long as there is a hint of the event that created that subject, the subject will come forth. For example: when I started playing *World of Warcraft* I created the subject that plays this game, faithful to the experience it provides. That subject plays *World of Warcraft* within the parameters that make the game an event that creates a subjectivity, but I also reflect upon my gameplay and interact with the community, thinking about the situation according to the game. The fidelity to the game extends to all those situations that can be thought of and/or acted in by the subject of the game. When participating in the community discussions I am also a subject true to the event of the game, even though I am not immersed in actual gameplay.

The player-subject is not limited to the game experience once it is created: it operates as a relevant subjectivity in every situation in which the subject can be successfully faithful to the game. The game as actuality—the experience of the game—is larger than the mere gameplay sessions: the game is every situation in which the subject that is created is operational. What this implies is that there is a connection between the player-subject and the other subjectivities present in our daily life. Being a player is just a subset of our being as multiple subjects, and what I am describing here are the necessary conditions for this specific subjectivity, the player, to arise. In this sense, the player-subject is not an isolated moral agent but an agent in constant dialogue, evaluation, and interpretation within the experience of the game situated in a world and in a culture.

Summarizing, the player as subject exists when it is operational, when the event it is faithful to is true. And that need not happen exclusively in the phenomenological experience of the game; it can happen outside the game as well, when the subject sports claims that are true for the game, but not true for any other world. For instance, if I talk about the importance of urban representation in *Half-Life 2*, I am speaking as a player-subject, because the statements and the frame of mind I am using are true for the game *Half-Life 2*. This extends the influence of games, and of their ethics, beyond the act of playing and into the realm of cultural behavior.

What are the ethical foundations of this subject? They are the ethics of truth, the ethics of aspiring to good, which Badiou identifies as the ethics of keeping faithful to the event. What is interesting about Badiou's ethics is that they presuppose that the subject that comes into being in the event is an ethical being, a being committed to doing good, where good is the fidelity to the event. The subject that comes into being is a moral agent, and is entitled to moral judgment within the event, and to apply the principles of the event.

This does not mean that players are mechanical beings that mindlessly follow instructions. In *Quake*[37], players found that if they took the rocket launcher, aimed it down, jumped, and then shot, they could jump higher, thus obtaining certain tactical advantages. Some could argue that these players were not being faithful to the game because their bending of the rules seems to contradict obedience to these rules. Nevertheless, the "rocket jump" is a part of playing *Quake*, another strategy. I will say, then, that the fidelity of the player is present as long as her actions are coherent with the game rules and the game world, and do not contradict a rule.[38] Rocket jumping in *Quake*, then, is an action that is both coherent in the game world and according to the rules of the game, and it does not contradict any rule. As such it is faithful to the game as event.

On the other hand, the reaction to cheaters shows the ethical nature of players as subjects. Player communities and game designers tend to see this type of player as a source of discomfort, and they stress that cheating has to be avoided and punished. Cheaters are perceived as such because they are subjects unfaithful to the event. A player of *Counter-Strike* who uses a software cheat to be able to see through walls, granting her the maximum benefit when playing against other players, is not being faithful to the event that created that subjectivity. A cheater perceives the conditions of the game not as an event, not as a ludic experience, but as something that can be modified with or without considering the possible harm caused to other players—they do not think about the situation according to the event. They break the game experience by refusing to become a subject and, instead, pervert those conditions by which all the other members of the community are constituted as subjects.

Summarizing, a player is the subjectivity that is created from the conditions of a game experience, and who is a part of a larger culture and community of players who are also subjects. The player-subject exists in fidelity to the game, to its rules and the experience that it creates, a fidelity that is related to the in-game coherence of her actions and choices and the noncontradiction of any game rule. This implies that the player will act in ways that preserve the fidelity of this event, thus becoming a moral being, capable of reasoning about the ethics of the process that created it as a subject.

I have used Foucault's concept of power structures to establish the ontology of the game as moral object and the player as subjectivity, stating that the actuality of computer games operates as a productive network of power that generates a subjectivization process. I analyzed that process of subjectivization with Alain Badiou's philosophy of the subject, which led me to conclude that players as beings are subjects created by and related to the game as a productive event; subjects need to be faithful to the game in order to become players. Badiou's approach also allowed the introduction of the player as an ethical subject, as the subject ought to have the inclination to preserve her subjectivity within the event.

Nevertheless, there are some objections to these theories that need to be fleshed out before constructing a comprehensive approach to the ethics of computer games. The main objection to Foucault is that his theory of power does not allow for any kind of ethical research that does not fall into relativism. Foucault advocates the end of the modern conception of the subject as a unified entity. Instead, the subject is a multiplicity of subjects who occur when inserted into different power relations. Thus it is not possible to state any ethical approach that might contribute to the understanding of the relevant ethical questions in a general way.

In this book I am not advocating such a relativist perspective. From the very outset, I have stated that computer games have ethics that can be analyzed and determined. Furthermore, I argue that computer game players are ethical beings who use a series of ethical tools in their experience of games. I argue for the consideration of the ethics of computer games as a set of beliefs, values, and practices that can be understood in a rather general, while not totally universal, way. The ethical analysis I am presenting here will be flexible enough to approach ethical dilemmas in computer games across cultures, and thus Foucault's moral relativism is discarded.

Alain Badiou's work, on the other hand, operates as a very functional explanation of the process of becoming a player within the set of rules and practices of the game. Nevertheless, when it comes to ethics, Badiou's work has to be handled carefully since in the original work the subject that takes place in the event is a moral subject, a subject to and for ethics, but whatever is outside the event is "the human animal";[39] that is, beyond the categories of good and evil. For Badiou, ethics only exist in the act of the event, while without an event there are no moral dimensions to be discussed.

This radical approach to ethics poses a series of problems when applied to computer games. Essentially, it would be odd to justify an ethical approach that only considers the subject ethically accountable and responsible when it takes place in an event. Players are subjects, but they are not detached from the larger set of subjectivities that constitute who we are. That is, outside the game as event we are also moral beings. Just this caveat would not be enough to justify these lines shaping my use of Badiou's philosophy. But it also seems to be out of order to understand the subjectivity of the player as totally detached from the moral subject we are as cultural and embodied beings. The fact that we play when immersed in a ludic experience does not mean that the created subject is impermeable to the ethical presence of the larger ethical being of which we are a part.

For example, when playing the first-person shooter *Perfect Dark*[40] for the Nintendo 64, I discovered that I could shoot the guards I knocked out, thus preventing them from waking up and catching me by surprise. On one occasion I used a scoped handgun to kill the lying soldier. Once I shot him "dead," the digital body crudely simulated the muscular spasms of a body when killed in this way, as popularized by cinema. That simulation disgusted me to the extent that I quit the game, and I never repeated such acts again when playing *Perfect Dark*. If the player is subject to the ethics that take place within the event of playing, why did I react like this? Why is a game like *Custer's Revenge*[41] considered an aberration? Why do some users of *Super Columbine Massacre RPG!*[42] react so violently in the discussion forums against this game?[43]

When playing a game, the player creates a set of ethical values inspired by the game, derived from the game culture and community, and strictly applicable within the game situation, including participation in the different layers of involvement of the game community. But the player is also limited by the fact that she is a culturally embodied being, and her own ethical values and practices cannot be easily suspended. In more Aristotelian words, we cannot avoid being moral animals.

Therefore, to understand the possibilities that reflecting about the player as subject gives to the ethical research of computer games, I will now argue for an expansion of the notion of player as subject. To do so, I will use Barbara Becker's theories on embodiment to provide a first step for the analysis of the player as a moral subject.

3.2   The Player as Ethical Skin

The player is a subjectivity that arises when faithful to the event of a game. But as I have mentioned, this approach does not take into consideration the ethical subject *outside* the event. The player-subject would be detached from her culture and her embodied presence, and as such the ethical risks of playing games would be obvious. The player-subject is only a subset of the larger cultural beings we are—we cannot avoid bringing into the game experience as much as we take away from the game experience. I will now propose a way of understanding the relations between the player-subject, its process of generation, and the larger cultural and embodied set of subjects that we all are. To do so, I will draw on the work of philosopher Barbara Becker,[44] especially her phenomenological understanding of the body-subject as a relevant experiential/phenomenological being.

My central argument is that the agent of the ludic experience, the player, is not an animal beyond morality. Players are subjects that take place when ethical beings play a game; when there is a moral being who voluntarily and freely engages in the experience of the game. We must take this into consideration when analyzing the ethics of the player; otherwise, we are giving absolute moral agency to a subject that takes place only within the boundaries of a game experience. We need to clarify how the player-subject comes into being within the experience of a game by a moral being, and how these subjectivities correlate.

For Becker, the issue of the body in cyberspace has to be taken into consideration from a phenomenological perspective, which yields an interesting result: "we find the concept of the double existence of the body. It is simultaneously an external being that can be experienced and an internal being that experiences other, and thus it is ambiguous, somewhere between a material object and a pure consciousness, an intermediate phenomenon between nature and culture."[45] This body with double existence is what Becker calls the "body-subject." The body-subject, at the same time perceived and perceiving, experiencing and experienced, is not self-generated, but created both intrinsically and extrinsically by the experience of the world: "the body-subject therefore does not only depend on individual self-creation and self-determination, but is also governed by the strange and unavailable laws of the world."[46]

The body-subject takes place in the world of experiences, both passively and actively, by means of the act of touching, "simultaneously giving and perceiving meaning."[47] To touch is to instantiate this body-subject, to give it a conscious place in the experience from which it comes: "touch is never the product solely of a controlling intentional subject. It can only be understood at the point of its emergence."[48] By touching, we constitute ourselves as body-subjects in the world we experience, but doing so is not to be free of those affordances of the experienced world, affordances that can be in human agents or in objects: "touch is an act of responsivity, a resonance, because we are always answering to the atmosphere and the affordances given by the objects or persons with which we are in touch."[49] Becker's phenomenology returns the physical body to a place in philosophical discourse through the poetic use of the concept of skin and touch.

Similarly, I argue that the player as subject is a body-subject; it does not have a full body, real or simulated, but it does present some qualities of embodiment. The complex and highly detailed process of avatar creation in games like *City of Heroes*[50] is a symptom of this fact. In *City of Heroes*, the player is encouraged to create her avatar in grand detail, using multiple options for customization. For some players, the way their avatar looks is extremely relevant. And this high level of detail in customization is present in many contemporary computer games, from *EverQuest 2*[51] to *The Sims 2*[52] to *The Elder Scrolls IV: Oblivion*,[53] where the customization options are so many that creating the avatar could possibly take hours. In the light of these examples, I would argue that the detail that computer games provide to the player when it comes to customizing the virtual body's physical appearance is related to the necessity of creating a skin that is both "oneself" and "other," because it has a component of strangeness that puts the player in contact with the virtual world, the "other" world.[54]

This is not to say that there is a correlation between the player as body-subject, the player as skin, and the avatar's virtual appearance. The fact that we can modify our avatar's looks is a symptom of the larger process of subjectivization into the body-subject that plays. The player as body-subject has to be understood as the subidentity created during the play experience. The subjectivity of the player is our skin when interacting with a computer game: it marks the boundaries of the subject, but also determines how much we can interact with the digital world. Playing is putting on the player-skin and experiencing the world and the game world within it.

When playing, we are a body-subject that becomes the significant element in our relation with the game world in the broadest sense, including the game community and the other players. Understanding the player-subject as a skin is a useful metaphor because it connects the internal, individual subjectivity of the player with the larger communitarian, cultural, and historical subjectivities of the contemporary self. This player-skin includes both our subjectivity as a player and how it relates to the larger being that is affected by this process of subjectivization, separating our being from the experience of the game. This subjectivity, which keeps the culturally embodied being both together with and separate from the player-subject, is related to, but distinct from the cultural being in which it originated. It keeps us close to the fact that players do have a body, both real and virtual, and that the body matters, be that the body of the avatar or the real body, as they are constituents of the player-subject's skin. But it also indicates a fundamental tension between our values and our values as player-subjects; a tension that is at the heart of the ethical issues that computer games raise.

When I play *Fahrenheit*, I relate to that fictional world by the subject that follows the rules and experiences the game world. In that context, my player-subject is created, and I interact with *Fahrenheit*. But the situations and some of the choices this game puts me through affect my player-subjectivity: the game is designed so that players grow attached to some characters. *Fahrenheit* is designed to provide elements that make us use that subjectivity in a rational and emotional way. The fact that the game uses quick-time events as a means of interaction (a polemical design decision) could be interpreted as a tool for strengthening the physical relation with

Figure 3.2
Fahrenheit: A Matter of Moral Choices

the player, trying to embody the act of playing by means of interface design. In action scenes the player has to follow some on-screen indications as to what controller input needs to be given in order to pass the level, what is popularly known as a "quick-time event." That input consists of pressing the buttons, manipulating the joystick, and combinations of both, following a certain sequence. It seems like such an odd choice for controlling the action sequences of an adventure game, which has its origin in the intention of "embodying" the player to a greater degree via the use of the console controller.[55]

When experiencing a game, the player-subject is created as a skin with a set of functions: it both separates and connects the cultural embodied being from which the player is generated from the player-subject; it also creates the game experience as it is created by it; and, finally, it operates as a sensitive organ that is affected and affects the experience of the game. It is possible to speak of a game situation even when it comes to Internet forums or other social environments in which we wear our player-skin and thus remain in touch with a player experience.[56]

The player-subject, in touch with the larger cultural and embodied set of subjectivities that forms her self, can relate to the affordances of the object by which it is created and which it phenomenologically experiences. In this sense, the player's body-subject is created to fit and mold, as a flexible organ, to those affordances and constraints in the behavior that the game as object presents. A player is a body-subject created in and by the experience of a game. Phenomenologically, the player-subject as skin acts as a being that creates the game and is created by the game, in a process of dialogue in which the player uses moral reasoning in her relation with the game world and with other players. Ethical judgment is necessary to preserve the integrity of the body-subject and the fidelity to the game event, and to contribute to the flourishing of a player community where the player's body-subject can achieve excellence without being broken or harmed. To understand that use of moral reasoning, it is necessary to delve deeper into the phenomenological layer of the game as experience.

3.3   The Phenomenology of Playing

If the player is a subject that comes into being when playing a game, then the ethical nature of the player must be placed in the context of that experience. The phenomenology of playing informs the ethical being of the player and how these processes of mutual creation and experiencing work are related to ethics. In particular, Gadamerian phenomenology provides a framework for the analysis of the player as ethical being and for the understanding of the ethics of computer games. The essential questions about these two processes will be approached in three different and consecutive stages: I will first draw on phenomenology to explain playing as a process; then I will focus both on the hermeneutics of becoming a player and on the hermeneutics of games; finally, I will make the transition to the ethical discourse by using the Aristotelian concepts of *praxis* and *phronesis*.

Let's start with defining play as a phenomenological process. I read about the experimental independent game *Passage*.[57] I access its website, read the author statement, and understand that the software I am about to download and play intends to create the experience of a *memento mori*, a work of art that intends to make me experience the fragility and futility of life. I start the game and am presented with a narrow, elongated game world where I control a little avatar that can move around in four directions. I explore: I find treasures, and eventually a partner, a computer–controlled character who will follow me. As the game proceeds, I can see progressively more of the map I am leaving behind, and less of what I have ahead. After five minutes of play, and after the death of my partner, I die and the game is over.

Passage creates a moral and philosophical game experience—playing the game is realizing the perception of time and how it relates to potentiality, to the loss of possible lives that happens when we grow old. And it does so not through the artist statement, but through the game as such—the evolving perspective of the game, where we progressively see less and less of the future until we die, and by the ultimate acknowledgment that the score system is futile. There is a tradition of memento mori in art history, but *Passage* is unique because it is, to my knowledge, the first time this experience of the fragility of life and its times takes place in the phenomenological experience of game. In other words, is it only as a game that *Passage* is meaningful art, or is it only because it is a game that *Passage* is experienced as art?

Computer games are about becoming the player that the game allows, directs, and suggests that we become. A more prosaic example comes from *Guitar Hero*,[58] which wants the player to feel like a guitar player of

Figure 3.3
Passage: Death and the Game

rock-star magnitude, and as such the game is bundled with a guitar as its physical interface. Like in other rhythm games like *Donkey Konga*,[59] the player can actually manipulate the game with a standard controller, but the game is only understood in its full actuality when played with the guitar, when the player lives through the whole body and machine experience.

Stated more precisely, games are the experience of being a player—without this experience, the game is *just* an object designed to provide the means for a subjectivization process; a process that will result in a ludic experience that actualizes the game. The game as object is just the condition by which the player comes into being, and with her the game. The game, then, has to be understood as an experience and not an object when the player is taken into consideration, as Gadamer had already hinted at: "the mode of being of play does not allow the player to behave toward play as if toward an object."[60]

To understand the player and the game from this experiential perspective we will use the concepts and method of phenomenology, within the tradition of Heidegger and Gadamer. Phenomenology is a fundamental ontology that interprets an experience, relating it to the context in order to understand its mode of being.[61]

Phenomenologically, the player is the subject that experiences a ludic situation originated by, but not limited to, the game as object. For the ludic activity to exist, the player has to come into being within the limits and extensions of the ontology of the game.[62] Phenomenologically, the player has to be considered as a subject within an experience, a player-and-game involved in a procedural operation of being,[63] a subjectivization process by which the player comes into being as a body-subject.

A music player in a band, for instance, is both a part of the music group and only one instrument. For the music to be played correctly, the musician has to be a subject in the experience—that is, both an individual producing a set of sounds with her instrument, and a part of the larger experience of the music as performance. For a spectator, the musician need not be *a subject*, but a part of the process of creating or interpreting the music; for the musician, there is a duality in her mode of being within the performance experience. The spectator may see an orchestra; the player experiences her own performance *and* her performance as a part of the orchestra.

Playing a single-player computer game like *Super Columbine Massacre RPG!* presents the same mode of being: as a player, I am experiencing the game not as an object, but as a process that regards, rewards, and punishes my interaction with it. What I experience is my subjectivity as a player with the ergodic agency of the computer game. In *Super Columbine Massacre RPG!* I have to control Eric and Dylan, the troubled young sociopaths who perpetrated the Columbine massacre, on the day of the events. Moreover, I have to play those events through the conventions of classic role-playing games. As a player, I have to enter the high school, plant bombs, and massacre students and teachers with a crude turn-based combat system. The game as experience creates me as a player who becomes "forced" to gather tokens and resources in the game while eliminating opponents, but those tokens and resources and opponents, despite the retro-aesthetics of the game, are teachers, students, and other victims of the massacre. The ludic experience of *Super Columbine Massacre RPG!* takes place for that subject who is forced to perform these actions that, at the same time, are rewarded by the system with new possibilities and expansions of my capacities as player within the game world.

Of course, most players will probably evaluate this tension as uncomfortable. Even though the game is not different from other classic

Figure 3.4
Super Columbine Massacre RPG!: Playing the Unthinkable

role-playing games, it *feels* different. There is a strong tension between the player-subject and the subject external to the act of play, a tension generated by the contradiction between the fidelity to the game experience and the cultural meaning of the actions, which we give from a perspective external to the player-subject. This tension is crucial for understanding the potential of computer games as ethical experiences, and can be analyzed by applying hermeneutics in the Gadamerian sense, which will help in singling out the being of the player in the experience of the game—explaining how the player operates as a reflective, moral being.

I will return to *Super Columbine Massacre RPG!* in later stages of this book. For now, I will focus on a less controversial example: the computer game *Daigasso! Band Brothers* is a simulation of a musical orchestra in which the single-player version tries to simulate the process of playing a tune, while the multiplayer version puts every player in charge of an instrument. *Daigasso!* provides a very interesting insight into the process of playing a game, becoming a player, and experiencing the game in a phenomenological sense. Using some of the most interesting hardware capacities of the Nintendo DS, *Daigasso!* is a game built around an orchestra simulator. The player is faced with a certain number of training tutorials that, simulating the progress of a musician in the development of skills, allow her to play more and more complicated songs. The gameplay is exquisite for its simplicity: the player is faced with abstracted sheet music in which, instead of notes, there are keys that have to be pushed following the rhythm. In single-player mode, the player interprets a different number of instruments in each song, much like in any other rhythm game.

The multiplayer version of *Daigasso!*, on the other hand, presents other interesting aspects. The DS is equipped with Wi-Fi capability, which theoretically allows a number of consoles to connect wirelessly in order to share information, chat, or play. More interestingly, with many DS games it is only necessary to have one physical copy of the game to start a multiplayer session. That is the case with *Daigasso!*—with just one copy of the game it is possible to create a small network of players. And the multiplayer version of the game is rather remarkable, for players can actually join in and play one of the songs, and each player individually interprets one instrument. It is, then, a collaborative simulation of a music band in which all participants have to take part in order to recreate the song and achieve individual points. In this sense, it is possible to say that all players are at the same time a unity, for they all play the same game united in the desire to achieve the same goals, and they are individual players because they will be evaluated for their actions. From a phenomenological perspective, *Daigasso!* multiplayer mode is the experience of individual play and of individual player-subjectivity, as well as collective cooperative play, in which it could be argued that there is a "player of players," a larger play subject that is composed of a number of players experiencing the same game at the same time, with different procedures of play simultaneously.

What hermeneutics actually explains is precisely the operational properties of the player as subject within the game experience; that is, those ontological capacities that make the player as subject come into being within a game. The act of experiencing a game—making a game object actual—is an act of interpretation of what that situation demands for creating a subject. Playing is interpreting our ontological situation as players within the borders established and agreed upon by the game as object; but playing is also a process of self-reflection and interpretation of our own being as players, within those parameters of the community or group of players, our culture, and those values and ideas that inform our real-life existence.

Gadamer and Heidegger provided an ontological turn to hermeneutics within the limits of phenomenology by stating that what we understand from an object or experience is already somehow in the object or experience; or, rather, understanding is partially derived from what is understood. In the case of computer games, the player repertoire (the fact that we can infer the rules of most unknown games by using our past experience as players) seems to suggest the same conclusion: playing is giving to the game object an interpretation derived at least partially from our own cultural and game-cultural background, inferring the being of the game from our own interpretational capabilities applied to the game rules. In that circular process the game and player come into being within a ludic experience.

This mutual (re)creational process, in which the player constitutes and is constituted by the interpretational process of playing a game,[64] calls for the use of the hermeneutic circle, which explains the process of understanding a part of the text and how that affects the understanding of the whole. Within Gadamer's theory, though, the circle becomes more than an interpretational tool: "The circle, then, is not formal in nature. It is neither subjective nor objective, but describes understanding as the interplay of the movement of tradition and the movement of the interpreter . . . thus the circle of understanding is not a 'methodological' circle, but describes an element of the ontological structure of understanding."[65] The ontological turn implies that for Gadamer the circle operates as a way of acquiring knowledge about the modes of being of understanding, and, by extension, of the modes of being of the subject who understands.

Returning to *Daigasso!*, when starting to play the game, the player-subject comes into being, and so does the game as experience. Then the player uses her culture and tradition as a player to find ways of experiencing this particular game. Knowledge of the genre, reviews read in magazines or online, or personal interaction with other players provide the initial interpretational tools. Once the player figures out the key elements, it is possible for the game to become a fulfilled actuality through and with the player. In the case of *Daigassou!*'s multiplayer mode, we have to take into account the player community that is created—how the player is integrated in that community, and what role(s) she has. Finally, the act of playing is evaluated and understood via the culture, values, and traditions of the player outside the game, because that is the way in which we acknowledge the particular seriousness of games, their specific ontological being separated from and distinct to other types of experiences.[66]

The process of experiencing a game as a player-subject takes place in interpretational layers that provide different yet complementary ontological feedback to the process of becoming a player. It begins with an ontological move voluntarily made by the player: accepting the game as object and its conditions for success. Then the player interprets those conditions, actualizes them, and becomes player-subject within the game experience. This subject is then interpreted by the player culture as player; that is, by the tradition in which she has been a player. In the case of several players within the ludic experience, the player also takes into account the created community. Finally, the acts and experiences of the game are evaluated by the real-life self, her culture and subjectivity, in a circular process that returns to the player-as-being, the initial constituent of this situation. It is in this hermeneutical process where the ethical being of the player-subject takes place and finds meaning.

Gadamer's reinterpretation of hermeneutics is heavily grounded in Aristotle, and, more specifically, in the concept of *phronesis* or practical wisdom.[67] For Gadamer, hermeneutics is not only a mode of understanding, but also a mode for self-understanding, developing what Aristotle considered a key value for the ethical development of the individual as a moral being. Aristotle believed that humans are moral beings, roughly because we have a rational mind that guides us in pursuit of happiness.

The hermeneutical process operates as a way of self-understanding within the parameters of phronesis. Considering that, for the player-subject, playing games is a hermeneutical process, I argue that in those situations the player informs her interpretational process of the becoming from a moral perspective. The player can be, then, a moral subject who rationalizes the game experience with the tools and parameters of her ethical wisdom, which is (as I will show later on) both a cultural and an individual property. But before stepping into those layers of the player-subject, I will focus on the ethical turn of the hermeneutics of becoming a player.

Aristotle considered ethics a practical science—beyond a theory or a set of empty discourses, ethics had to be practiced by those who wanted to achieve the virtuous state in which life was balanced at the moral level. These practices had much to do with the specifically human capacity for moral reasoning, which was anchored in moral wisdom as a practice, or phronesis. What phronesis gives to this approach to the player-subject is the connection of the ethics of the game as object with the ethical nature of being a player, the two main elements for the configuration of the ethics of computer games.

Let's consider the act of playing *Black & White*.[68] This game puts the player in the role of a god who is in charge of a civilization, with which the god communicates both through direct actions in the environment and through a gigantic creature that the player trains. The way the player treats this creature will determine its behavior: an evil god, for example, will create a scared and enraged creature, while a benevolent god creates a more pleasant creature. Playing this game is the act of interpreting the game rules by means of the knowledge amassed by the player of previous games within the game genre—in this case everything from the classics *Populous*[69] and *Civilization*[70] to the software toy Tamatgotchi. But it is also the act of interpreting that tradition within the new elements of this game; namely, the fact that the player *is* a god that will be evaluated according to the choices she makes. And it is also the act of interpreting that the player-subject has to adopt the logic of a god in the game, and how that might relate to real-life values, ideas, and cultural settings.

To play a computer game is a cultural process in which we grow up and mature as players. A *Manhunt* player who is not familiarized with computer games will not only have a hard time navigating the environment, but she might feel shocked by the gruesome acts she is compelled to play. A more experienced player, I argue, will understand that the game is actually designed to make the player enact an unethical experience, showing that there is no fun in committing these acts, but rather mirroring the lack of morals and the desperate situation of the main character in the fictional game world. The player of *Manhunt* will go through an ethical experience, unless her own ethical values, her cultural embodied being, despises the game so much that the subjectivization process breaks down. Experienced players have a better chance of understanding *Manhunt's* ethical conundrums because the more we play, the more literate we are in the rhetoric and play styles of computer games. We better understand the design decisions, and we are able to penetrate the game as object in different, more complex ways during the process of subjectivization.

Playing computer games should be considered as a praxis, an act of choices and decisions, a voluntary self-evaluation and creation of a subject. It is my argument that a game has to be understood as an object experienced as a praxis of moral wisdom, in a process of interpretation and self-interpretation. The player is the subject that culminates the transition of computer games from object (potentiality) to praxis (actuality). And, by introducing it in the realm of practices, players become subject to self-scrutiny, the evaluation of and reflection on the very same processes of being and becoming players. In the praxis of playing computer games, players become ethical subjects.

3.4   Players as Moral Beings

It is time now to close this phenomenological turn and introduce the perspective of virtue ethics applied to the subject of the player. To do so, I will start by putting players in context, showing the similarities and differences in playing alone and playing together. I will then introduce the perspective on the player as moral being that I believe defines the player as ethical being: the virtue ethics perspective, in an Aristotelian fashion. I will define a number of virtues for the player, and illustrate them with references both to literature on players and to actual games. Finally, I will define what the nature of a player is from an ethical perspective, and how this affects the overall consideration of the ethics of computer games.

But first, an example. The settings of *Counter-Strike: Source* allow for a detailed search of what kind of server the player wants to join. One of the filters for the search engine is the availability of anticheat software: if a player wants to make sure that there will be no use of any kind of cheats or exploits during gameplay, she will certainly choose to play on a server in which this anticheat system is present. Furthermore, once a protected server is chosen and while the connection between client and server is established, the player will read on her screen a rather harsh warning: "Players who cheat will suffer an immediate and permanent ban." And such is the case not only with *Counter-Strike: Source*, but also with many other online first-person shooters. Similarly, players who exploit the rules of other online games, by cheating the economic systems or "farming" resources, have seen their accounts banned, and the community reacts quite aggressively against these kinds of acts.

Stepping a bit away from digital games, if we reflect on the practice of collective or multiplayer games, patterns emerge. When playing soccer or basketball in a social context, certain kinds of behaviors are regarded poorly by the community of players, or directly rejected. In soccer, for instance, nobody likes an individualist striker who does not help in defense, and in basketball noncooperative players who just want to score all the points are often regarded as spoilsports. And like these two examples, most team-based sports and games tend to have implicit codes of conduct that are enforced by the players in order to preserve the well-being of the game in progress.

When we play with other people, we want to experience the game, and we demand that nobody spoils that enjoyment. Therefore, we care about those behaviors that threaten the experience. Playing is not only experiencing a game, but also preserving the ludic flow of that experience. And playing with others is also a matter of demands: we demand behavior from other players that ensures the game will not be spoiled by those who do not want to follow the rules, or those who believe that winning is the only desirable outcome of a ludic experience. Playing is also learning those codes of conduct that tell us what can we expect from other players, and how we should behave if we aspire to contribute to the well-being of the player community.

Becoming a player is the act of learning the practices that the historical community considers desirable and undesirable. Playing is learning to be a good player, to care about how to participate in the game. This is not to say that players believe that goals are more important than means, or that there are no practices of playing that consider cheating a desirable behavior,[71] but in general cheating and other spoilsport behaviors are seen as practices that should be avoided.

These phenomena are not limited to playing with other players. Playing a single-player computer game is also an act of moral relevance. A player introducing cheat codes, for instance, affects the game balance and the carefully crafted game experience, thus shattering the game experience as it was intended and optimized. Playing, for instance, *Half-Life 2* in "god" mode, where your avatar cannot suffer any kind of harm, is somehow amusing, but also slightly boring, unless of course it is done with the sole intent of finishing the story of the game. In an example I have already suggested, I pointed out that *Grand Theft Auto: Vice City* warns players who save a game in which they have cheated that this action may compromise the stability of that save-file, risking the loss of all the data of the game progress up to that moment. Besides, at the moment, those games that actually pretend to simulate the importance of morality in gameplay, like *Fable*[72] or *Knights of the Old Republic*, are single-player games.

Playing a computer game is still the act of enjoying a ludic experience, and being a player, even in a single-player game, is taking the responsibility for playing the game in enjoyable, sanctioned ways. This does not mean blindly following the rules. After all, some of the most creative computer games in history, from *Elite*[73] to *Grand Theft Auto IV*, are sandbox environments where the player exerts her creative capacities in her interactions with the world. But this creativity comes with a responsibility, both for players and designers: ensuring that the game is a pleasurable and balanced experience. The player should not be considered a passive element of gameplay, a mere trigger of situations placed there by the designers. Players of computer games also have the stewardship over the game system, the software, and its informational integrity.

The process of becoming a player is also the process of creating, accepting, and developing that stewardship. Being a player also implies becoming, or aspiring to become, a good player from a moral perspective. To define what a good player is from an ethical perspective, I will use Aristotelian virtue ethics, since it provides a well-defined theoretical framework wherein it is possible to give a clear picture of what it means to be a good player.

Being a good player is being a virtuous player. A virtuous player is the one who engages in a game and enjoys its ludic experience, but it is also she who, in the face of a moral challenge, uses the practical wisdom acquired by playing that game, and all those games that form her repertoire, in order to make the most ethically informed choice. These moral challenges can be either experienced by the player-subject or by the out-of-game subject. For instance, in a situation where two players of different skill levels are playing *Pro Evolution Soccer 4*, the challenge for the most skilled player is to choose a different difficulty level than her opponent. In doing so, it will be more difficult for the skilled player to defend. If both players do so, there is a larger chance that the simulated football match will become an enjoyable ludic experience. As a matter of fact, the act of tweaking the gameplay in a casual setting, such that it is possible for players of different skill sets to enjoy a common ludic experience, is rather common when we play games, and is a symbol of how as ethical players we behave toward others in the pursuit of a successful gameplay session.

What is, then, a virtuous player? To define more clearly what I mean by virtuous player, it is necessary to define virtue. For Aristotle, "Virtue then is: a state apt to exercise deliberate choice, being the relative mean, determined by reason, and as the man of practical wisdom would determine."[74] I define virtue applied to computer games as the capacity for a player-subject to make a gameplay choice informed by her practical wisdom and understanding, taking into account her membership in a player community and her self outside the game. A virtuous player uses ethical reflection based on her virtues when playing a computer game.

This is too much of an abstract definition, and requires a more precise approach to what virtues players should have. In the *Nichomachean Ethics*, Aristotle expands on a list of virtues[75] that, in his mind, define the virtuous citizen. Additionally, those virtues are explained under the Doctrine of the Mean.[76] A virtue is a mean state between the absence and the excess of virtue, the classic example being how the courageous person is the optimal virtuous being between the coward, who is dominated by fear, and one who foolishly puts his life in danger. The virtues spelled out by Aristotle need to be complemented with what the virtues of the player-subject in a game experience should be.

I will elaborate on these virtues, taking as a premise the player types categories suggested by Richard Bartle.[77] These player types broadly define play styles any player can adopt in a multiuser dungeon (MUD). This account of how players behave, what their motivations are, and what defines them can cast some light on an initial set of virtues that are present in game players. Given the assumption that virtues are, roughly said, the ethical modalities of gameplay sported by players, it is of interest to understand what kind of play types are present in virtual worlds, and from them deduce the related virtues.

There are, though, two caveats that need to be mentioned: first, Bartle's work was originally derived from the study of MUDs, and only later extended to other online worlds like *Ultima Online*,[78] or to social spaces like *Second Life*.[79] Even though there are differences between virtual worlds and single-player games, and between these and multiplayer local-area network games such as *Daigasso!*, I will advocate for a more integrated view, arguing with illustrative examples that Bartle's player types are relevant for the description of the player's virtues.

The second caveat has to do with my definition of player. I have defined the player-subject as a subset of the self that comes into being when experiencing a game. And I have argued that this player-subject is a body-subject, related to the cultural, embodied, and temporal self outside the game. Nevertheless, I am here presenting specific game virtues, which can have a different meaning when playing games. Being courageous in an online match of *Halo 3*,[80] for instance, is not different from being courageous outside of the game, for acting too cowardly will not allow the player to score points, and rushing into action will probably kill you, losing online status in both cases and forcing some undesired waiting time.

There is then a connection between the virtues external to the game and the virtues that are appreciated in a game. But there are some virtues that are only relevant within the game experience. For example, players who do not try to communicate at all in a MMORPG like *World of Warcraft* will have a hard time experiencing the game, because it is a game in which communication is essential for achieving certain goals. Likewise, a player who just enjoys the linear achievement of goals will most likely not fully enjoy the expansive, almost living world of *Grand Theft Auto IV*, because in that environment the gameplay—the linear action—ends up being quite dull. Finally, the classic example is cheaters: most players do not like cheaters in multiplayer games. Conversely, most players do like players who behave in ways that are perceived as positive, sharing knowledge of behaving with sportsmanship.

Bartle's player types, as interpreted in light of virtue ethics, provide an understanding of how players interact with the game and with others within a virtual world. Bartle distinguishes initially between four types of players: achievers, who "regard points-gathering and rising in levels as their main goal, and all is ultimately subservient to this;" explorers, who "delight in having the game expose its internal machinations to them;" socializers, who "are interested in people, and what they have to say;" and killers, who "get their kicks from imposing themselves on others."[81] These four types refer to dominant play styles that determine the type of players that a virtual world presents and the dynamics of the interaction between them.[82]

What player types show is different ways of engaging in gameplay, ways that are specific to games and that can be interpreted within the perspective of virtue ethics. I will now proceed to deduce a basic set of virtues for players, relating them with player types. I am considering player types as extremes from which virtues can be deduced.

Achievers demonstrate that we can consider legally attempting to achieve the goals of the game a virtue. For instance, it is virtuous to try to win a race in *Project Gotham Racing 2*[83] using the given cars, unmodified, and depending only on one's skill at the wheel or, in this case, with the gamepad. This wish to complete the game and face the challenges can also be considered a virtue. In excess, this trait would create a player who does not respect any social rule or protocol in order to achieve the goals (in the case of *Project Gotham Racing 2*, this player would try to crash other players), while a player who lacks this trait would probably choose the slowest cars, impeding other players' ability to enjoy the competition in equality.

The first virtue would then be achieving, which is present in those players who compete fairly against the challenges of the game and against other players, respecting the social norms and rules, and for whom victory is a desirable state in the game but not the most desirable—for that would be enjoying the game, alone or with others.

Players like exploring the boundaries of game systems, realizing at once their belonging to that experience, their being as players, and the relatively safe nature of these environments. Players of *The Sims* have actually tried different ways of killing their avatars.[84] Similarly, some players used the open and modifiable universe of *Deus Ex* until they discovered that by using adhesive mines they could climb some walls and avoid conflict, a classic example of emergent gameplay.

Exploring the game system and the possibilities of interaction is a player virtue. In excess it can make players forget about the goals of the game, ignoring the designed gameplay process. In *The Sims*, for instance, a player who just explores the many ways of building a house and how complex it can be is setting aside a crucial gameplay element: the house is just the container where the game action takes place, and the possible ways of creating houses are determined by the gameplay.[85] On the defect end, a player that only sees *The Sims* as a game, and does not explore the building possibilities, will most likely find the simulation boring because it is indeed repetitive if we don't consider the multiple possibilities of customization that the game offers.

The socializers seem to be the backbone of contemporary role-playing online worlds, but they are not limited to these environments. Socializers create and move communities by caring about the players within the game as much as for the players outside the game, and they do so by using means of communication, from fanzines to the Internet, to make communities cohere. Socializers care about other players and about the game, and they express their care by, for instance, attending game forums where they actively participate. In the case of *Shadow of the Colossus*, many players have cared enough to complete the game's voluntarily incomplete fiction, since there are many questions about the game's characters that are never answered. These players provide fan fictions that contribute to a vibrant game community surrounding this single-player game.[86]

In excess, the virtue of socialization can encourage players who act despotically within the community, players who may believe that the game is just secondary to their participation in a community that, needless to say, makes sense only within the shared experience of the game. But by default, a player can ignore these communities, which in itself is problematic. For instance, players in multiplayer games who do not take into account the presence of a strong and coherent community may participate in unethical actions (as determined by social rules) and they would do so because they ignore, or do not give importance, to the fact that players do have a culture of their own, surrounding specific games and beyond that. The socialization virtue defines those players who participate in a player community, contributing to their culture as players, but who acknowledge that this community is a part of a game experience, and that it is the game, or the shared event of being a player, that makes the community exist.[87]

At first glance, it may seem that killers do not sport any virtue—how could a killer be virtuous? Nevertheless, it is possible to consider killers as somehow virtuous players. Killers only exist in multiplayer environments, and they are only present in those games, from persistent worlds to online multiplayer match games like *Counter-Strike*, in which player-versus-player gameplay is a sanctioned practice. In the case of *World of Warcraft*, a killer would inhabit a server where she could engage in combat with other players. But, as I will show in my analysis of that game in chapter 5, *World of Warcraft* changed its design by implementing an "honor system" that added a set of ethical affordances to the game. This system did actually disrupt the gameplay very much, and even now, after a number of developer-originated solutions, the forums related to player-versus-player gameplay are full of complaints about the honor system, the "battlegrounds," and how killing other players is rewarded.

To kill other players has a "balanced aggression" virtue. By it, players may have the right to attack and kill other players, but that gameplay should be balanced, regulated, properly rewarded, and be interesting from a gameplay perspective. In the case of *Counter-Strike*, for instance, when joining a server it is possible to allow the computer to balance the teams automatically, so the matches have an even number of "terrorists" and "counterterrorists." This adjustment is made so that it is possible to enjoy balanced gameplay with the right number of players. The defective presence of this virtue explains why some *World of Warcraft* players who joined a player-versus-player server complain about being attacked while doing quests: they do not understand that an implicit part of playing in such a game mode is to be targeted as hostile by the opposite faction, and thus possibly get killed. And the excess of this virtue would lead to griefing; [88] that is, to players that use the player-versus-player enabled environment to harass other players without considering the rewards or the logic of allowing player-killing.

Bartle's player types are abstract categorizations of different play styles, and thus they show generalizations of how players actually play. I have used them here as a source for describing the virtues of the players, deduced from these player types. I by no means try to make a correlation between player types and player virtues—in my interpretation, Bartle's player types show which is the dominant virtue of a player in a given situation or world. But ideally, all these virtues should be present in the ethically good player: sense of achievement, explorative curiosity, a socializing nature, and balanced aggression. Yet these are not enough, and there surely must be more of them.

The notion of game balance is closely related but independent of the player virtues. The Doctrine of the Mean can be translated, in the realm of digital ludic environments, to the act of seeking balance in gameplay, or, better stated, to the need to preserve game balance. Game balance is what Rollings and Adams define as a game where it is only the skill of the player that determines the success factor.[89] In a virtuous sense, players ought to preserve the game balance, thereby making it a fair game for all the parties involved. In a more phenomenological fashion, I would argue that the virtue of preserving game balance has to do with the preservation of a successful game experience for all players and agents involved in the game.

In the case of *Project Gotham Racing 2*, a more skilled player is not obliged to choose a worse vehicle if she is playing against less-skilled players, be those computer agents or humans, but she would definitely be a better player from a virtuous perspective if she did so in order to create and preserve a successful ludic experience. By choosing a less desirable vehicle, she would have to use all her skills and her mastery in order to win the game, and the less-skilled opponents would stand a chance in the competition.

Game balance in this sense has to be understood as the balance perceived by players, and not necessarily, like Rollings and Adams suggest, the formal property of the game system. As I will explain in my analysis of *Bioshock*[90] in chapter 5, a game can be unbalanced, yet still both playable and ethically relevant. A brief example can be taken from *Passage*: the choice of having a partner prevents players from exploring the world, while not giving any specific systemic reward. This imbalance is actually appealing to the ethical player, who will understand its meaning beyond the actual design of the game. In those cases where the game is voluntarily and creatively imbalanced, the virtue is then to preserve the game balance both in terms of the system, and in terms of the experience of the system.

Finally, I will briefly consider the issue of sportsmanship as a player virtue. Most of the work on the ethics of sport[91] has clear roots in the virtue ethics paradigm, defining what is to be a good sport, or, more specifically, how and why sportsmanship is a virtue for players in sports. These authors start from an implicit, yet pervasive point, the golden rule of sports:[92] "Always conduct yourself in such a manner that you will increase rather than detract from the pleasure to be found in the activity, both your own and that of your fellow participants."[93]

A good sportsman is one who is capable of following this golden rule. Sportsmanship is a specific virtue that has more to do with the ontological status of the player-subject and the relations it establishes with the game experience than with the fact that the player is immersed in a ludic experience that creates the player-subject. The virtue of sportsmanship, then, "is a mean between an excessive seriousness, which misunderstands the importance of the spirit of play, and an excessive sense of playfulness, which may be called frivolity and which misunderstands the importance of victory and achievement when play is competitive."[94]

Sportsmanship is a virtue related to the subjectivization process of being a player, and therefore it is different from and complimentary to respecting, protecting, and enhancing the game balance. I have argued that becoming a player is a process of subjectivization deeply related to the acceptance of a set of rules. An agent that fails in this subjectivization process but engages in the act of playing regardless fails to follow the virtue of sportsmanship.

This may seem a conceptual contradiction with the classic concept of sportsmanship, which intuitively refers to the capacity for making the right moral choices within gameplay. Let's observe a situation in which we would need to use the concept of sportsmanship: when playing *Diablo II*[95] online, I was approached by another player who had obviously used a hack to enhance her powers. This player invited me to join her guild, offering me access to the aforementioned hack, and also wealth and good weapons. A good sport would decline the invitation, we would say, because cheating is wrong. It was the realization that such a promise of wealth and power could only mean that suddenly the game would become more boring, and more focused on harassing those who did not want or have these powers, that led me to turn down the offer. And of course, to be griefed for a while by that other player.

Similarly, when playing a game like *Grand Theft Auto: Vice City*, a player can face the dilemma of using emergent strategies to solve missions. For instance, one of the game's missions consists of taking a motorbike and jumping from roof to roof in order to get some tokens. But as the game is an open environment, it is also possible to complete that mission using a small helicopter available for the player at another location. If the player has completed the mission in this way, she did not take the challenges of the game seriously, therefore she has been a player, albeit not a virtuous one.[96]

Sportsmanship is, then, the virtue that determines the degree of success in the subjectivization process that takes place when playing a game. A player can still be considered a player-subject if she is not a good sport, but she would be a worse player-subject, due to her detachment from the game rules, and certainly not a virtuous player.

Returning to Aristotle's definition of virtue, there is an element that needs to be considered in order to define the player as a moral being, and that is practical wisdom. Aristotle defined virtues as related to what "the man of practical wisdom would determine."[97] This practical wisdom, or phronesis, is one of the key concepts in Aristotelian ethics, and also one of the most discussed concepts in the history of philosophy. It is not my intention here to perform an exegesis of the word, but to define it appropriately for the player of computer games.

Phronesis is the central concept of Book VI of the *Nichomachean Ethics*. In this chapter, practical wisdom is defined as "a state conjoined with reason, true, having human good for its object, and apt to do."[98] There are several elements in this definition that need to be addressed in more detail. Phronesis is a capacity of the reason: that is, it does not concern feelings and it is not irrational or subconscious. Practical wisdom is an attribute of a reasoning mind. This reasoning mind aspires to be "good," good being the state in which all virtues are present, the state of maximum human flourishing.[99] Finally, practical wisdom is related to actions, to praxis. I have already mentioned that, for Aristotle, ethics is a practical science, and practical wisdom is the tool for the use of the agent's virtues in a practical situation.[100]

When a long-time player of *Counter-Strike* starts playing another first-person shooter, say *Battlefield 1942*,[101] she will most likely act much like she did when playing *Counter-Strike*—avoiding camping, enhancing teamwork, and all the other elements that her repertoire indicates are appropriate. But let's imagine that she faces a situation in which she doubts—it is not clearly a part of her cultural experience as a player, and she does not know how to react. Her actions will then be dictated, if she is a virtuous player, by her moral wisdom—she will try to make a decision informed by her experience as a member of a given human community as well as one or more gamer communities; a decision that maximizes her enjoyment of the game without hurting the experience of any other players. She is using her ludic practical wisdom.

In the case of a game like *Super Columbine Massacre RPG!*, players are forced to use their ethical practical wisdom in a different way. In this game, ethical reasoning, the practical wisdom of players, is of foremost importance. Practical wisdom is used to interact with a game as a player-subject, reflecting on what the game suggests that we do, what we can actually do in our interaction with the game world, and how that affects the moral integrity of both the player-subject and the self outside the game experience. In the case of *Super Columbine Massacre RPG!*, the game is consciously designed to provoke moral reflection by using the conventions of computer role-playing games to make ethical comments about the act of playing a game, being a player, and their influences on real events. In this game, players have to incarnate Eric and Dylan and follow step by step the process that ended in the Columbine massacre. By forcing the player to commit these acts, the game designer forced players to reflect on the meaning of actions: as a player, you want to win, but as a human being, you have to think about what winning means, and what the actions that are being simulated meant. As I have already mentioned, it is in this tension where thinking about the ethics of computer games is productive, and shows the potential of computer games for creating rich moral experiences.

It is games like *Super Columbine Massacre RPG!*, *Manhunt*, or *September 12th* that draw on the fact that players present moral reasoning, a capacity for applying ethical thinking to their actions within a game, not only to take the most appropriate action within the game in order to preserve the game experience, but also to reflect on what kind of actions and choices she is presented with, and how her player-subject relates to them.

In this chapter I have argued that players are moral beings whose ethics when playing a game can be understood using virtue ethics in a classic Aristotelian framework. I have identified a number of virtues that players should have:

- sense of achievement
- explorative curiosity
- socializing nature
- balanced aggression
- care for game balance
- sportsmanship.

All these virtues are put into practice when playing a game, forming players' practical wisdom, their phronesis, defined as the gameplay choices taken by players following the virtues in order to become good game players from an ethical perspective. I have also argued for a hermeneutic understanding of the phenomena of playing, in which a player interprets the game situation and her role in that situation using those values that are a part of her gamer culture, of her gaming community, and of her real-life presence.[102] I have argued that the player-subject is a skin subject in contact with the world outside the game, which in return does have influence over how a player experiences a certain game.

What these reflections on the ethics of the computer game player show is that the act of playing any computer game is a moral act. A player who comes into being within a game experience wants to preserve that phenomenological experience, and to do so she will engage in certain actions and avoid other practices that, even though they are possible, work against the balance of the game experience. Players decide which values, practices, and discourses are morally desirable, making the act of playing against other player agents, be those artificial or human, a constructivist act: a process of creating the desirable behaviors and practices within the game experience.

Games as objects can condition what the ethical practices and values of the players will be through their affordances and constraints. For example, physical aggression in soccer is strictly forbidden, and those players who engage in violent actions are seen as spoilsports. On the other hand, Australian football is rather permissive with some aggressive behavior, pushing the boundaries of what is acceptable and what is not in sports. This shows that it depends on how the game as object is designed; the experienced game will encourage certain player behaviors, as well as making others unethical or undesirable for the players and the player community because they disrupt the phenomenological experience of the game and its being.[103]

Nevertheless, the game object, as I have hinted before, is not exclusively responsible for what players believe is ethical or unethical. Players interpret the game experience from their game cultural background, making ethical choices that affect the way the game is experienced. The player as ethical being is constructed first, individually, by her interpretation of the game object as projected into her experience; then that ethical being is modified by the player's interpretation of the game experience from her viewpoint as a subject immersed in a player culture. Finally, players take into consideration, when creating their ethical values in a game, what other players do and consider correct; a player is a part of a moral community.

Players are body-subjects, cultural and embodied beings that take place when playing a game. Our cultural values also play a role in the construction of the ethical subject of the player. The Atari 2600 game *Custer's Revenge* sported hideous gameplay based on avoiding arrows so the player avatar could reach a tied-up female avatar and rape her. Beyond almost any game that has been publicly criticized for its content, *Custer's Revenge* broke all taboos, turning itself into one of the most shameful examples of game design ever made. It is not the player-subject who makes this game's ethical evaluation: the degree of moral perversion in this game makes many players immediately suspend the player-subjectivity and evaluate this with their own personal and cultural values.

Players use phronesis as a practical ability for the configuration of their being in the game. This moral wisdom is applied both to the experience of the game and to the other agents that are immersed in it. Other players' well-being has to prevail in order to enjoy a successful game experience; also, the game experience's well-being has to be respected for the experience of the game to take place. Winning is not always the most rational choice. This might be derived from the fact that players are moral beings who care for other players, acting with moral judgment when creating the game experience.

But are players *always* ethical beings? From the virtue ethics perspective, the answer is partially negative. For Aristotle, ethics and virtue are not something we have, but rather a practice—one in which we can improve.[104] Our goal as beings trying to flourish as moral beings is to first cultivate the virtues and then develop the practical wisdom that will allow us to make virtuous choices in different situations. Similarly, playing games is a matter of maturing our capacities to create the player-subject and its moral reasoning.

A game like *Fahrenheit*, in which some of the choices the player has to make concern personal relationships (of love, of brotherhood), is addressing a player who can reflect upon the ethics of these choices and how they may affect the branching structure of the game. *Fahrenheit* targets its gameplay to a player population that understands that game choices have as much to do with ethics as with the optimal strategies for proceeding in a game.

Players need to play games in order to develop their own culture, but also to develop their virtues and their capacity for reacting with practical wisdom to any situation within a game. This is a process that takes time, much like the learning process that any other art requires.

It is possible to imagine the following counterargument: because players are subjects that take place in the experience of a game, they are exempt from ethical consideration, for their existence as such only takes place within the game. I have argued against this point of view by using the concept of body-subject: players are not encapsulated in the game experience, they are immersed in a culture and they do have a bodily presence that can affect their ethical judgment and configurations. Players are not exempt from ethical scrutiny just because they are subjects that take place in the game. Precisely because games can be moral experiences, players have to be taken into account as agents who use ethical thinking not exclusive to the game experience, but related to their being in the world.

Let's return to Liberty City to understand, in detail, who we are when we play *Grand Theft Auto IV*, and how this game is designed for an ethical player. I have pointed out the essential tension between Niko Bellic's wish to begin anew (the noninteractive fiction of the game) and the players' interest in interacting with the game and making the story progress (the gameplay). The Niko we see in the noninteractive scenes regrets the past and the violence; the Niko we play to complete the story is a violent, merciless criminal. Niko is a tragic hero, and, as Heraclitus put it, his character is his destiny. But what is his character?

We, as players, decide Niko's destiny. We, as players, have the choice of not engaging in violence. We can work as a driver, we can flag taxis instead of carjacking, we can forget about the story and just dwell in Liberty City. But that is not playing *Grand Theft Auto IV*. As players, we have to engage in the values of the game, in the ethos of *Grand Theft Auto*. As players, we have to make Niko a criminal again so our experience of the game is complete. If we want to become players, and ethical players, we have to play this game. Our virtues, as players, are a part of the experience of the game. When engaged with *Grand Theft Auto IV*, not playing is unethical.

As players, we have the ethical capacities to interpret the game and the decisions we make in it as a part of the process of creating our subjectivity. This means that we will understand the game as a simulation, as a process in which our values relate to the values encouraged by the game. That means that the ethical player of *Grand Theft Auto IV* will build values based on the values of the game: values that imply, ultimately, that Niko has to be a criminal. Of course, this could be interpreted as an argument for considering *Grand Theft Auto IV* a reasonably unethical game: our values as players are created by a game that simulates the life of poor criminals in a big American urban environment.

But that's where *Grand Theft Auto IV* becomes a true ethical masterpiece. As players, as ethical agents, our ludic phronesis acts as the evaluation method of the appropriateness of our actions and values. We think, and play, as ethical agents beyond being players, but also as cultural beings. We play as body-subjects. That's why playing *Grand Theft Auto IV* becomes an exploration of meaning and purpose, of values and actions. Previous iterations of the *Grand Theft Auto* series used humor to distance the player, to allow her a moment of reflection to interpret the game as subversive satire. *Grand Theft Auto IV* does not use humor, but tragedy: we empathize with Niko, yet we are forced to drive him to crime. Do we really want to do that? Further, will we also be criminals when we can play in free-form, when we don't have to complete the missions in the game? What does this power say about who we are as ethical beings?

Playing *Grand Theft Auto IV* is, among other things, exploring the relation between the values we have as players and how they relate to who we are outside the game. The *Grand Theft Auto* series is only suitable for mature audiences, not only because of its violent content, but also, and more importantly, because it is appealing to who we are as consumers of computer games: our values, our behaviors, our conscience. *Grand Theft Auto IV* is a game designed for the ethical player, since it is a story about ethos and destiny—about *our* ethos, and *our* destiny.

The act of playing is concerned with the well-being of the players and the success of the game experience. Players create codes of behavior that grant that their actions, as well as the actions of the other players, will respect and enhance the game experience. Players act with moral wisdom and can be considered moral beings who take place when experiencing a moral object. It is in that phenomenological process where the normative approach to the ethics of computer games will find its meaning, as it is there that the ethics of computer games take place.

4   The Ethics of Computer Games

Metal Gear Solid 3: Snake Eater[1] is a stealth game. The player controls a soldier commanded to infiltrate and eliminate renegade Soviet and American units in a 1960s alternative universe. Even though players are presented with a heroic character, Naked Snake, trained for combat and survival, the game does not encourage violent solutions. By using nonlethal surrendering techniques, players can accomplish the mission killing only those enemies the game narrative requires. *Metal Gear Solid 3* encourages intelligent use of environments and resources, where violence tends to be the least optimal strategy.

The freakish world of *Metal Gear* is inhabited by characters beyond humanity, in touch with other fragments of reality. The most interesting character in the third iteration of the series is The Sorrow. When we meet him, he is already dead, and we are clinging on to life. After barely surviving a great fall into a river, Naked Snake awakes in a shallow river of burning trees and nightmare skies. He will soon meet The Sorrow— the ghost of a powerful psychic who reminds us that the world of *Metal Gear* is a world of sadness. The Sorrow will remind us of death and the meaning of combat actions: Naked Snake will have to walk up the river, against the stream of all those he has (or we players have) needlessly killed.

The Sorrow remind us, the players, of all the deaths we have caused. We will walk up a river, facing the spirits of the dead, walking our memory. If we have played the game as intended, as a tactical stealth challenge, and we haven't killed more than those required to make the story progress, we will only face a few ghosts. But if we have been reckless, if we have executed soldiers who needn't have died, then we will have to face them. We won't die, and they won't kill us, but the trip up the river will be slow and painful and it will take much longer to finish this sequence. We will have to face the consequences of our actions.

This gameplay sequence is one of the most accomplished translations of the ethical possibilities of games into actual game design, and is the perfect introduction for the core chapter of this book. Let's analyze it within the perspective of the two previous chapters: from a design point of view. The Sorrow is a clear ethical affordance in the design. Players ought to engage in stealth more than in combat. The more soldiers they kill, the less accomplished players they are, and as such they will be punished with a slower game progression. This ethical affordance indicates that killing soldiers is unnecessary, and the experience of the game will be altered accordingly. Through a rule, the game is communicating a series of values about how the game should be played.

From the perspective of the ethical player, this rule is translated into ethical values during the game experience. *Metal Gear Solid 3* encourages a number of virtues, all based on the stealth mechanics. If the player fails to build these virtues, she will be faced with the tortured ghosts of all those she has killed. Actions now have consequences, and appeal to our ethical mind. The Sorrow, as a villain, can only be understood from the perspective of the ethical player: the character is designed for reflection and redemption, two qualities that can only apply to a moral agent. This trip through the river of the dead, resonant of classical Greek mythology, appeals to the ethical player, understood both as the agent that interacts with the game world to complete goals following rules, and the as the body-subject who understands the semantics of these rules and goals and the ethical meaning of the game.

The Sorrow punishes us for being unethical players, and that punishment affects our gameplay experience (the game is longer and more tedious), as well as our moral reflection. The Sorrow reminds us of who we are as ethical players, and how games can be ethical experiences.

In this chapter I will take these lessons and formulate a comprehensive ethical framework that can be used to understand, analyze, and perhaps even predict the ethical issues computer games pose, as well as the possible solutions that developers, players, and theorists can apply.

As a general method for the analysis of computer game ethics, I suggest first defining games as experiences, then applying an ethical theory that can be used to identify the relevant ethical issues taking place in that game experience, and how they relate to the different components of the phenomenology of the game (player, object, community).[2] I interpret the ethical problems posed by computer games by applying two consolidated ethical theories, virtue ethics and information ethics, each providing a specific analysis of these ethical questions. Nevertheless, these theories present a number of shortcomings when strictly applied to computer games, which leads me to argue for a framework that can surpass those limitations and operate as an ethical analysis method specifically tailored to computer games.

After this framework is presented, I will put it to use in concrete analyses of games (chapter 6), as well as in the explanation of academically and culturally relevant topics (chapter 7) and in a more practically oriented application of the theory for game design (chapter 8). As with all comprehensive frameworks, there may be aspects that need deeper argumentation, but it is my ambition to provide an operational framework from which detail can be derived. Some examples of how to extend the original framework can be found in those aforementioned chapters, though other approaches and issues will be left unresolved in this book.

This chapter ties together and puts in perspective the notion of games as designed ethical systems and the arguments for considering players as ethical beings. Most of the theoretical work has already been done—it is now the time to consolidate these points into a unified theoretical statement. But first I will apply the two ethical traditions that will inform the arguments of the framework presented in this book.

4.1 Virtue Ethics and Computer Games

I will now introduce the analytical notions that virtue ethics provides to the study of computer games, introducing as well the shortcomings of an exclusively virtue ethics approach. I will argue that this theory is of the most use when applied to the relations between the game object and the player-subject. The analysis of game ethics from a virtue ethics perspective will conclude with an interpretation of Gadamer's hermeneutical circle that will describe the ethics of computer games. This hermeneutical circle will be the legacy of virtue ethics to the ethical framework presented later on in this book. I will conclude with an outline of the limitations of this approach.

Even though Aristotelian virtue ethics were already present in the last parts of chapter 3, I will now introduce ithem in a rather more comprehensive manner. The reader will nevertheless be already familiar with some of the concepts presented here.

4.1.1 Defining Virtue Ethics for Computer Games

Virtue ethics is one of the oldest schools of thought in moral philosophy. Reaching back to Plato and Aristotle and spanning from the Fathers of the Church to contemporary feminist philosophy, virtue ethics has proven to be one of the most solid yet flexible ethical theories of the Western world. Roughly stated, virtue ethics attempts to define the ethical virtues that human beings and human communities should aspire to exercise in order to be ethically sound. Virtue ethics is an ethical theory about the practice and development of the moral characteristics and practices that make human beings moral animals who aspire to the good.[3]

Virtue ethics provides a cross-cultural connection to the Eastern world, because much of the ancient ethical thinking in the East, such as Confucianism, shares principles and rhetoric with virtue ethics. Without being a universalist theory, virtue ethics provides a framework that can be understood and translated to different societies across physical and cultural boundaries. This characteristic itself could arguably justify its use in the study of a global phenomenon like computer games, in which the importance of the Eastern world and culture is undeniable.

Virtue ethics as applied to computer games are essentially focused on the act of playing. From this perspective, the ethics of the game as object are a condition for the morality of the experience, but not a central issue. The game as object, the system of the game, may have embedded values, but this virtue ethics approach will only focus on those values that are actually experienced in the game. Thus, the importance of the connection between this approach and Gadamer's hermeneutical phenomenology: it is in the experience of the game object where we shall find the ethics of the game. That experience is a process of interpretation of the game system, the game situation, and of the very subject of the player, considered from synchronic (while playing the game) and diachronic (as all the games ever played) perspectives. In that hermeneutical interpretation the use of practical wisdom, the Aristotelian phronesis, provides the basis for computer game ethics as a ludic experience.

It is possible to describe which values a game may enforce via design, but it is only when the game is experienced that those values can be analyzed, described, and prescribed. As an example, the possibility exists of winning in a strategy game like *Age of Empires*[4] by building a Marvel (such as a pyramid), and it may lead to a nonviolent resolution of the game.[5] Nevertheless, most players do not perceive that possibility as a valid strategy in the multiplayer version of the game; therefore it has little relevance in the ethical experience of the game. Because the system is designed to encourage conflict, players don't perceive other strategies as valid possibilities. The Marvel is a very expensive unit, and it requires a large amount of resources that are usually needed just for securing the borders of the empire. The fact that nonviolence is an option for the players is interesting, but its embedded values of nonviolent problem solving are denied by its actual impracticality as a game strategy. Players do not experience *Age of Empires* as a game that can be won by nonviolent strategies, and in that experience virtue ethics finds its research space.

This virtue ethics approach is essentially player-centered, both from an individual perspective and from a player-community perspective. It defines players as virtuous beings who make gameplay choices informed by their practical wisdom, guided by the presence or absence of a number of player-specific virtues. Surprisingly though, game designers consider players those final necessary elements in their ludic architecture, trained users who will trigger the predetermined actions they have so carefully designed.[6] While many game designers do respect players and give them a lot of importance, this discourse of the player as a somewhat passive figure,[7] whose interaction with the system has been already plotted and is rather constrained, remains dominant.

This is a paradox because games need players to exist. The presence of a player/user who actively engages with the system is crucial for understanding the ethical configuration of the game experience. Players are not passive receivers, and they are not just bots clicking on the button to get their ludic fix. Players are reflective, virtuous beings; they think about their strategies in more ways than just trying to figure out the success criteria and the best ways of achieving these goals. Players act in a game as ethical beings as well as goal-oriented, rational players. There is a responsibility in their actions; they are not passive victims but active moral agents when they play.

For example, playing a game like *Grand Theft Auto: San Andreas* is an ethical action of several dimensions. First, given the sheer size of the game, the player may be compelled to cheat in order to unlock some of the world's interesting items, such as vehicles or locations. But *Grand Theft Auto: San Andreas* is also a game known for its violence. Choosing to play this game, and to engage in the acts of simulated violence that are a crucial part of the gameplay, is also an ethical action. A player can actually play *Grand Theft Auto: San Andreas* without committing any crimes,[8] just exploring the virtual world of the game. That is a gameplay choice derived from the ethical reflection of the player-subject.

Being a player and being immersed in a cultural community of players is also an ethical action. Our relations with other players, within the same game experience or in the social instances that surround the game, is a practice of playing a game; a practice that, I argue, is moral. It is moral because being a part of the game community implies creating the shared values by which this game will be experienced, both alone and in the company of others. There is a responsibility in how players construct the ethical environment of the player community, how players relate to others, and what kinds of practices they allow or disallow in the game experience.

When defining the player as a virtuous being, I use the Aristotelian concept of practical wisdom, or phronesis, to refer to how a player determines which choices can further develop her virtues as a player. I define ludic phronesis as the moral wisdom that is developed as players experience games, which is used in evaluating the actions and dilemmas players are confronted with when playing and when being members of the community. On one level, being a player is also an act of learning: of learning the rules, how to achieve the goals, and in which ways we can and should relate with other players. There is a learning of the ethical maturity needed to play games, not only due to the complexity of the game systems, as it is not the same to play Tic-Tac-Toe as to play *Eve Online*, but also due to the relevance of other players in our experiences as game players. Playing games, alone and with others, is also the act of developing the ethical wisdom that helps solve those dilemmas we face when playing games. Ludic phronesis is, in this virtue ethics context, the operative ethical knowledge present in the act of playing games, which evaluates the morality of the player's actions. This practical wisdom related to games will not only develop the ethical maturity that can inform the decision-making processes during a gameplay experience, but it will also act as an operative mark of the player-subject as body-subject.

Ludic phronesis operates on two levels: one, within the player-subject, determining the player's best choices and behaviors in order to preserve the game experience, and making it pleasurable as well as relevant for the development of the player virtues. And two, ludic phronesis operates the ethical triggers that dismiss the player-subject when the game experience actually forces the player to make choices that are deemed unethical by the being who is external to the game. We stop being players in the middle of a gaming session when our practical wisdom connects the player-subject with who we are as ethical beings outside the game experience. This double functionality of ludic phronesis is of crucial relevance for understanding the issues related to the simulation of unethical activities in computer games.

Good judgment in computer games, meaning the correct development and application of ludic phronesis, enhances the virtues of the player-subject as a user of a designed environment. The correct use of phronesis strengthens the ethical relevance of the player-subject, and is of paramount importance to the player in the ethical experience of the game. A good player from a virtue ethics perspective uses ludic phronesis to preserve her ethical integrity both outside the game, via the critical interpretation of her acts in the game experience, and inside the game, making those choices that enhance her virtues and the well-being of the player community.

Virtue ethics applied to computer games can be defined as a player-centric ethical discourse that gives the most importance to the player as ethical agent within a game and as a part of a community. Players' responsibilities are evaluated as the praxis of ethical virtues that leads to the development of a kind of ludic phronesis. The player as moral agent is an embodied, ethical agent in a culture outside the game, which affects the ethical interpretation of the game and the game culture and how it is reflected in the moral character of players.

4.1.2 Virtue Ethics and the Computer Game as Moral Object

Even though the virtue ethics approach taken here will make the player the focal point of the reflection on the ethics of computer games, it is useful to consider the moral nature of the game as an object and how it relates to the more player-centric virtue ethics perspective. Computer games are moral objects. If the game object becomes a game experience and contributes to the player's subjectivization process, then it is relevant to think about the relations established between the player-subject and the game object, and how virtue ethics can cast light on the ethics of the game object.

As I have previously argued, computer games are moral objects because they present values embedded in their design. Those values can be found in design choices as well as in game world simulations. It is the combination of both the system and the world that makes games interesting objects. For example, in the case of a game like *World of Warcraft*, where players of different factions cannot use the chat function to communicate with each other, it is possible to argue that this design choice implies a series of ethically significant constraints and affordances.

In *World of Warcraft*, the fictional world and the developers' intent to feed the endless war, creating the game's central topic, provide an explanation for these communication affordances. By imposing such a constraint, the developers have stated that players in opposite factions will have a hard time trying to settle their differences, or uniting against computer-controlled characters of extreme power. The gameplay, the experience of the world, and its fictional level are highly conditioned by a design affordance that constrains possibilities for the players.

This brief illustration shows how games are, above all, systems designed to create and facilitate practices. These may not be neutral or, as I shall argue later on, the player or the community of players may not interpret them as morally neutral. Within the ethical approach of this book, this means a type of agency-constraining design that focuses on limiting the behavior of an ethical agent with reflective capacities concerning her actions. It is important then to keep in mind that players act in games within the boundaries defined and allowed by the system. In this virtue ethics framework, players are not to be taken as passive subjects, but as active ethical agents. Nevertheless, it is also necessary to remind ourselves that players are actually constrained by the voluntary experience of a system designed to create, enhance, and enforce behavior. Players can evaluate that behavior from an ethical perspective, using their moral judgment, but they are still constrained by what is possible and what is not within the game.

Even though players of *World of Warcraft* might want to make a truce in specific areas, such as high-level instances, so gameplay can be more satisfactory by eliminating the need to fight the computer-controlled characters and players of the opposing faction, the game is designed so that this communication is hard to establish, if not impossible. As such, it would be incorrect to say that players do not want to solve their differences in nonconfrontational ways—rather that players actually cannot easily engage in that kind of communication because the system is designed to thwart that possibility.

From a virtue ethics perspective, the game design is relevant when the origin of an ethical dilemma can be tracked back to it, as in the case of *World of Warcraft* and cross-faction communication. But it is the players who, as active agents, have the responsibility in the process of accepting and experiencing those ethical values.

There is a relevant perspective that virtue ethics can provide to the understanding of the game object: to analyze the design of the game in terms of the constraints and affordances that allow players to reinforce their good virtues, first as players, and second as human beings. Virtue ethics could argue that a game like *Manhunt* fosters the development of ludic phronesis because in its design it takes into account how the player is constrained in order to make choices in the game, and how those constraints are parallel to the fiction of the game. The *Manhunt* player is, by design, encouraged to explore the limits of her player-subject—how far can she push the ethical boundaries of her subjectivity before her actions in the game are deemed unethical by the ludic phronesis, effectively halting her experience of the game?

The ethical values embedded in game design are of interest for the virtue ethics approach to computer games, as they are relevant for understanding how experiencing the game can foster the player-subject's virtues. Moreover, there are some principles that virtue ethics can suggest to game designers in pursuit of ethical games; principles that affect not so much the game design per se, but the game design in interaction with a moral agent. These principles have to do with the inclusion in the design of options for players to practice their ethical understanding of the game, changing them from guided users into informed practitioners of the ludic experience. Virtue ethics provides a solid framework for understanding the game as object when put in the perspective of players as moral beings.

4.1.3 The Heart of a Good Game: The Ludic Hermeneutic Circle

From a virtue ethics perspective, the player has to be understood as a virtuous being. When immersed in a game situation, players use their motor skills, their capacities for abstraction and logic, and their intelligence to solve the challenges posed by the game. And they also apply their ethical reasoning. This implies that players are responsible for their acts in computer games. Players have the moral responsibility of creating values in the experience of computer games; they are the ones who will create the experience that will make a game ethical or not beyond the limits and constraints of its design. The responsibility for the affordances in the design is still the developers', but players must be considered responsible for the game experience and for how that game experience creates values for the community.

A virtuous player reflects upon her actions not only in the strategic, goal-oriented sense that we traditionally associate with games, but also in a moral sense. The virtuous computer game player ought to critically and ethically reflect on her actions as well as on the design of the system she is engaged in. The virtuous player is so in her reflection about her actions, alone or in the community, and through her behaviors in the game experience. Also, the virtuous player is one who seeks to participate in a virtuous community.

There are, then, three elements at play: the game system that conditions the players' capacities, the player's individual reasoning and ludic phronesis, and the player as a member of a community. It is in the interplay between these three, which can be effectively understood as the core of the virtue ethics approach to computer games, where the ethics of computer games is to be found, and more specifically where the virtuosity of players can be clearly outlined.

Within the perspective defended by virtue ethics, the ethics of computer games are the ethics of the agent who engages voluntarily in the game. Two issues have to be then taken into consideration: one is concerned with the relationship between the ethics of the game as agent and the ethics of that agent when not being a player; the other is concerned with the relations between the player as moral agent and the game as moral object. It is in these relations where the ethics of computer games is to be found, and it is by means of these relations that ethical issues related to computer games must be solved.

These two issues will be explained using an adapted version of the hermeneutic circle as applied by Gadamer. I shall call this adaptation the ludic hermeneutic circle. Gadamer's hermeneutics, due to the influence of Heidegger, go beyond classic hermeneutics and become an ontological tool for the understanding of the being and the being in history. His use of the hermeneutic circle as a conceptual exercise is based on his dialogic understanding of perception and experience: the circle stands for a codetermination of the experience and the subject who experiences, or in the case of texts, of the text and the reader, or the work of art and the observer. This codetermination, the fusion of horizons,[9] makes the being of the work of art and the observer into a whole. The circle is the process of understanding beyond methods, as an almost intuitive practice.

Ludic phronesis is an ethical resource in the process of interpreting the game experience. Ludic phronesis can be defined as the ethical interpretation of a game experience in light of the player-subject and the cultural being outside the game; it is a crucial element for understanding the applicability of the ludic hermeneutic circle. The circle I will propose here as a tool for understanding the role of the player is a game-centered close interpretation of the principles of practical knowledge and dialogue that permeate Gadamer's work, inspired by Aristotle and adapted to computer games as ludic experiences.

The ludic hermeneutic circle, then, is a model for describing the process that takes place when an embodied, cultural human being becomes a player, and how that player relates to her subjectivity, the game experience, and the subject external to the game. By embodied and cultural human being I refer to a person that actually has a body, bringing forth embodiment and gender issues, and who lives in one or more cultures. The player is not only the subject that is within the game; it is also the body-subject that makes the game come into being as an actual experience by interpreting the game system and the game situation. This process of interpretation is a dialogic instance between the game system and the player. By constraining choices and affording practices, the game encourages behaviors that the player has to evaluate in order to successfully experience the game.

Playing any game can be understood as an act of interpreting the game system and choosing the appropriate strategies, which need not be the optimal strategies. The missing step in game research has been to link this process of interpretation with the ethical nature of players. Ethics play a role in that interpretation process: the analysis of the game system and the possible strategies that can be chosen are also evaluated from a moral point of view. It is precisely those players who participate actively in creating the values of the community who should be taken into consideration when analyzing it. And, incidentally, all players should aspire to participate in the game community and create those values.

The ludic hermeneutic circle operates as a layered interpretational moral process, which starts with the becoming of the player and goes through a series of interpretative stages that conclude in the development of the ludic phronesis. The interpretation process begins with a cultural subject external to the game that becomes an agent by experiencing a game system. In the first step of the ludic hermeneutic circle, the game system conditions the player-subject. The player interprets the affordances and constraints of the game as necessary boundaries that have to be accepted in order to become a player, and so she does. This initial player-subject, the zero state of the player as ethical being, is uncritically engaged in the game's ethical values and discourses.

By referring to a zero state, I am not referring to the concept of "blank slate" in behaviorist theory. The player-subject is created anew in the game experience, but that subject comes from a cultural self and from a previous tradition of playing games. The initial subject is open to the specificities of the game experience she is engaging in, but she is not isolated from her past as player, nor from her self outside of the game. In other words, the imprint of the game system determines the zero-subject of the player, the zero-subject being the initial condition of the player as subject for that game experience. That choice is not necessarily ethically informed, but it creates a subject that is conditioned by the game system's ethical affordances.

Once that zero-subject comes into being, the moral interpretation process of the ludic hermeneutic circle starts. If players were reduced to mere zero-players, mindlessly and amorally determined by the game as object, we wouldn't find reactions in response to reflection on the design and the fictional world of the game, like complaints about the content or imbalance of a game, or elaborate community-driven policies. The second step of the ludic hermeneutic circle is a moral reflection of the player as player-subject; that is, as a subject that takes place and interacts with a game world designed for her ludic enjoyment. Players reflect on the act of being committed to the power structure of the game. The experience of the game is not unidirectionally system to player, it is a dialogue between the system that imposes restrictions and affords behaviors, and a player who reflects upon those.

This player-subject is not only that who can win the game, or achieve more of the goals in the case of games without a clear winning condition, it is also a virtuous player who is capable of adapting her behavior to the situation of the game as well as to the goals and constraints it creates. What kind of player somebody wants to be is not determined by becoming victorious, but by how to win; that is, the virtuous player will try to win by playing virtuously, using her ludic phronesis to assess the strategies and choices made.

This is the first level of the ludic hermeneutic circle—one in which the player uses her own ludic phronesis in order to interpret her presence in the game world and the actions she should take, starting to develop her own subjectivity for that game experience, the individual layer. But, as I have stated before, being a player is also being a part of a synchronic and diachronic community of players. This community plays a crucial role in the process of experiencing a game, and thus it has to be included in the ludic hermeneutic circle.

We have all played, and we can always share game experiences with other players, even if those experiences are of different games, precisely because we share a common culture as players. Our player-subject, who starts as a zero-subject but is modified by a dialogic reflection upon that subjectivity, is also in a dialogue with the game community, even in the case of single-player games.[10] The relation between the individual and the community of players can be used to address topics such as cheating in single-player games, or hardcore gaming.

It could be argued that players do not cheat in single-player games because a part of being a good player in a player community is surpassing the challenges posed by the game, garnering a skill-based achievement.

One can righteously claim victory over a game in front of other players only if that victory is legal, so other players can see it as done within the boundaries of the game rules. Likewise, hardcore players—for example, those who strive to achieve the 100 percent completion rate in a game like *Grand Theft Auto: San Andreas*, which may involve more than 100 hours of playing—do it not only for personal satisfaction, but also to become recognized in their communities. Even in single-player games, then, we are a part of a community. Community is an ever-larger part of multiplayer games because of the presence of institutionalized, systemically embedded representations of the community, such as guilds.

What this second stage of interpretation does is to situate the player in the larger context of the player cultural community—cultural because different communities of players create different traditions in games that affect the interpretation of the individual virtuous player. For example, Italian soccer coaches and fans seem to be very keen on extremely defensive tactics, the so-called *catenaccio*,[11] thus making the virtuous player one who is both disciplined and relevant to the game's overall defense. On the other hand, Brazilian soccer fans enjoy the beautiful game, the *jogo bonito*, which demands great individual skill and not necessarily a lot of tactical or collective sacrifices. This is a crucial difference for the understanding of football cultures. While catennacio makes order, sacrifice, and teamwork the basis for the appreciation of a game, jogo bonito insists on individualism and imagination, catering to thoroughly different expectations from the observers and the players. For these two communities, virtuous soccer players require different values and interpretations of the game. It is within this culture that the player enters an interpretational dialogue, participating as one among many who create the ethics of a game. The individual player and her reflection upon her own subjectivity under the rules of a game can be modified by thinking as a part of a community, thus the importance of the community in the configuration of the individual player's ethics and the game as experience.

There is a final element in the ludic hermeneutic circle, an element that broadens the perspective and possible application of this concept of the understanding of computer game ethics: players and player communities are cultural and embodied outside the game experience, where other values that are not those of the game as object, the player, or the player community are dominant. Ultimately, our actions within the game, as members of a player community, are to be interpreted under the light of our own existence as moral beings in the world outside the game. That world and our physical presence in it are an important factor in the configuration of the ethics of a computer game. There are cultural taboos, and there are firm beliefs that cannot be overruled by the commitment to the game world. Being a player is maintaining a part of what makes us moral beings in the real world as a reference.

This is not to say that there is an easily distinguishable boundary between the player as subject and the self from which the subject originates. It is not possible to place an arrow pointing at the limits between the two ways of experiencing reality. I have argued that a player comes into being only when immersed in a game experience, be that playing the game or participating as a member of a game community. When not in any of those situations, there is no active player-subjectivity; we are not looking at the world with the eyes of a player. This distinction, as with many operational tools in philosophy, is hard to prove empirically, and yet it is logically sound and analytically productive. There is a player-subject who is evaluated by a cultural, embodied, moral being who has accepted the rules of a game, thus becoming a subject but never losing its presence. Being a player is also being evaluated by who we are as moral, embodied, cultural beings.

This whole process of interpretation, starting with the zero-subject faithful to the game and ending in the dialogue between the player-subject and the moral being, constitutes the ludic hermeneutic circle. It can be argued that I have only depicted the harmonious side of the ludic hermeneutic circle, and that there are players who actually engage in deviant gameplay and enjoy doing so, harassing other players, cheating, and griefing. That is where the importance of the player community manifests itself: an individual player may develop a judgment of her self in the game in which griefing and cheating are acceptable. On the other hand, the player community, historically speaking, tends to treat cheaters and griefers as elements of disruption who need to be avoided or punished for the well-being of the community. This does not mean that the community of players consists of zealous defenders of the gaming orthodoxy—the player community consists of players who collectively and historically have developed a sense of sportsmanship and values that good players, both in skill and in morals, should sport. The game community is effectively powerless—

they can cast away players, but they cannot influence, punish, or reward them, unless the game designers include the game community as an institution inside the game structure.   ·   ·

This dialogic procedure of interpretation of the game, along with the actions of the player within the game and the community and her relation to real life is what creates the ludic phronesis that informs the virtuous player. This includes the capacity of experiencing the game within the dialogic interpretational procedures of the ludic hermeneutic circle. Ludic phronesis is the ethical interpretation that takes place in the described stages of the ludic hermeneutic circle. It is a character trait and a knowledge that we develop. Learning to play games as an interpretational process of who we are and how we behave is the process of developing this moral reasoning. Because games operate in this circle of interpretation, we can have political and ideological games—the player develops a moral reflection of her actions that is somehow processed and evaluated by her real-life values, an evaluation process intrinsic to games, and a proof of the moral nature of computer games. This is a model of the ludic hermeneutic circle:

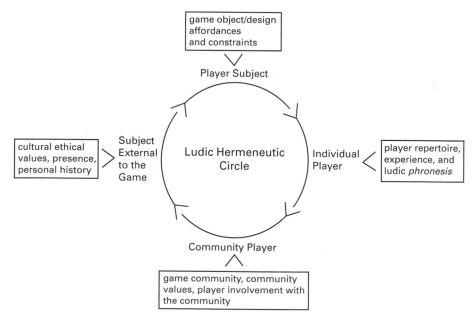

Figure 4.1
The Ludic Hermeneutic Circle

The ethics of a computer game are the result of the ludic hermeneutic circle, the outcome of a game experienced by moral agents who reflect upon their actions and upon the design of the game using their ludic phronesis.

4.1.4 The Ethics of Computer Games According to Virtue Ethics

Understanding the ethics of computer games from a virtue ethics perspective gives players a great amount of responsibility when it comes to dealing with moral issues in computer games. A common mistake when analyzing the ethical dilemmas that computer games pose is to consider the player as a passive element, abandoned by her moral intuitions in a labyrinth demiurgically created by the game developers. Virtue ethics challenges this perspective, situating morally aware players in active dialogue with the game—a process made possible by the player who is responsible for the ethical nature of the game experience in which she willingly engages. Players are the bearers of computer game ethics, the act of playing computer games being a matter of interpretation within virtue.

Individually, players are affected by the game design. To play a game means to initially accept the affordances and constraints that a game presents; in this process, players come into being—they become an ethical subject capable of reflecting on the in-game choices and strategies. A player experiences a game in a ludic hermeneutic circle, a process of procedural moral interpretation of the game experience. This process is also a dialogue between the player as a moral being and the game. In this dialogue the player has not only to interpret the game, but also to provide ethical behaviors of her own to the experience. Therefore, an ethical game by design is that game in which the designed system does not constrain the possibility for the player to afford ethical values into the gameplay experience. Those affordances have to be meaningful for the gameplay, relevant and agreed upon by other players. An ethical game is that which acknowledges, respects, and encourages the ethical being of computer game players.

This does not mean that a game has to be molded according to the values of its players, or that players ought to be free to choose whatever ethics should rule in the game. The ethical dimension of the game as object, according to virtue ethics, relies on the openness of the system—a game by design ought not to interfere with the ethical affordances that players may want to provide to the game, both on an interpretational level and on a more practical level. Nevertheless, it could be argued that there are examples of games in which this openness does not happen, and yet they can be considered good games from an ethical point of view. In the case of *Manhunt*, for example, the game designers performed a rhetoric design of subtle mastery: by being aware that the player is a moral being, the game design reflects the game world, translating it into the game experience. More clearly: in *Manhunt* the experience of the horrible actions the player has to commit is unavoidable, and the player is forced to go through that experience. *Manhunt* seems aware of the procedures of the ludic hermeneutic circle: because the player cannot behave in any other way than committing those actions, her experience matches that of the game fiction, thus creating a moral experience.

This implies an open path for political and satirical games, as well as for games used for social and political commentary: a game design may not want to let the player introduce ethical values into her gameplay—but that has to be done with a clear design plan in mind, being conscious that it will provoke a strong moral reaction in the player, an ethical awareness that may bring games the possibility for new forms of expression. The possibility for political games lies here: acknowledging that there is a player with ethical capacities and interests who is willing to engage in a ludic experience that will make her reflect on the actions she is taking within the game. Players would not be given information—they would experience the political dilemmas, because they are active agents engaged in the production of meaning in the game.

This virtuous player engages in gameplay conscious of the process of ethical interpretation. A virtuous player is defined as a moral being with the capacity to interpret and reflect on the game as object, on her behavior, and on her presence in the game world and in the game community. A virtuous player develops and uses the player virtues and ludic practical wisdom when playing computer games, a kind of moral reasoning that takes into account its specific being and meaning within the game experience, and acts upon those values. This is also a process of maturing, a process of developing the necessary ethical skills to ensure that the experience of the game is ethical. A player is responsible for her moral well-being in a game experience, as well as for the values she enacts. A player has to behave virtuously and develop the moral knowledge to do so.

The virtuous behavior of a game player is that behavior which shows an understanding not of the best strategies and actions to win the game, but of the gameplay processes that ensure a satisfactory game experience. The ethical goal is to win by respecting the game and other players, by doing what is best to preserve the ludic engagement in the game. A player who decides not to engage in player-versus-player gameplay against weaker characters in *World of Warcraft*, for example, is showing moral reflection on the structure of the game—her behavior is ethical by nature, sporting in her gameplay those virtues she believes the game must have.

But players are seldom alone. The role of the community in the development of the ethics of computer games is as important as the role of the individual player. Player communities have the responsibility of creating the implicit and afforded codes of interpretation and conduct that define what a good game is, thus placing those who disrupt the well-being of the game experience outside the moral goodness of the community. A game community has importance in the ethical configuration of a game, how it is understood, and how ethical behaviors are enforced and respected by all the players. When an ethical issue arises, the player community should be able to provide answers and create open discussions, empowering their opinions and actions in their experience of the game.

The player and the community, then, are partially responsible for a game's ethical values, together with the ethical affordances and constraints that the game may have in its design. A player is responsible for her acts in a game, for the way she behaves, and for what she makes of a game in her experience of it. The ethical issues that a game can create are the responsibility of the player to the extent that the game designers have allowed players to create and afford their own values in the game. This is not to take away the importance of the design affordances, because the player as subject is to some extent conditioned by those affordances. In other words, the design is relevant from this perspective because the game should foster the development of the player's virtues. If it doesn't, from a virtue ethics perspective we would be talking about an unethical game.

The moral maturity of players, and the way they relate as such to the game, plays an important role as well. Players have to develop virtues in order to become good players, and make the games good. By being part of a historical game community, and by playing games, players develop this moral sense of playing, creating the ludic phronesis that determines the ethics of games. This phronesis is created through time, which is one of the reasons why not every game is suitable for every player. Players have to develop the moral maturity to understand the specifics of a game and how to interpret them. Given that a game's ethics are partially dependent on the players' ethically interpreted actions, it is of utmost importance that these players present moral maturity, so that the game becomes an actually good, ethical computer game.

The ethics of computer games is dependent on the ethics of the players because the players are the ethical centers of the ludic hermeneutic circle. A good computer game is that which fosters virtuous players, a game designed to create player-subjects who can understand and develop their ethical values, and where those values can be reflected. The player is responsible for becoming the virtuous player that the game is designed to encourage. The virtue ethics perspective on the ethics of computer games puts players in the center of the picture by expanding the presence and importance of ethical norms and experience with the ludic phronesis, the capacity to morally interpret the act of playing from a perspective derived from previous experiences and belonging to a game community.

4.1.5 Limitations of the Virtue Ethics Approach

While virtue ethics seems quite fit for explaining the ethics of computer games from a player perspective, it presents some limitations that have to be taken into consideration. The strongest problem has to do with the importance given to the community. Games are a voluntary activity, and digital games are a voluntary activity that depends on access to a computer and, in some cases, to Internet connections. The material conditions for playing computer games are subject to social and economic constraints: not everybody has access to the best computers or the fastest Internet connections. Furthermore, not everybody has time to spare participating in game forums because of the limitations of their connections. Therefore, putting so much responsibility on the community may give rise to some problems. I believe the most relevant among these is related to the constitution of the community. If the community is comprised exclusively of those who can afford to log onto the Internet regularly and/or spend vast amounts of time participating in the common creation of the game culture, then there may be silent web-less majorities that do not follow the values of the community, therefore distorting the values of the game as they can be perceived. That is, the values of a game as deduced from its community may only be the values of an elite group with time and technical knowledge and capacities.

This is perhaps the most important ethical dilemma computer games can face from a virtue ethics perspective. These are participative systems because players actually have a large degree of effect on how the game must be played. But the fact that the design and mechanics of the game are out of reach, and that developers ultimately have control over the game, leads to the discarding of coparticipation in creation of the actual game design, or game object. Game communities solve this problem by being creative and productive, adjusting with their imagination and their values to the closed framework in which they were created. But if a minority of users creates these communities, then that elite dictates the values of the game, forcing other players to accept values they may not endorse, but which they have to accept due to material constraints.

This limitation needed to be mentioned here as evidence that I am not arguing for an exclusive virtue ethics explanation of the ethics of computer games. Virtue ethics provides answers to those ethical issues in digital games related to players, player behavior, and the role and importance of ethical practice alone or with other players, in the context of a game. But its scope is limited, and it can only explain to a certain extent the ethics of computer games. As ethicists and players, it is our task to point out the limitations, and formulate what may be developed as solutions. Such formulations are beyond the scope of this book, but they must be mentioned for the sake of completeness in this virtue ethics approach to the ethics of computer games.

4.2 Information Ethics and Computer Games

So far the computer games-centric analysis presented in this book could still be applied, with few changes, to any type of game. Nevertheless,

I have stated that my main interest is the ethics of computer games, especially in the perspective of computer ethics. Virtue ethics has been successfully applied in that field, and I have argued that it is also a useful framework when analyzing computer games. Still, it is of interest to apply a philosophical ethical theory that is related to the ethical problems created or changed by the use of computers and digital systems of information.

This theory is information ethics, which provides an alternative reference framework that both places computer games in the tradition of computer ethics and can be applied to the analysis of the ethics of computer games both as objects and as experiences of an ethical agent. Information ethics has the potential to cover the analysis of most of the elements that make computer games ethically relevant, from the design of the game system and game world to the implications of community creation and individual behaviors of players in the information-rich environments of computer games. As such, it is a core component of the ethical framework I will present in later stages of this book.

4.2.1   Key Concepts and Method of Information Ethics

The ethical theory I have chosen to represent a closer computer ethics perspective is information ethics as defined by Luciano Floridi, Jeff Sanders, and others.[12] Information ethics is a radical perspective on computer ethics that takes into account the nature of computing as well as the presence of human and software agents in digital environments. Furthermore, it shares with virtue ethics a certain constructivist approach. It is my goal to provide an answer to computer game ethics that draws on the common grounds of those theories, but also to use and exploit their specific conceptual strengths.

In Floridi and Sanders's words, information ethics "is an Environmental Macroethics based on the concept of data entity rather than life."[13] Information ethics defines itself as a macroethical approach, a framework that expands the responsibility of moral agents by defining existence as informational existence: we are all data entities. Every biological life is a data entity, but there are more data entities than life-forms: there are artificial data entities that need to be respected and that can be harmed. For instance, databases containing our credit card data and records are data beings that need to be preserved from harm. These data entities share an environment that needs to be ethically protected. Information ethics expands our moral universe to include everything informational, and the relations that we establish and that are established with us. Furthermore, information ethics is an "architectural ethics," an ethics addressing not only the users but also the creators and designers of the "infosphere."[14] The infosphere is an ecological environment of informational agents, patients, and their mutual relations. All elements of the infosphere are in one way or another mutually connected, precisely like in an ecosystem, and the balance of this system can be affected, leading to harm and thus defining what unethical actions or relations are. The infosphere is defined as "a context constituted by the whole system of information objects, including all agents and patients, messages, their attributes and mutual relations."[15] The infosphere is a key concept in information ethics, since it makes clear where we can find data beings, how their relations constitute their ontologies, and what can harm them.

Computer games are infospheres. In a specific level of analysis, or level of abstraction, a game like *World of Warcraft* (which I will analyze in more detail in chapter 5) is an infosphere: the product, the developers, the servers and their technology, the players, and the online resources. But a specific server is also an infosphere, depending on the level of abstraction necessary for the analysis. The infosphere could include the player-versus-player server where I played, as well as the Internet forums hosted on the official web page, for example. Other analyses may need to define different operational infospheres, always depending on what is relevant for the research question to be explained.

Information ethics takes into account the necessity of operating within different informational perspectives by using the concepts of level of abstraction and gradient of abstraction.[16] The use of these concepts is closely linked with the ontological nature of information ethics. According to this theory, data beings are capable of agenthood. The problem is that if there is no threshold of agenthood, everything can become an agent. Thus, a formal approach is needed to specify what beings present agenthood under which circumstances. The method of abstraction, from which the concepts of level of abstraction and gradient of abstraction are taken, provides a serious logical framework that allows a clear specification of what reality is being observed, and how it is being observed.

A level of abstraction "is a finite but nonempty set of observables, which are expected to be the building blocks in a theory characterized by their very choice."[17] A level of abstraction determines the features of the observed object we are focusing on. The whole set of different observables used in the research yields the gradient of abstraction, "a way of varying the level of abstraction in order to make observations at differing levels of abstraction."[18]

Information ethics has an object-oriented approach to ontology: an object is informationally, and thus ontologically, defined by the objects with which it constitutes the infosphere—their relations, capacities, and possibilities.[19] By using the phenomenological concept of system and relating this to the procedures of information constitution and exchange of computer systems,[20] information ethics describes a moral universe in which not only is no being alone, but every being is indeed related, *morally* related to other beings, because in their well-being is connected the welfare of the whole system. Agents are systems that affect larger systems with their actions, affecting themselves as well, since other systems are procedurally and informationally related to them.

Information ethics considers moral actions an information process. It is worth pointing out that the agent and the patient are, in this level of abstraction, not necessarily human. Information ethics allows an operative level of abstraction without human agency. In fact, information ethics suggests artificial agency as a key element for the understanding of morality in the infosphere.

Also of interest for this ethical framework is Floridi and Sanders's concept of *homo poieticus*, central to information ethics' anthropology.[21] Both information ethics and virtue ethics are constructivist approaches, but while the latter could be accused of promoting an anthropocentric approach, the former takes into account a much wider system. Information ethics expands the ethical universe, increasing the degree to which we are morally responsible for the world we live in. According to information ethics, the moral scope has to be expanded to take into consideration any informational being that is present and has importance for the well-being of the infosphere. Furthermore, as human agents we have the task, the ethical duty, of using *and* producing virtuous environments. For the environment to be ethically sound, we need to be ethically responsible as users and producers.

The strong object-oriented background of information ethics implies that every agent in the infosphere, to some extent, is a producer as well as a consumer. In a system such as the one suggested by information ethics, interconnectivity is not enough to explain the degree of interdependence that every element of the infosphere presents to the other beings of that infosphere. As informational beings we are coparticipated by every other being in the infosphere, both in a material and in an informational way. Thus, the responsibility of producing and sustaining the infosphere's well-being is extended to each and every one of its participants, be they human or not. The concept of subject that is present in this approach is, beyond the *egopoietic* approach of virtue ethics, *ecopoietic*; that is, it assumes that the agent creates the environment and participates in its generation and sustainability, and thus is ethically responsible for the preservation of its balance as well as for its adequate use and development. We are all developers and consumers in the infosphere, and in this regard we must behave ethically and preserve the well-being of the system.

Information ethics expands our moral universe so we are responsible for the act of participation and co-creation of the informational worlds with which we are engaged. This may seem a highly theoretical, complex understanding of computer ethics. Nevertheless, I will argue that information ethics fits computer games especially well, and its application provides insights on the morality of computer games and ludic experiences that place their analysis in the field of computer ethics.

4.2.2 Information and Games

To understand the ethics of computer games from an information ethics perspective, the first condition that has to be met is that the computer game, both as an experience and as an object, has to be considered an infosphere, the informationally rich environment where moral agents and patients engage in informational relations that affect and change their states. It is an environment where all beings are informational objects, and their relations are determined by the system and implemented by the creative agents.

Let's use a popular example: *World of Warcraft* as an infosphere can be described as a computer-coded state machine[22] that hosts a number of agents who can interact with the world in an exchange of information aimed at modifying the informational values of agents, patients, and environments in predesigned but not predetermined ways. In other words, *World of Warcraft* is a system programmed to react to informational exchanges from a number of agents simultaneously accessing and inhabiting that environment. The changes in the state machine are available to everybody in that environment, and may also be suffered by everybody. Within this perspective, the subjectivization process of becoming a player is nothing other than reprocessing our being into informational values that are relevant only for that infosphere.

If we see *World of Warcraft* as a whole, we can describe it as an environment in which we interact with other agents by exchanging meaningful information aimed at influencing the state of the game, and we can do so only because as players we have become informationally relevant for the system in which we are immersed. The game world, without the presence of the player community, is a construct of data, some of which is passive and noninteractive, but most of which presents interactive functionalities—something that could be defined within the information ethics perspective as data beings. These data beings are informationally relevant, and thus perceived as beings by those agents that are immersed in the game in order to play it. To play a game, then, is to exchange information in an infosphere specifically designed for such exchanges. The informational space of *World of Warcraft* is a place designed for play, an environment where these agents and patients exchange information in order to experience the system in a ludic way.

When entering these systems, a player accepts a limitation in her information being in order to be able to exist and participate in the infosphere. This infosphere is a designed environment that demands certain informational capacities from its players, imposing restrictive rules as to what is and is not possible for the agent in the world. The infosphere design can have an impact on the informational being of the agents that voluntarily come into being in it. This shaping of the agent's informational being implies an ethical participation of the game system in the configuration of being, and thus it becomes a source of ethical dilemmas. In other words, the way the informational system is designed to create and allow informational beings to exist and participate in the informational world has to be analyzed from an ethical perspective, because the design affects the well-being of relevant informational beings, and it may therefore influence the overall ethical informational balance of the game, hence the relevance of games as designed ethical objects.

It is import to here remember the ontological nature of players as informational beings. Information ethics is an ecological ethics—it defines the well-being of a network of interconnected elements, in this case informational beings, and how it should be protected. Informational beings are related and determined by the other informational beings in the infosphere. For example, in a role-playing game the level of a player is both an internal characteristic, as it is forged through gameplay, and an external characteristic that reveals relevant data about that player. In player-versus-player situations, level is used for assessing the chances of a victory in a duel, or for calibrating other gameplay options. It is also the cue that determines when an action is potentially unethical, like corpse camping a lower-level player.

This implies that players are actually dependent on and affected by not only other players' informational natures, but also by the way the infosphere articulates and facilitates those interrelations. Understanding this ethical balance of the game, and how the informational relations between the agents and patients of the infosphere shape the ethics of the game, requires using the concepts of levels of abstraction and gradient of abstraction, since they show relevant aspects of the informational complexity of computer games as infospheres. This method is similar in concept to the ludic hermeneutic circle, but it pertains to the informational being of the game and the relational capacities of the system instead of placing the importance exclusively on the interpretational capacities of the human agent. In this sense, the use of the method of abstraction for the informational analysis of computer game ethics provides a more thorough framework than that proposed by virtue ethics.

There are some levels of abstraction present in all computer games. These are not the only levels of abstraction that can be used to analyze games, but they are dominant when analyzing their ethics as infospheres:

1. The game system as informational environment: the game as a designed infosphere, and how it shapes interactions and behaves as a state machine.

2. The player as informational being: how the player becomes relevant to the infosphere by becoming an informationally relevant being, capable of exchanging information within that infosphere.

3. The player as an informational being related to and determined by other informational beings in the infosphere: that is, how the player behaves in relation to other players and the possible artificial agents in the game, and how those informational relations shape the environment of the infosphere.

4. The player as a *homo poieticus*: how the player creates the values of the infosphere not only by behaving ethically, but also by constructing those values that should make the infosphere of the game an informationally ethical place, a place where information exchanges take place in a moral way.

Within any of these levels of abstraction, an unethical action would be that which modifies the infosphere's informational structure, creating an imbalance in the experience of the system—any unwanted informational asymmetries. An informational asymmetry, in the context of computer games, is a situation in which one or more agents have an influence on the infosphere that is seen as illegal by the rules of the game. The case of cheating, for example, implies a modification of the infosphere that introduces informational asymmetries into the system, corrupting the well-being of the game.

In computer games, informational well-being can actually be clearly defined: a game infosphere is healthy when its informational structure, its game design, allows players to undergo a ludic experience in which they can participate. This experience is designed and limited by the system. In other words, the game infosphere is in balance when all players can experience the game's designed system successfully. This implies that a healthy game infosphere is one in which the player can actually create and enforce her values within the game system, and in which the implementation of those values does not alter the informational structure of the game.

Also, in a healthy game infosphere, players exert their creative stewardship. Creative stewardship means, in the case of computer games, to act responsibly and ethically, preserving the game experience and the game system as an infosphere (for example, not cheating), while exerting a level of creativity within the game—creating new strategies, improving as a player, cooperating with others, and exploring the world. Let's take the example of emergent gameplay in *Deus Ex*. In this game, players are placed in open-ended levels that they can navigate in almost any way they want, making use of their knowledge of the game and the tools and mechanics provided by the designers. One of those tools was a mine that could be stuck to the walls. Cleverly enough, some players discovered that, with the right amount of skill, these mines could be used as ad hoc ladders, which allowed players to avoid potentially fatal enemies.

Did the players cheat? No—as a matter of fact, this is a great example of creative stewardship in a computer game: players understood the infosphere, how it functioned, and how they related to it as players within the game world so well that they could devise an unforeseen strategy that, while preserving the logic of the game, was also a symbol of their own capacities as players in the world. In other words, players appropriated this world and made it theirs, preserving its original structure and functions, but extending it by means of reflecting on their agency. Creative stewardship in games takes place in all instances in which players contribute to the game beyond the mere manipulation of the basic input procedures required for the game to be played: building communities, helping other players, or devising strategies and gameplay patterns are all examples of this type of ludic creative stewardship.

In summary, a game is an infosphere designed to create an experience by a number of players who are interrelated in their informational being. Information ethics provides a way of understanding why these design choices, which at some levels (the system as such; the player devoid of other agents) may be considered harmless, are actually a source of harm and thus unethical. For any informational system to be ethical, it has to be open to the creative actions of its agents. Otherwise, the system is prone to imbalance, and thus has a tendency toward becoming an unethical system.

4.2.3   Information Ethics and the Ethics of Computer Games

A computer game is a ludic infosphere, created with the intention of making possible a limited and combinational number of informational exchanges between agents, patients, and informational objects. The game is then not only the game world, but every world in which the informational being of the system and its agents, the players, is both possible and meaningful. Information ethics takes into consideration this game world, the game situation, (e.g., the living room), and the game community (e.g., *World of Warcraft* forums). All these layers of the infosphere are determined by the initial informational value of the infosphere, as it is this value that determines if the informational exchange is relevant. In other words, the conditions that create the infosphere also determine its boundaries and thus the applicability of the information ethics method.

A player is an informational being relevant in the infosphere; an informational being that has constructivist values, not only participating in the infosphere as an agent, but also acting as a creative steward who has to be responsible for the informational well-being of the system. Information ethics has a strong object-oriented approach, meaning that players, or by extension any agent in the ludic infosphere, are never atomized units of information: their being is dependent and modified by the being of other informational beings in the system. What a player can be is determined by what the system allows her to be, and how she can relate to the system. Like in classic text-based adventure games, in which there was only one keyword that could trigger the game's progression, players can relate to the infosphere in only a limited number of ways, some of them allowed by the game, some a consequence of the constructive capacities of the player in her interpretation of the game's informational values.

Information ethics' object-oriented approach supposes a radical change of perspective. Every being in the game is related, interconnected, and relevant for some other being, or for all those beings. And this not only accounts for what is actually programmed or coded: the game community, the individual player, and even the media or elements traditionally considered to be external to the game play a significant role in the ethical configuration of the game, because every being in the infosphere can and will eventually be related to and determined by another being of that same infosphere. This explains the players' repertoire and their community culture, but also those discourses of the media and of institutions that affect the informational status of the game. When the United States military praises the capacities of computer games as virtual web-based environments for training, they are effectively adding value to the *America's Army*[23] infosphere: it becomes a propaganda tool and a recruitment device. And they add this propagandistic or political meaning because the nature of their discourses is informationally relevant within the game infosphere, and thus becomes a part of the game experience.

This leads to the concept of distributed responsibility, which is the great contribution of information ethics to the understanding of digital games.[24] In a computer game, every informational being that plays a role in the infosphere has a shared role in the ethical values of that infosphere. The responsibility is not univocal; there is not one single element of the infosphere that can be held responsible for the ethics of a computer game—not the designers, not the players, not the player community, not the media. Every informational being, including computer-controlled agents, has a role in the infosphere and thus has responsibility for the well-being and ethical soundness of the system. Distributed responsibility implies that ethicists have to look at which informational stakeholder is relevant for any ethical issue that arises within the infosphere of a game; it also implies that we have to look for the distributional and relational structure of those responsibilities: who is responsible for what, when, and to what degree. There is no single bearer of responsibility in a game because a game is an object-oriented informational structure where many elements can be interconnected in their ontological existence in that infosphere. To describe the ethics of computer games, then, it is necessary to identify the distributed network of responsibilities relevant to a specific ethical issue, determine the structural relations in terms of responsibility of that structure, and suggest solutions for the ethical problems found.

Distributed responsibility is of crucial importance when we think about the importance of players and nonplayers[25] in the ethical configuration of the ludic infosphere. The responsibility that the agents and participants in the infosphere have relates to the previously introduced concept of creative stewardship, by which the agents of the infosphere are entitled to exert their creative capacities within the infosphere, while they must at the same time preserve its integrity (in the case of games, the successful experience of the game).

It could be possible to relate to virtue ethics using the concepts from the object-oriented approach of information ethics, which also relates to the notion of distributed responsibility. Agents can be defined as informational objects with a number of data structures and methods.[26] Those methods determine how objects relate to others. For instance, the capacity of players to create their own codes of behavior that adapt to the virtual environment in *World of Warcraft* may be considered a "positive" method, one that allows players to directly intervene on behalf of the infosphere's well-being.

It can be assumed, then, that there is a relation between those methods that contribute to the infosphere's well-being and the virtues of players as described previously in this book. The interesting aspect of information ethics, though, is that while the virtue ethics approach tends to limit the development of these virtues to the player,[27] in the distributed responsibility perspective all stakeholders should contribute to fostering these virtues, these methods that contribute to the well-being of the ludic infosphere. Information ethics expands the moral universe to take into account all the beings that can affect or suffer harm within the infosphere.

The gradient of abstraction of any research on the ethics of computer games from an information ethics perspective defines the network of distributed responsibility by the method of abstraction: harm to the informational balance of a particular game has to be defined in a number of levels of abstraction, creating the gradient of abstraction in which the ethicist should place the network of responsibilities. Once these elements are identified, the ethics of a particular situation in an infosphere are ready to be analyzed.

The ethics of computer games from an information ethics perspective has two crucial elements: first, distributed responsibility implies that the consumers of the game are equally responsible as the game designers, or sometimes even more responsible. Thus, its concordance with the *homo poieticus* approach, by which active agents in a game ought to be creative and responsible for the well-being of the game and the game community, players are creatively responsible for their experience in the infosphere.

Furthermore, distributed responsibility expands the moral orbit of the ethics of games, including those stakeholders whose discourses are informationally relevant for a game, even though they are not agents in the game. The media discourse, and other discourses and agents, are also part of the informational nature of the game and ought to play a role in the game's ethical soundness.

Second, by defining informational balance as morally good, this adaptation of information ethics places a great deal of responsibility on the design of the system, and indirectly on the designers. A bad game design is unbalanced, making the game experience flawed or negating the constructivist capacities of the players and the players' communities. Bad design is an unethical practice. A game poorly designed is, in principle, an unethical object, because its dysfunctional design interrupts and harms the ludic experience, damaging the infosphere as a network of ecological relations. A game that is impossible to win, or the camera design in *Shadow of the Colossus*, which sometimes does not allow the player to actually see where her target is, are examples of bad design that create a frustrating experience, affecting the well-being of the agents in the game.

There are degrees, though, of unethical design. A game that is poorly balanced, extraordinarily difficult, or terribly unplayable is unethical, but it is so in an intrinsic way; that is, it is unethical in its design but not toward the players. On the other hand, a game that constrains the constructivist ethical capacities of the players by not allowing them to bring their own values and practices into the game, dismissing or disempowering them, is an extrinsically unethical game: it affects the well-being of the infosphere by affecting the agents and their informational capacities. Most MMORPGs that follow the *Ultima Online* tradition, from *EverQuest* to *Dark Age of Camelot*,[28] tend to present instances of unethical design in the way their players are occasionally unable to play by the values they create, as I will argue in my study of *World of Warcraft*. Not every game, though, needs the presence of players' values—but every game can present intrinsically unethical design, as they are all designed objects.

From an information ethics perspective, to understand computer games it is necessary to take into account the game design and the game object, players, and other elements that can be considered, at some relevant level, informationally relevant for the game as infosphere. Furthermore, the relevance of the concept of information and informational being also opens up the possibility of understanding the moral responsibility of the fictional layer of the game.

The semiotic layer of the game, what Juul would call the fiction of the game, is a part of the informational structure of the infosphere, and it should be analyzed as such. Thus, it might be possible to say that the game's fiction can also be highly responsible for the game's ethical values. For instance, a game like *Manhunt* could be deemed unethical by its fictional level, because the actions that the game simulates are clearly unethical. Nevertheless, the fictional element of the game is only a part of the informational structure if it is relevant for the designed experience of the game. In *Manhunt*, the violent actions are a part of a design that creates interesting ethical reflections in the confluence of system design and game world simulation, as I have argued before.

Games are processes, and we have to understand their ethics as such. This is also true when it comes to their fictional layer. Everything that is not a part of the informational exchange between agents, patients, and the system, but which is fictional, is of no interest for the ethics of computer games; but if a fictional element is relevant to the way the game design configures the informational exchange, then that fictional element can be a part of the distributed network of responsibilities in an ethical analysis of the game. For instance, the impossibility of cross-faction communication in *World of Warcraft* is an element that does play an informational role in the game via design, thus, it should be analyzed from an ethical point of view. On the other hand, the fact that Mario in *Super Mario Bros.*[29] is a small Italian plumber is not ethically relevant, as it plays no role in the game's informational exchange.

Information ethics can provide a comprehensive theoretical framework for the understanding of the ethics of computer games, a framework that expands our capacities of analysis of game ethics by also expanding our moral universe. From this perspective, computer games are ecosystems of information in which users and producers are responsible for the well-being of that given environment. Nevertheless, this perspective presents some limitations.

4.2.4   The Limits of Information Ethics

Information ethics is a bold attempt to provide a theoretical framework by which some problems posed by computer ethics can be solved. It does so by using information theory and logics in a way that can metaphorically resemble the technical nature of hardware and software. The use of an object-oriented approach, and the use of the method of abstraction applied to the infosphere, map the inner core of computing in a way that makes information an ontology. All of this roughly constitutes the core of information ethics as a theory, and it gives it its theoretical strength, which is its assumed capacity for taking computer ethics issues and solving them as particular ethical problems derived from the use of computation. But this strength is also information ethics' main weakness in its application to computer games.

The limits of this approach as a tool for understanding the ethics of computer games are located in its highly theoretical nature. I have attempted to adapt some of the core concepts to the field of computer games. This adaptation seems to be operational, providing new insights into computer game ethics. Nevertheless, it can always be argued that these key notions are not necessarily applicable tools, but more conceptual paradigms by which we can understand research fields related to computer ethics. The problem with a theory that does not necessarily commit itself to application is that, while it can operate in the logic field with doubtless strength, it may be flawed when its concepts are taken into practice. Information ethics has just recently begun to find applications in the study of privacy-related ethical issues,[30] but there is work to be done before information ethics can effectively be regarded not only as a strong theory, but also as a tool for understanding and solving computer ethics issues.

The main conceptual problem in applying information ethics to computer games is the use of the concept of infosphere: understanding a game as an infosphere and giving to any element in the game the category of being because it is informational might seem a far-fetched application of the concept. Perhaps the biggest problem comes with the expansion of the moral responsibility that the use of this concept brings. By determining that the game is an infosphere, every element of the game, from design to artificial agents, is responsible for the moral fabric of the game. The problem is what an infosphere is, and how we can determine it. By defining an infosphere as the place where information exchanges are meaningful and by determining the ontological being of the agents and patients in that infosphere, we run the risk of opening the paradigm so wide that everything may be considered as a part of the infosphere, and thus we potentially jeopardize our results.

Nevertheless, the relatively closed nature of games provides a good environment for testing this theory. It is possible to outline some clear boundaries as to where information is relevant for the game experience, thus giving us the ability to define the infosphere quite clearly. Whenever the information exchanges are meaningful within the game experience—that is, if they are logical within the world of the game—then the infosphere is an appropriate tool for understanding the ontological and ethical status of the game, the players, and the software.

The limits of information ethics are determined by the fact that its concepts have so far seen little application outside theory. Information ethics intends to redefine the scope of computer ethics with a new understanding of the ethical processes that configure computing systems. To do so, it has provided a strong theoretical framework in which this radical approach is based. Applying this framework to a specific object may always bring forth issues of applicability and scope of the concepts. Those are the limits of this theory. Nevertheless, I have applied it to computer games and it has been proven to be of use. It is then simply a task of pushing the boundaries of these limitations so that information ethics can be defended as a successful and resourceful approach for the understanding of ethics in computer games.

This act of pushing the boundaries, of combining the insights of virtue and information ethics, informs my own theoretical approach to the question of computer games and ethics. In the next section I present the framework that can be used to effectively analyze the ethics of computer games, as I will illustrate with case studies in the following chapter. This introduction will be highly abstract and rather formalistic, with the intention of creating not an infallible theory, but a vocabulary and a framework for the understanding of the ethical issues of computer games.

4.3   The Ethics of Computer Games

The framework I am now going to present has to be understood as a practical application of the theory, derived from virtue ethics and information ethics. It is an applied ethics framework that goes beyond the dependence on one theory and toward its possible implementation in actual ethical concerns related to computer games, some of which will be presented and analyzed in the next chapter.

Most of the work that has been done on ethics and computer games has focused on the content of computer games as the factor by which their moral value has to be determined. The fundamental flaw of this approach is precisely its focus on the content. It is not the game world or the fiction that makes a game ethical or unethical. Or, more precisely, it is not only, not even primarily, the fiction of the game that determines the ethics of the computer game.

I am not trying here to downplay the importance of the fictional level in computer games when it comes to their ethical nature. The fiction of the game—the way the game world is presented to the player—does play a role in the ethical construction of the game. If we take, for example, *Counter-Strike* and *Under Ash*,[31] two games of similar gameplay and design, it is possible to argue that *Counter-Strike* is a highly de-ideologized game (which, in itself, is highly interesting from an ethical point of view, as terrorists and counterterrorists are identically defined for the game). The representational layer of *Under Ash,* by contrast, calls for an ethical reading of the world it depicts, since it is a first-person shooter that simulated the Palestinian-Israeli conflict from the perspective of a Palestinian combatant.

Fiction plays a role in the ethics of computer games. The content of a game, its story, backstory, character description and visualization, and game world have significant relevance for the game's ethics. But they are not central to the ethical construction of meaning in a computer game, because computer games are objects and experiences beyond their fictional nature. The limits of content analysis applied to the ethics of games come from the initial colonization of the field of game studies by disciplines like narratology or film and media studies,[32] which had tools for understanding other kinds of objects and experiences significantly different from computer games. The uncritical use of the same methods,

Figure 4.2
Counter Strike versus. Under Ash: Meaning and (Political) Games

concepts, and approaches for films and computer games is a methodological mistake that can only provide limited understanding of the ethics
of games.

While the content of the game plays a role in the ethics of games,
it is not enough to accurately describe them. Only if we take into account
that games are designed objects that create experiences for players
will we have a starting point for analyzing the ethics of games. Understanding the ethics of any computer game involves researching the interplay between a designed moral object, a moral experience derived
from that object, and the moral agent that experiences the game.
The relations between these three elements determine the ethics of computer games.

Because the computer game is a designed object in which the
player usually cannot directly exercise moral reasoning over the game
system, modifying it accordingly to her own values, the design of the
game is morally responsible for the ethical experiences it might create.
Poor design, unbalanced features, or a biased balance of the game
system, in which some agents have unfair advantages, are elements
of unethical design, even in the case of unintentional flaws. It is so
because games as objects create ludic experiences that may be harmful
for the player as a moral being. Bad design,[33] then, is to be considered
unethical.

An example of bad design that harms the player's experience of the
game is the ethical affordance in *XIII*, an example of unethical design

because it is inconsistent with the game world and the experience of the game up to that point, and it imposes on the player a contradicting rule: until the first game sequence where there are policemen, everything on screen was shootable. But, once the policemen are on stage, they are not to be made targets. If what the designers wanted to do, with good intentions, was to avoid having the player shoot policemen, then both the fiction and the game design should have alerted the player and guided her toward making that choice as a moral agent in the game world, by implementing, for instance, a level design in which shooting policemen would actually be either impossible or too demanding and impractical.

Not only bad design is ethically relevant; the design of a game as object is also the ergodic structure by which players access and experience the fiction. The representational level, the simulated game world, is important, but only if we consider it linked to the design of the game. It is in the informational structure of the game as state machine that we can find the ethics of computer games. Those computer games that try to convey political or social commentary values, such as *September 12th* or *Disaffected!*,[34] do so not only by creating a fictional world in which the political or social commentary has a role, but also by creating a world in which the designed interaction will create ethical meaning. In the case of *September 12th*, it is the manipulation of the game rhetoric, from the impossibility of a victory condition to the ironic reflection on game interface convention, which makes the ethical and political dimension of the game relevant. These serious games are actually so because it is in the interplay between the design of the game and the content of the game that their political and ethical values arise.

Computer games are also experiences, the phenomenological creation of the gameplay by means of interaction with the state machine of the game. The ethics of the game as experience are closely related to the ethics of the player, as well as connected to the game system that is designed to create that experience. An ethical game experience is one in which the player, a body-subject that exists and experiences the game system, can interact with that system as a moral agent; an experience that allows for the player's ethical behavior, interpretation, and, in the best possible case, contribution to the value system of the game experience. Gameplay ought to reflect, affect, and motivate the ethics of the player as a creative agent whose values are represented in the game, and who is partially determined and affected by the values that the game system has.

Traditionally, players go through this ethical experience by modifying the rules or the gameplay of a given game depending on the adversary, the situation, or other variables. The example already mentioned is the master who is playing against a neophyte: modifying some of the rules may imply a shared successful experience. Nevertheless, in the case of computer games these modifications of the game system or rules are either not possible, difficult due to the technical requirements, or predetermined by the game designers, like choosing a difficulty level. Thus it is important that the game as an experience can include the ethical presence of players as agents; it is of importance for the ethics of computer games to allow players to create a moral experience, or, in the case of games developed with the intention of creating a particularly ethical experience, the game as experience has to reflect clearly the values and the reasons why players' choices are constrained. An ethical game is that in which it is possible to apply ethical reasoning to the game experience in order to achieve a successful ludic experience.

In this perspective on the ethics of computer games, it is the player who has a new ethical dimension and role. The figure of the player tends to be seen as that of the victim, or the guilty victim to be more precise: the player engages in an unethical experience in which she passively suffers conditioned training and manipulation, and she does so by actively engaging in that experience. The ethical understanding of computer games I argue for gives a different role to players, a role that is significantly more demanding, but which also reflects the complexity of the ludic experience of a designed system. In this perspective, the ethics of computer games are highly dependent on the ethics of the players as creative and proactive value-bearers; on an ontology of players that has values and a culture which they look forward to expanding, protecting, and experiencing. The player of a computer game is a moral agent who plays according to a set of values partially created by the ethical nature of the design and the game experience, but also by the individual, communitarian, and cultural values that inform her ethical being. A player uses ethical reflection, phronesis, and her creative stewardship to evaluate her actions in the game, an ethical reflection that is part of her own previous experience as a player, as an individual, and as part of a larger cultural community of players.

The player is an ethical subject who develops moral training in the playing of games precisely by playing games. The more games we play, the more we understand their ethical implications and how to behave and interact ethically with them, not only because we learn to understand games as systems and experience, but also because we become a part of a player community that is rooted in our culture. Players know how to relate to other players, they know what the essential values that a good player must represent are, and they know what players should avoid in order to create balanced game experiences. This means that not every game is for every player. Playing games is also a process of moral maturation in which we learn how to play the game and how to understand these ethical systems. In other words, we learn to behave ethically in games by playing them, developing our moral understanding of games and our ludic phronesis in the same process.

Summarizing, the ethics of computer games has to be approached from three different but interconnected elements: the ethics of the game design, which comprises the game as object from its systemic to its fictional elements; the game as experience, or how the ethical values of the game as object are projected into an experience in which the agent(s) have moral presence, relevance, and influence in the ethical landscape of the experience; and the player as a moral body-subject who can interact with the game using moral reason, and who creates the values of the game as a cultural object by means of her interpretation and subsequent behavior in the sphere of the game, considered as both the game system and the game culture.

This multidimensional description of the ethics of computer games requires a conceptual tool that can represent the interwoven relations of system, experience, and agent in the creation of computer game ethics. To do so, I will again bring forth the concept of distributed responsibility as a functional theoretical tool for the analysis of computer game ethics.

Distributed responsibility refers to the fact that in the game experience there are a number of elements which share in nonproportional ways the responsibility for the game's ethical content. It is a tool for analyzing what the ethics of a game are, and what the roles of the different elements in the game situation are, from the players to the designers, including the game as designed system. All these elements of a computer game have a weight in the moral configuration of the game. Distributed responsibility is a concept that should be used as the initial step in the method for understanding and solving the ethical issues raised by a game. Distributed responsibility is informed by the ecological approach of information ethics, as well as the communitarian values of virtue ethics; it also takes into account the phenomenological ontology of the player as a relational body-subject that comes into being in the experience of a game, as a part of a community of players.

Because there are different relevant actors in the ethical construction of a computer game, and thus in the possible ethical problems it may raise, the first step is to plot the ethical interrelations of these actors. But these actors' responsibility should not be considered individually, or isolated from the presence of others. The ethics of computer games is networked by nature. Any ethical issue concerning computer games may have the design of the game as the source, but it is not independent from the other agents and their presence in the system. An ethical problem created by a design issue affects the game experience and all the agents in that game experience. Furthermore, because players are ethical agents capable of moral reasoning and action within the game experience, it is also, to some extent, a matter of their behavior and interpretation of that ethical issue in the game. Therefore, there are no clear boundaries, no isolated layers in the description and analysis of ethical issues of computer games.

The concept of distributed responsibility acknowledges this. In fact, it is at its very core: a game is a system where ethical issues are distributed over a network of ludic systems and game agents. The goal of the research on the ethics of games is to identify an issue, establish the network of game elements involved, and map the different degrees of affectedness and responsibility. That overview of the weighted network of ethical responsibilities in a computer game is what constitutes the distributed responsibility of that game.

Distributed responsibility intends to be a practical tool for the analysis of which elements are relevant in the ethical configuration of a certain computer game, or relevant to one of its aspects. By recognizing that a computer game is a complex experience in which there are many interrelated elements of importance that share the possibility of affecting each other, this concept can be of practical utility both in the analysis and in the development of computer games. Understanding the network of responsibilities in a computer game is taking one step toward systematizing the design of computer games with ethical gameplay, and it is also a tool for understanding the ethical issues that digital games raise.

In the following chapter I will apply this ethical framework to different relevant ethical issues concerning specific computer games.

5   Applying Ethics: Case Studies

It is now time to put my ethical framework into practice. So far, most of the argumentation has been purely theoretical, with a number of examples that specifically illustrated the key arguments of this method for describing the ethics of computer games. In this chapter and the ones that follow, I will apply the framework to specific issues, starting with a close reading of the ethics of three games: *Bioshock*, *DEFCON*,[1] and *World of Warcraft*. These games will also be used as illustrations of more general reflections on the ethics of single-player, multiplayer, and online game worlds. The analyses are not exhaustive, but serve as an illustration of how to analyze computer games from an ethical perspective.

5.1   *Bioshock* and the Ethics of Single-Player Games

The mainstream computer game industry can sometimes be rather conservative. It is true that games push the boundaries of technological development, and they often use the most advanced resources afforded by computing research. In fact, it is possible to claim that computer graphics as a discipline benefits very much from approaches that have an origin in computer game needs. Nevertheless, as much as it is an innovative technological field, the game industry is culturally conservative. The degree of innovation in the technology is seldom coupled with innovation in gameplay, storytelling, or virtual world creation.

Of course, there are economic reasons for this, based on the large budgets game development companies require to produce a high-quality title, and the risk aversion of the investors that provide those budgets. But sometimes there are companies that dare to try something new, and the games that result from this combination of daring, innovation, and talent are often heralded as the symbols of what computer games can contribute to both the popular and the fine arts.

Launched in 2007 to critical acclaim, and heralded as the definitive step of mainstream games toward the artistic and expressive capacities of media like cinema, *Bioshock* constitutes one of the most significant examples of what the mainstream game industry understands as a game that pushes the boundaries of game design expression, targeting mature computer game players. Furthermore, thanks to its storyline and game mechanics, *Bioshock* was also received as a game in which moral gameplay would be of extreme importance for the game experience. It is therefore of interest to analyze this game in light of the ethical theories I have presented in the previous chapter.

In this analysis I am not going to describe some elements that could be of interest in outlining *Bioshock*'s ethics, like the online communities around the game, the technical problems that the game suffered on release and how they affected some players, or the game's reception by its core target audience. *Bioshock* is interesting because it both failed and succeeded in the task of creating an interesting ethical single-player computer game experience. Understanding this duality and what it teaches us about the development of ethical games is of extreme interest. I am also aware that *Bioshock* is very much a successor to the classic game *System Shock 2*,[2] but again, there is little in that comparison that can inform my interest in the particular ethical experience that this game creates, and how it illuminates the range of ethical gameplay possible for single-player games.

Bioshock is an example of a large-budget production aimed at creating something different and recognizable as worthy of merit even by those who are not interested or invested in computer games. The art direction, combining the impressive graphics technology with a unique vision of how the game world should be experienced, immediately distinguished *Bioshock* from all the other first-person shooters in the market. Nevertheless, this is a rather conservative game in terms of gameplay design: it is a conventional first-person shooter where the player navigates a 3-D environment using weapons and special powers to eliminate enemies. These enemies' resistance increases the more the player explores the game world, with the occasional "boss fight" against a particularly powerful rival. The innovations in the basic mechanics and rules of the game are superficial: players can acquire genetic powers that work in combination with the environment, allowing an "ecology" of weapons, a set of tools that encourage tactical combat. Nothing radically new, but interesting and rather well implemented.

What makes *Bioshock* unique is the game world where the actions take place, and its consistency as a designed experience. Unlike most other first-person shooters, *Bioshock* does not take place in a space station, the enemies are not aliens, and the protagonist is not a space marine. As a matter of fact, as players we know very little about the main character's past: we do know that the enemies were once human, and that the year is 1959. *Bioshock* builds its unique aesthetic in blending futuristic technology, such as intelligent robots and genetic engineering, with the fictional space of a hypothetical 1950s art deco underwater city. The world of *Bioshock* is unique and refreshing.

But it's not only the world that makes the game interesting. Its storyline has to be taken into consideration, since it is relevant for the ethics of *Bioshock*. The game starts with a plane crash, and the discovery by the only survivor, adrift in the middle of the ocean, of a strange access gate to some kind of underwater facility, called "Rapture." Soon the story unfolds: Rapture is an underwater utopian city created by a man named Andrew Ryan, a Randian objectivist who believed in rational self-interest and a kind of extreme libertarian capitalism where all humans are equals and mankind is the only God.

Figure 5.1
Bioshock: Welcome to Rapture

But Rapture is a dystopia, where the deranged citizens fight for meager resources, their minds forever lost due to the excessive use of genetic manipulation. There is also a latent conflict between Ryan and a mythical character called Atlas, who resisted the forms of despotic order that ended the initial dream of Rapture. The protagonist is drawn into the last efforts of this resistance, and he is progressively guided by Atlas toward the murder of Ryan, and thus the end of Rapture. But of course, interesting plot twists reveal the protagonist to be a pawn in a larger power struggle that only ends with the closure of the dream at the bottom of the sea.

This is a rough summary of the main elements of *Bioshock*'s storyline, which is of course more complex and detailed, and rather compelling in its character-driven depth. Its use of environmental cues in the ruins of Rapture configures a classic and very well thought-through computer game narrative. What makes *Bioshock* the target of this ethical analysis is the importance that the developers gave to moral choice and moral reasoning in the game. The story is of course important, but it is oriented toward a certain reflection on the modes and motives of player agency in the game world. In other words, *Bioshock* was designed as an ethical experience, and it is thus interesting for what it will illuminate about the ethics of single-player game experiences.

The main reason why *Bioshock* is interesting from a moral perspective is its insistence on choice as the game world's reason to exist. Of course, choice is related to the particular interpretation of objectivism the game proposes, but also to the experience of the game. Choice appeals to the ethical player, who has to reflect on the meaning of her actions and their consequences. *Bioshock* has two significant ethical devices oriented toward that ethical player—two methods of creating moral gameplay that I will analyze, in their relative success and failure, in order to cast light on the ethics of single-player computer games.

The first interesting ethical design element is based on the story of the game and how it mirrors the gameplay experience. As I have mentioned, the player is put in the middle of a conflict in Rapture, a conflict between the founder of the city, Andrew Ryan, and Atlas, a mysterious character who, well into the game, reveals his true identity and motives. It is quite clear from the beginning that one of our main missions will be to kill Andrew Ryan: all the actions in the first half of the game are oriented to disable the defenses behind which Ryan is hiding. As players, we suspect that Ryan will be a boss fight and that we will have to eliminate him using the powers and knowledge we acquire.

But the more information we gather, the more we suspect about Atlas's intentions, and the more the narrative paces us toward questioning the purpose of our actions. We think: maybe we would need to hear him, maybe we should actually ally with him . . . and then the interesting ethical mechanic takes place: we cannot avoid killing Andrew Ryan. Throughout the game, up until that moment, we have been controlled by Atlas, who had implanted some kind of mental domination system that could be triggered by uttering some words— the same words we as players heard in the briefings for the different missions up to that point. In a moment of stellar writing, a cut scene gives meaning to all the previous gameplay, and challenges our experience of the game so far. And it is precisely this intense manipulation of player agency that makes this sequence in *Bioshock* an interesting, successful ethical experience.

Before analyzing the game in detail, it is important to describe some of the less stellar aspects of *Bioshock* as a computer game. The choice of the first-person shooter genre, and the strict allegiance to its tropes

Figure 5.2
Bioshock: A Choice between Two Evils

and figures of style, makes *Bioshock*'s innovations relative: the game still plays like a conventional shooter, and there is no advance of the genre in terms of mechanics. The worst problem, from a design perspective, is that this focus on classic shooter mechanics seems to have come at the expense of game world exploration: Rapture is a fascinating environment, but as players we are only allowed to explore some parts of it, while the rest tempts us from behind the windows and in drawings and stories placed in the environment. *Bioshock* feels more like a theme park and less like a game—the environment is limited, focused on very concrete experiences, very carefully designed, and as such the capacity to explore the rest of the world is secondary. This means that for most of the game, the player merely moves from checkpoint to checkpoint, completing missions in order to unlock new spaces. Rapture seems a theme park, and not a world.

In classic shooters of this structure, player agency was rather limited in terms of thinking about the meaning of the actions that were taken. It is a genre convention not to think about the world around the player and to just focus on moving from one series of challenges to another, much like in the classic *Half-Life*.[3] What makes *Bioshock* ethically interesting is how it intertwines the narrative with this design convention in order to explore the ethics of choice. As players, until the moment when Ryan is murdered, we basically follow Atlas's instructions in order to advance and "finish" the game. When confronted with Ryan, the moment in which the truth is finally unveiled, the process of playing the game comes into new light: the instructions were part of a mind-control scheme, and all the actions have led to a morally questionable conclusion, the death of Andrew Ryan.

This manipulation of player agency is what gives this design choice its ethical nature. As I have argued, a player is an ethical subject that has the capacity to reflect on the meaning of her actions, and of her values within the game. Most computer games do not challenge those values: the player is the hero, the actions are consequent, and there are no moral dilemmas, no need for a deep reflection on means and purposes. *Bioshock* builds on this tradition, as said, in an intelligent use of the player repertoire. We don't expect these missions, the close path we are following, to be anything other than the reflection of the actions the designers and developers want us to experience, in the order they want us to experience them. We can reflect on what they mean, but we cannot do anything to change them. This is precisely what the narrative of *Bioshock* is actually saying: we had no choice, at all moments we were guided by a force more powerful than our own will. All of a sudden, our actions become moral actions while we are facing Ryan, the character we are supposed to kill.

There is a further mechanical refinement in terms of ethical player agency: as soon as we meet Ryan, our agency becomes even more limited— we can move around, but we cannot interact with the game world, and we are deprived of our weapons. We have no choices, and the game resorts to a computer-controlled scene in which we witness how we kill Andrew Ryan. The change from actor to spectator, from agent to passive being, marks what should be read as a designed ethical experience: we are powerless, contemplating a horrendous act of which we are mere witnesses, yet that we have caused by our previous actions.

The understanding and manipulation of the network of distributed responsibility is what makes *Bioshock*'s mental control plot a brilliant example of the ethical capacities of computer games. Throughout most of the game, it seems that players are central agents in a world designed by the developers to be interacted with in a specific way, shaping in this way a two-way relationship in which developers have the responsibility for the game world and the freedom of the player within it, while the player is responsible for the actions taken within the game. But when the moment of killing Ryan arrives, the balance in that network shifts: suddenly the player is not an agent, but passive in the hands of the computer, which acts with the values of the narrative. By introducing a new element in this distributed responsibility network and showing that there was no choice or freedom, we are forced to reflect upon the meaning of the game and our actions; that is, our weight in the network of responsibilities of the game experience. We are not empowered beings, but mere agents in a larger system in which the extent of our agency will be questioned. And this is precisely the root of an ethical experience: the reflection upon the meaning of the previous actions and our being as players in the world of Rapture.

This design decision in *Bioshock* is particularly fascinating because it presumes a moral agent. I have argued that computer game players are moral beings, but we seldom find a game that appeals directly to our morality as agents. *Bioshock* requires an ethical player to understand the design decision of depriving the player of control at a specific point, but also of forcing her to reflect upon the meaning of the previous actions taken in the game, all consequent with her player repertoire but clearly unethical in the context of the game narrative. By appealing precisely to the ethical player, limiting her choice and agency in the game world, and creating a simulation structure that mirrors the ethical issues of choice and consequence raised by the narrative, *Bioshock* has a strong ethical component in its configuration as game experience. This argued requirement of a reflective ethical player brings the closed, linear world of Rapture to a dimension of moral experience that defines the game as an interesting blend of narrative, gameplay, and ethics. And it does so by combining the narrative aspects with a moral reflection on the nature of game mechanics and how they are mapped onto the player repertoire.

Bioshock's marketing campaign was focused on another element of ethical gameplay—one that, as I will argue in the rest of this analysis, is both questionable and much less innovative than the narrative-based approach I have just described. This second element was centered on the presence in Rapture of girls called Little Sisters and their importance in the gameplay progression. The alleged moral dilemma focused on the convenience or not of killing these girls to harvest some resources, but the implementation of this mechanic was not successful, for reasons that are closely connected to the merits of the mind-control ethical gameplay.

Little Sisters are genetically modified young girls with zombie eyes and a large syringe. They are always protected by a Big Daddy, a biomechanical monster out of Jules Verne's worst nightmares. Little Sisters are in charge of collecting Adam from corpses, one of the key substances in Rapture's genetic nightmare. Their apparent fragility is compensated by the presence of the Big Daddies, a true challenge for any player who wants to take them down. Little Sisters are precious because the Adam they harvest can be used for buying new upgrades for the player's genetic powers. But to obtain these resources, players first have to kill the Big Daddies, then eliminate the Little Sisters. And this is designed to be the central ethical gameplay mechanic of *Bioshock*—will you kill the Little Sister and harvest her resources, or will you let her live, and survive with fewer resources but with a cleaner conscience?

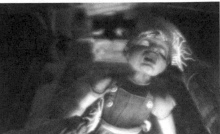

Figure 5.3
Bioshock: Harvesting versus Rescuing a Little Sister

Initially, this type of decision seems to appeal to both the player as subject in the game and to her ethics outside of the game, since the Sisters are portrayed as harmless girls. It could also look like an ethical choice: it involves life or death and reflecting about consequences and actions, involving the player as an ethical agent in the game world. But the Little Sister mechanic turns out to be an incomplete implementation of an ethical mechanic due to the misinterpretation of the game's weight as a designed system in the ethical configuration of the player and her relations with the game world.

Let's analyze this mechanic in more detail: from a purely formal perspective, players are faced with the choice between fewer resources and more resources, depending on a decision that the game's semantic layer insists on telling us is of moral nature. These resources are potentially linked to the difficulty of the game, and how much the player can do to beat it. So far, it seems quite clear that a design of this type would surely yield interesting ethical gameplay, involving the player in the larger experience of the game world and empowering her to take a moral standpoint in her ways of inhabiting it. In this sense, this is a good lesson to learn in terms of the design of ethical computer game experiences: if the player's choices are closely tied to survival in the game world, but those choices about resources will affect her position in the network of responsibility of the game, then we will most likely have an ethical game. More clearly, if the players' choices concerning resources have an impact on how the world perceives and responds to the players' values, then we will have ethical gameplay.

But this is not the case in *Bioshock*, due to a problematic design choice: there is barely any difference between letting the Little Sisters live or die, since the player will receive Adam as a gift if they are left alive, in a quantity similar to what she would get after killing the girls. Furthermore, the decision to let the girls live or die only has an impact on the ending of the game, and not on its progression, much less in the way the game world reacts to the player's ethical stance. Rapture, it seems, does not care much about the ethics of its inhabitants, and all choices are deprived of meaning—which in itself is an interesting topic to explore, as the mind-control example shows, but not in the way implemented in the Little Sister mechanic.

The problem with this mechanic is that it trivializes the moral capacities of the player to reflect on her actions by depriving the choice of any consequence to her relation with the world. If the inhabitants of Rapture reacted in varied ways to different paths taken with Little Sisters, or even if they acknowledged the difference in these choices, then there would be meaning for this action. If the game design is going to afford a decision as ethical, then it has to implement consequences, subsystems of rewards tied to the initial choices. Otherwise, players will react to the dilemmas not with a moral stance, but with their player logic, focused on achieving their goals in the game experience.

In the case of the Little Sisters, players will most likely decide if they want to kill them or not based on how much Adam they require to explore certain genetic power trees, or if they want to see any of the alternative endings of the game, or if they want to calculate how much Adam is it possible to get, provided the different gameplay paths. Furthermore, those players that may want to experience the game ethically will not receive any kind of feedback for their actions besides the differing amount of resources gathered. In *Bioshock* there is no experience of the player-subject as an agent with creative capacities, constructing their own values within the game world and living by them. The game turns their alleged key ethical decision-making mechanic into a resource management process that does not require any type of moral reasoning for the player to succeed.

It is precisely this that makes *Bioshock*'s Little Sister mechanic an unethical design choice: it taunts the values of the player. It seems to put the player in the central position of the network of responsibilities within the game, as a master of her own ethical presence in the game world. But in the end, there is no meaning attached to choice, and the player sees her own ethical agency deprived of any content or capacities. It is the developers who have already decided how the world will respond to her actions, in a binary system of outcomes: either she kills the girls, or she doesn't, and if she does so, there will be a negative ending, and in the other case a positive ending. And the resources will be roughly the same, so the gameplay progression is not affected by moral choice.

In most ethical games, gameplay progression is affected by ethical choice. Every choice taken by a player has to reflect her values in the game and see those values reflected in the game system, in terms of resources, mechanics, and the behavior of other computer-controlled or human agents. The fact that the result of the choice between the life and death of the Little Sisters is more or less insignificant deprives the player of any interest in applying her ethical capacities to the game experience, which in turn will make the game less interesting from a moral perspective.

I would like to push this analysis one step toward the field of game design. As I will argue in chapter 7, there are tools and techniques that allow us to analyze, and potentially create, ethical gameplay. What *Bioshock* illustrates are two facts that can hamper the design of any game as an ethical experience: the dominance of the narrative and the obsession with gameplay balance.

Admittedly, the story in *Bioshock* is of very high quality, almost unseen in computer games. Its references to objectivism, dystopian literature, and art deco are a relief in an entertainment form dominated by examples of poor, derivative science fiction narratives. Nevertheless, if what we are interested in is computer games as ethical experience, even good narratives have to be subordinate to the player-system relation and its ethical implications. A story must not prevail over player agency, unless that story brings something to the player as ethical subject: the example of the mind-control plot is effective because it forces players to see actions and consequences in a different light. But the lack of significant consequences when facing the Little Sisters dilemma deprives the game of interesting ethical outcomes, only because there is a story that needs to be told. Any story, then, in any single-player game that wants to become an interesting ethical experience, should be either subordinate to the ethical actions taken by the player, or should illustrate the actions taken by the player, forcing her to reflect on the meaning of her presence in the game world.

Similarly, any action that ought to be understood as a moral one in the game has to be supported by the game design; that is, reflected by the game system and providing a sufficiently distinct outcome so the player feels that her actions are of a moral nature. This means thinking about game balance in a different way than classic game design theory has reflected on. A game needs to be balanced in its overall experience, but it does not need to be balanced in the particular outcomes of ethical choices; furthermore, imbalanced outcomes are a particularly relevant tool for game designers to make statements via game design. If *Bioshock* feels ethically dull it is because there is little to no difference between saving and killing the Little Sisters—players don't need to think about their actions, since the outcome of the design always benefits them.

In classic conceptions of game balance, this is probably a positive thing: the game is balanced to different play styles. But when it comes to developing ethically relevant games, this balance is ineffective, since it is disconnected from player agency. There is, then, the possibility of thinking about some kind of ethical balance, a design choice that needs to be made when creating the game system, and that is related to how the game reacts to actions in which the player's ethical agency is at stake. In this sense, game imbalance can yield interesting ethical balance—and of course the task of the game designer is to allow for the game to be playable, despite these imbalances. Developers interested in creating ethical gameplay experiences with single-player narrative games should consider classic game balance principles as a tool, a guide toward establishing an interesting relation between players, game worlds, and stories.

Bioshock is a worthwhile game, a bold attempt at pushing the boundaries of computer game expression. Its art direction, the carefully crafted, yet sometimes too obvious narrative, and the thrilling world of Rapture make this creation depart from most conventions in the world presented to the player. But the player's experience is unfortunately mediated by an overly conventional take on first-person shooter mechanics. And the same allegiance to conventions harms the otherwise noble intention of turning *Bioshock* into an interesting ethical experience. If *Bioshock* is interesting from an ethical perspective, it is not because of its alleged moral game mechanics, those related to the choice of letting the Little Sisters live or kill them for their resources. *Bioshock* is interesting from an ethical perspective precisely when the player is devoid of choice, when an interpretation of game conventions and the player's repertoire are used to cast light on the meaning of actions in the game world and the overall nature of choice. The mind-control sequence is probably one of the most intense ethical experiences a computer game developed with commercial intent has ever created.

The failures and successes of *Bioshock* in its attempt to create ethical gameplay point to the two main aspects that any single-player game that wants to create ethical gameplay should consider. A single-player game places the player, as ethical agent, as the sole and most important agent in a system that is designed to react to her input. The relevance of the player's ethical agency in the network of distributed responsibility is high: the player has to feel empowered to either apply her own values to a world that acknowledges them, or to live the values of the system and reflect upon its consequences and meanings. In other words: choice has to be meaningful and the system has to react to it in moral ways—the game design has to acknowledge and support the player as an ethical agent. Or it has to be designed to reinforce the values the player has to live by, the ethics of the persona she is becoming in the game world.

A single-player game experience is, from an ethical perspective, the exploration of the meaning of choice and values in the game world by an empowered moral agent. *Bioshock* succeeds in turning the experience of the game into a reflection on actions and consequences, but it fails to give meaning to choices. Its ethical discourse is somewhat contradictory, and not supported by the game design. Any single-player ethical game is a system designed with a moral agent and an ethical experience in mind, and classic notions like game balance, difficulty, or even replayability are secondary. The design of single-player games that want to create an ethical experience is a challenge, an exploration of the player alone in a game world destined to be its ethical counterpart. A single-player ethical game is the exploration of who we are as ethical players.

5.2 *DEFCON* and the Ethics of Multiplayer Games

Historically, single-player games are somewhat an anomaly—if we look at both digital and analog games in our culture, we will notice that a vast majority of them are, in one way or another, multiplayer. Single-player computer games are mostly the outcome of the simulation possibilities of computers applied to the creation of semi-intelligent autonomous agents that can be used to wrap and enhance a particular mode of player interaction with the game world. Multiplayer games, on the other hand, tend to fall short on the narrative or fictional side, and focus much more on two classic forms of multiplayer game design: cooperation versus competition.[4] What is interesting about multiplayer games is not the story, or the world, but how that story or that world foster either of these basic elements of gameplay experience.

It is not my intention to write about the ontology of multiplayer games as opposed to single-player games, despite the obvious interest of that subject; my goal is to analyze a multiplayer game in the light of the ethical theory I have presented, with the intention of introducing some of the key elements that need to be taken into consideration when analyzing, and perhaps even designing, the ethical modalities of play in a multiplayer game. My focus is on games where more than one agent plays in nonpersistent worlds,[5] games like *DEFCON*, but also *Age of Empires, Civilization, Guitar Hero*, or *Dance Dance Revolution*. What is interesting about these games is not their online persistent world, but how gameplay sessions are experienced by multiple agents simultaneously.

My case study will be *DEFCON*, an independent multiplayer game developed by Introversion Software and launched to critical acclaim in 2006. Before introducing the game, I would like to add that *DEFCON*, as opposed to the other two main case studies I am presenting, is a game developed with a low budget, by a small team, and with different publisher/developer relations than the other two mainstream titles. Some could argue that the design decisions I will analyze here as ethical choices may have been a consequence of these production constraints. Nevertheless, any game that tackles the slightly controversial topic of worldwide nuclear war is making itself a target for ethical scrutiny, and as such my analysis of *DEFCON* as an ethical experience is validated.

Anyone who has seen the classic 1983 film *WarGames* will understand how to play *DEFCON*: the player is presented with a vector graphics representation of the globe, and the sounds immediately cue the fiction of an underground nuclear silo, a doomsday refuge in the advent of nuclear war. The game is played like a classic real-time strategy game:

players are given a territory and a number of units they have to manage while trying to eliminate most of their opponents. The difference is that *DEFCON* simulates nuclear war, and as such is a rather radical game: there is no victory, only degrees of defeat. The game world is there to be destroyed, cities will not produce units, and their populations are the mere statistics that generate meaningful strategies. Playing *DEFCON* is engaging in a dehumanized simulation of nuclear war where the goal is to lose the least.[6]

The basic *DEFCON* gameplay places the player as the commander of a specific territory, with a population of 100 million and a number of military resources that need to be deployed. There can be up to six other players in the game, competing for the best strategies of setting their attack and defense elements in place for the unavoidable conflict. The game goes through a number of states, named after different DEFCON codes: DEFCON 5 and 4 allow for the positioning of units, but not for attacks, nuclear or otherwise; DEFCON 3 and 2 allow for conventional combat, but not nuclear weapons; DEFCON 1 signals the last stage of the game, where nuclear missiles can be launched, and where the fate of the game is

Figure 5.4
Defcon: We're All in a Bunker Now

decided. Depending on the game type, the score is calculated on the basis of the number of population units that have survived, and the number of "megadeaths," or million population units eliminated by each player. The score is a result of the balance between these two numbers. In other words, the winner is not always who kills the most, but also who loses the least.

An interesting design choice, to which I will return later on, is the possibility of making alliances: players can create alliances between them, which grants them access to their allies' radar units, which in turn allows for a more detailed vision of the environment, since *DEFCON* also uses the classic strategy game mechanic of the fog of war, or the inability of players to see beyond their territory or the space their radar units can cover. But there can only be one winner: alliances are always broken at some stage in *DEFCON*, creating an interesting tension between players' wish for maximized information on their rivals, and the dependency on what they know is going to be a broken alliance at some moment. The social dynamics that emerge from these contradicting mechanics are also of relevance for understanding the ethics of *DEFCON*, and of multiplayer games.

DEFCON can be a game of patience, of tactical psychology, waiting for other players to make a move and predicting what that move will be so that it can be countered. This is a game that puts players in an isolated environment, but with the knowledge that there are other humans there, in front of similar maps, plotting similar strategies to get rid of the enemies. This sense of isolation dehumanizes the other players, but as players we know that they are human agents—this tension between how the game is played and how we understand it is, in my opinion, crucial to understand the depth of *DEFCON*'s ethical gameplay, as I will argue later on. But for now, it suffices to say that the game, in its audiovisual design, cues the player to think as if inserted in a bunker environment, isolated from humanity, in a place where population and enemies are just numbers that can be adjusted, modified, and deleted.

The reception for this independent game was quite positive, and many reviewers actually noticed a certain degree of ethical thinking in the design of the gameplay.[7] *DEFCON* is a shining example of the independent game industry: a well-made, original, independently produced title that brings some new experiences to players by means of cleverly manipulating genre conventions. These facts make *DEFCON* interesting from an ethical perspective as well. This is not to say that all good independent games are ethically relevant—*DEFCON* is interesting because its innovations, its essential mechanics, and the score system are ethically interesting.

But why is *DEFCON* so relevant, so enticing for an ethicist? First of all, it is a game about the ultimate war, about the annihilation of the human race by means of atomic weaponry—and it is fun to play. But beyond its topic, *DEFCON* is interesting for the game experience it creates around it: the feeling of isolation, the calculations of megadeaths and victory, the ultimate tension between detachment and attachment to the game world—all these elements configure a ludic experience of enormous relevance. In *DEFCON*, players are calculating how to maximize their nuclear strikes to annihilate as much of the enemy population as possible without suffering severe losses in the game's inevitable outcome. This calculation is part of a process of reflection on the meaning of the game world, and it appeals to players both as subjects in the game, and as ethical citizens.

Figure 5.5
Defcon: The Aesthetics of Atomic War

Two of *DEFCON*'s design choices require ethical analysis: the alliance system and the calculation of victory based on the number of losses in population. The alliance system regulates the behaviors of and relations between agents in the game system, and as such is of primary interest for the understanding of the ethics of *DEFCON*. The winning condition rule, on the other hand, brings forth the more direct implication of game designers in the value systems of the games they develop, and how they are projected into a specific game experience.

DEFCON is also interesting because it is a multiagent environment that pits moral agents against each other under the agreed and sanctioned rules of a game, following the mechanics afforded to them by the designers. Multiplayer games are ethically important because they are designed mediators of player interactions, and since both the design and the agents are ethically relevant, the ways they affect each other are of extreme relevance for understanding the particular ethics of a game experience.

In this chapter I am going to analyze the alliance system and the winning condition design in *DEFCON*. They will both illustrate aspects to take into consideration when describing the ethics of a multiplayer game, since they cover the way agents relate to the game world and to other agents in it, and the influence of game design in the experience of the game by these moral agents. My reflections will be based on *DEFCON*, but they will apply to multiplayer games in general, except those played in persistent worlds, which I will analyze in the next chapter.

We start with the alliance system: in *DEFCON* we have a plurality of agents competing for resources, in this case space, with limited time and opposing goals. There can only be one winner, so the domination of space and the deployment of units that allow for massive strikes and defensive networks are crucial. These processes are troubled by the players' lack of absolute information: the visibility of the map is rather limited, and choices have to be made in light of those limitations—unless, of course, players engage in alliances. Alliances are useful because they allow players to have a wider perspective on the playing field, sharing the radar visibility with the other players in the same alliance. Alliances also have their own, private, chat channel. These benefits make it a tactical advantage to establish alliances.

But alliances, as I have already pointed out, are counterbalanced by the fact that there can only be one winner, regardless of the alliances established during the game. Both alliances and the winning condition show the developers' special interest in creating a type of designed experience based on the equilibrium between information and mistrust, a balance crucial for understanding the historical balance of power during the Cold War, elegantly simulated by Chris Crawford in the classic game *Balance of Power*.[8]

From an ethical point of view, any multiplayer game designer will have the challenge of managing the presence of a number of moral agents in her game world. This challenge is twofold: on one hand, players need to be respected as ethical agents, capable of reflecting on the meaning of their actions and how they treat other agents in the game experience; on the other hand, developers have to ensure that whatever ludic experience they set out to create with that game is present when players interact with their game, and that this experience is, closing the conceptual loop, respectful to the ethical being of players.

DEFCON achieves the goal of creating a compelling moral experience with the combination of the two mechanics, showing a way of both respecting players and imposing on them, via system design, a specific behavior that will lead to desired, successful ethical experiences. Players of *DEFCON* see their ethical agency respected by allowing them a great degree of freedom in the selection of the strategies, especially in terms of alliances. Players can enact their values to a certain extent in the game experience, being collaborative or secretive; remaining individualists, helping other players, or directly conspiring against others. This degree of enhanced agency allows for the player's deep moral engagement with the game world.

We could argue that multiplayer games that want to introduce ethical gameplay as a part of the ludic experience need to design the patterns of interaction between players, allowing them to enact their own values, while guiding the ways these values can be used in the game world. In any system that manages the simultaneous input of different ethical agents, it is necessary to think about those modes of interaction in ethical ways: what types of ethical issues are going to arise, and how can players solve them, without a direct intervention of the system designers? Players can self-manage abusive alliances in *DEFCON*, since there is no rule that states that there cannot be massive alliances against one player; in this sense, the game empowers players to reflect about their own actions to others during the game experience, which is a desired outcome of any multiplayer game that wants to create an ethical experience.

This ethical experience is nevertheless created and guided by the designed system of rules. In the case of *DEFCON*, the relative openness to ethical agency of players in the game world is limited by the presence of a strong design constraint: there can only be one winner. While players are respected ethically, the developers created a very intense ethical experience by ultimately turning that freedom against their own intentions as players. Winning the game means to survive the strongest alliances and to break them at some moment. In this sense, the game is affording a type of behavior that can have interesting ethical interpretations by players. *DEFCON* wants, by design, to spiral down in a storm of broken alliances and treason, only to mimic, by means of design, the insane last moments before nuclear dawn.

Multiplayer games construct their ethical systems by means of modifying the behavior of the agents in the world through the use of game rules and game mechanics. The balance between the freedom of ethical agency provided by these and the constraints dictated by the winning condition and end state of the game are crucial to understanding the ethics of any multiplayer game. In *DEFCON*, the ethical experience is created by conflicting interests in terms of ethical player agency and the game system's end state: there can be alliances, but only one winner. These types of tensions, which are created by means of alternatively manipulating the players' intentions of cooperating and of conflicting by means of game design, can create relevant multiplayer ethical experiences, forcing us to reflect on what we have to do, and how those actions affect the other agents of the system.

The other ethical design choice that makes *DEFCON* relevant as an illustration of moral multiplayer gameplay is its understanding of the score system. As stated, *DEFCON* is a game about nuclear war From an ethical standpoint, nuclear war is absolutely evil: it not only indiscriminately massacres by the thousands, it also ruins the environment for future generations. And yet for many years nuclear warfare was considered a part of the legitimate arsenal of the Cold War superpowers, and the world lived under the shadow of a war that would, this time around, end all wars.

This absolute nature of nuclear war is simulated in *DEFCON* by means of its scoring system. Conventionally, the winner of any game is that who wins the most points. There are exceptions to this rule, but in general most games have a correlation between number of points and declaration of the winner. In *DEFCON*, playing in the default scoring mode, players win by accumulating megadeaths, but also by avoiding them. As a matter of fact, players who suffer severe losses, no matter how well they perform in their attack, will lose. In the Survivor scoring mode, players have to lose the least in order to win, no matter how well they perform in their offensive mode. And this reflects an ethical affordance in the game design: nuclear war is always lost.

I have argued that computer games are designed systems for interaction that can have embedded values. Some of these values, as in the example of the amnesic killer in *XIII*, are experienced as clumsy interferences in the ethical agency of players. In fact, it is not easy to create a game that is ethically relevant by means of design while encouraging its users to think and experience the values they play by. In *DEFCON*, this balance is created precisely because it is a multiplayer game, and the focus is not on the

Figure 5.6
Defcon: Endgame Score Screen

development of a narrative within the game world, but on the dynamics of interaction between players. This is not to say that it is not possible to create an ethical multiplayer game with a strong narrative—but interesting moral gameplay in these games takes place not in the way the story unfolds, but in the ways players relate to others through the system, thus the importance of looking at the game design.

DEFCON cleverly manipulates our conventions concerning victory conditions by changing the meaning of the final score and turning victory into a measurement of defeat. Of course, this choice has meaning within the semantics of the game world, but it is arguably designed to resonate in the ethical fabric of players: their actions, their strategies, everything done in the course of the game session is oriented to the extermination of their rivals' populations. And that fact is highlighted precisely by the scoring system. Any score is an evaluation by the system of the players' behavior, but it is also an enticement for players to optimize their behaviors following the rules of the game, and to play the game again. Pinball machines, with their scores in the millions, have largely set the trend in scoring design: encourage players to earn as many points as possible, and greet them not with 10, but with 10,000 points.

DEFCON modifies this rhetoric with an ethical approach: players are encouraged to score by the millions—actually, by millions of population kills. And not only that, but in two out of three game modes, players are also punished for allowing their own millions to be annihilated. What is relevant is both the fact that the winner is not who scores the most but who loses the least, and also the semantic layer added to the notion of points: these are not abstract units, but "population," a metaphor enhanced by the design of the user interface and the game world. Players own, protect, and destroy "cities" with populations of millions—those populations are their scores.

Of course, *DEFCON* can be played ignoring this metaphor, and it still holds as a cleverly designed multiplayer strategy game. But playing it that way is ignoring one of the reasons why this game is a fundamental example of multiplayer moral gameplay: *DEFCON* does not only appeal to the passive, button-mashing player, but also to the ethical player, who will play, and win, but still reflect on and be affected by the experience of the game. And that player is appealed to by the combination of game world design and game design, by the way the rules and mechanics are wrapped in an intense metaphor directly targeted to the thinking player.

Multiplayer games have to be analyzed as ethical objects and experiences, keeping in mind that these are multiagent systems where the network of responsibility, unlike in single player games, is not a process exclusive to the developers, the system, and the player. In multiplayer games, there is also an element of player-to-player relations that needs to be taken into consideration: the ways players relate to each other, the ways they compete, and how they determine the validity of their actions in the game world.

In the case of multiplayer games, though, the weight of the design in the ethical experience is of extreme relevance. It is by means of design that we relate to others during the game experience, and so they shape at least partially our moral agency in the game world. Of course, game design is a rather large task, and not all of it can be ethically relevant for multiplayer games. As I have argued using the example of *DEFCON*, there are three elements that need to be taken into consideration when analyzing the ethics of a multiplayer game design: the winning condition, the player-to-player specific mechanics, and the way the game world coherently reflects those mechanics. In *DEFCON*, the rule that states that the winner is the one who loses the least, the alliance system conditioned by a single winner, and the aesthetics of nuclear war as a desensitized experience all configure the game ethics. In any other multiplayer game, starting the analysis with these elements is a first step for the description of its ethics as projected by an object to a moral player.

This does not mean that players will blindly follow whatever instructions, goals, and mechanics the game affords them—players are, or ought to be, empowered users who can reject some strategies or actions that the game provides if they feel they are contrary to their values as players or as human beings. But this ethical empowerment has to be understood in connection to the importance of behavior design in multiplayer games: players will create their ethical values in the game experience oriented by the game design, and that can have a strong influence in the actual ethics of the game as experienced by ethical agents. In this process, the importance of player interaction design is crucial, and much more determinant than in single-player games, or even than in online worlds, since in multiplayer games there are no persistent communities, at least not with power and presence in the game world.

DEFCON is a rare gem, a computer game that feels and plays as a rather complex experience, a combination of the exhilarating features of multiplayer games coupled with the depth of reflection traditionally only present in other media. Despite some of its shortcomings, especially in terms of usability (for all its aesthetics, *DEFCON* is a rather complicated game to learn to play), this is a very interesting ethical computer game. It does not try to teach or educate its players, and it never renounces the goal of creating fun—but it does so by appealing to our rational, ethical minds. *DEFCON* is a multiplayer experience that makes us, its players, face our own values and thoughts—we are alone in its world, and the others are just blips in an impersonal depiction of a possible world. Many computer games are about exploration: exploration of worlds, of narratives, or of human relations and the sense of competition. *DEFCON*, a multiplayer game, is a game mostly about exploring our own values as ethical agents, while we push a button and the screen laconically informs us that New York is gone, and we have scored another five million deaths.

5.3   *World of Warcraft* and the Ethics of Online Game Worlds

So far, I have analyzed both single-player games and multiplayer games. It is time now to tackle the most complex of all contemporary gaming phenomena: virtual worlds designed for creating ludic experiences. But before I embark on this case study, there are two caveats that need to be mentioned: first, I am here analyzing those virtual worlds designed to be experienced as games,: that is, *World of Warcraft* or *Eve Online*, but not *Second Life* or *Habbo* (a social networking site). Second, this chapter should be read as an introduction to the analysis of the ethics of virtual worlds—the sheer complexity of these multiagent systems calls for detailed and exclusive analysis, deeper than what I will present here. Nevertheless, my intention is to provide a snapshot of the applicability of this framework, used for analysis of computer game ethics, to the understanding of virtual worlds.

I will use the MMORPG *World of Warcraft* as an illustrative case study. The phenomenal success of this game, which as of February 2008 had reached ten million denizens, has made it somehow the classic case study for online worlds—so much so that it could be possible to say that there is a burgeoning field of *World of Warcraft* studies. But my decision to analyze this game is not tied to its popularity, but to the fact that, while I was playing it, there was an interesting event that showed me in a very clear fashion the network of responsibilities at play in online worlds, and how that network affects communities and the moral fabric of gameplay.

Even though *World of Warcraft* is a rather well-known game, I will give a short description of it, including its universe, essential gameplay mechanics, and aspects of the game community. I will focus on the honor system, its implementation and how it affected the ethical being of the game. The honor system is a gameplay rule that rewards and encourages player-versus-player combat and its implications for the game experience. I will argue that the honor system is a perfect illustration of ethical affordances in the design of the game and how the player-subject may relate to them from a moral perspective. The analysis of the game I am presenting here is based on my personal experience playing, observing, and participating in the community. The portrait of the community I am going to present is based entirely on my observation and participation: no empirical data sampling has taken place, thus all the derived caveats should be applied.

I played *World of Warcraft* an average of three hours a day, from its European launch in March 2005 until December 2005, reaching levels 60 and 40. The period of time reflected in this case study description, though, comprises only a fraction of that time, between patches 1.1 to 1.7 (September 2005). The nature of an online virtual world like *World of Warcraft*, in constant development, suggested an approach that limited the timeframe of this research. I decided to stop my analysis of the world with the advent of patch 1.7. Since then, there have been interesting examples of ethical issues arising in the online world, and no doubt there will be more in the future, some of them related to the perception that Blizzard has of the player community and the use of its end user license agreement to pattern and control behavior.[9] Nevertheless, for the sake of this research, I have put some time boundaries on the description of the world. In this chapter, then, there is a description of *World of Warcraft* and a history and analysis of the honor system, since the public release of the game until the release of patch 1.7.

World of Warcraft is a massively multiplayer online role-playing game based on the *Warcraft* franchise, started by Blizzard Entertainment in 1994 with the launch of the real-time strategy game *Warcraft: Orcs & Humans*. This initial title, followed up in 1995 and 2002 with two sequels, as well as complemented by three expansion packs, created the game world of Azeroth, where the epic struggle between the Horde and the Alliance takes place. I will not describe here in full detail the mythology of *World of Warcraft*, but I would like to give readers an impression of the fictional layer of the game, which is important for understanding some design decisions that influence the gameplay mechanics and community values and practices.

Azeroth, the world of Warcraft, is a place where magic forces of good and evil are entangled in a battle for supremacy. The world was originally home to a number of races that cohabited in relative peace. The invasion of the "evil" orcs and other magical events destabilized this world, starting a never-ending war between the Horde (orcs, undead, trolls, and tauren)

Figure 5.7
World of Warcraft: Flying is a Pleasant Experience

and the Alliance (humans, elves, dwarves, and gnomes). These two main factions fight for control of the ruined world of Azeroth, but they are both threatened by the presence of other forms of evil, such as the Scourge (an undead infection of evil) and the Silicid (huge wasp-like insects). There is no time for solace or peace in Azeroth, as dangers lurk in every inch of this vast world.

World of Warcraft is played on servers divided by play style: player-versus-player, role-playing, or player-versus-environment, with the added combination of player-versus-player role-playing servers. Furthermore, there are important differences between the gameplay in the beginning of the game and in the end of the game. What I am about to describe is an account of the steps a player goes through in order to experience a fraction of what *World of Warcraft* offers as a game experience. This account will not be systematic, but focused on those elements that will be of relevance for the following discussion on the ethics of computer games. Also, it is worth mentioning that my own experience playing does not include some endgame content, such as large raids, simply because I never got to that level of involvement in the game. The following, thus, is a partial vision of *World of Warcraft*, albeit a reflective one.

The first thing a player of *World of Warcraft* will do is choose and design an avatar. At that stage, the player has to choose between the Alliance and the Horde. Once the faction is chosen, players have to choose one race out of four (currently five), and then which class they will play. Class is particularly important because it determines which kind of gameplay the player will engage in the most. These classes have different gameplay attributes: there are damage dealers (mages) and primary (priests) and secondary healers (shamans), melee damage dealers (rogues), ranged damage dealers (hunters), and so on.[10] Gameplay depends largely on the class of the player; any other choice (except that of faction, as I will argue further on) is more or less cosmetic. Nevertheless, it is important to mention that players grow fond of the physical appearance of their avatars, and that they use magic and enchantments to personalize, within very narrow margins, the look of their characters, by means of clothing or "glowing items."

Once all these aspects have been chosen, the player is inserted into the world of Azeroth. *World of Warcraft* is a huge environment with dozens of different settings, from deserts to high mountains, where day and night are differentiated, but where the world does not change—not even as an effect of the weather conditions. It does not matter what the actions of the players are, the world is immutable to them. Killing computer-controlled characters, even those that will be in charge of giving quests, does not have a lasting impact on the world, as they will eventually respawn.

In this world players can talk to nonplayer characters that will command them to do quests, which are rewarded with money or items and experience points. Players need equipment in order to improve their skills and thus their survival rate. The more powerful a player is, the more regions of Azeroth she will get to know. Accepting a quest usually implies going somewhere else and slaying some monsters. Players can also spend their time killing monsters outside of quests, because each kill usually gives some loot of different economic value, and experience points, depending on how difficult to kill or rare the monster is.

Acquiring experience points, money, and gear is the main goal of the game, and its mechanics are oriented toward it. Even though there are

Figure 5.8
World of Warcraft: A Gnome and a Cow, Two Faces of the Conflict

some players who enjoy the social aspect of meeting other players, or speculating in the in-game economy to make money, *World of Warcraft* is relatively unsuccessful in providing tools for expanding the gameplay beyond the repetitive actions of slaying monsters, together with others or alone, in search of better items or money that can buy them. Mastering *World of Warcraft*'s game mechanics means mastering the player's character class, both in playing solo and with others, so the chances of improving her gear and economy are better.

Combat and communication are then the two pillars of this experience. Combat is performed by activating the avatar class's powers in the most effective way according to the enemy at hand; meanwhile, the system calculates the success of the attack and the damage depending on statistical data related to the player's class, race, and equipment. In *World of Warcraft*, combat is dependent on skills like timing, coordination, and knowledge about the game mechanics and the rules of the game.

Communication, or socialization, on the other hand, usually takes place in those spaces where combat is less likely to happen, such as cities or villages. Communication is usually made via the text chat, complemented by emoticons or "slash commands," which trigger avatar animations related to the input command.[11] Communication is organized around a number of chat channels, some of them common to the world, meaning anybody anywhere in Azeroth can read them; some of them common to the world but exclusive to groups or guilds; and some of them limited to specific provinces or cities, and only heard in those spaces.

Essentially, *World of Warcraft* consists of a series of repetitive and relatively similar quests, which the player has to complete alone or in the company of other players (up to 40 if it is a raid instance, up to five if it is a normal instance).[12] Some of the quests take place in the persistent world, and other quests take place in instanced maps, which exist as they are experienced only by the group that enters them and only for the period of time in which they are inside. All high-level content takes place in instanced dungeons.

One of the most controversial aspects of the design of *World of Warcraft* is its player-versus-player mechanics. Allowing players to attack other players brings forth issues related to the values of the game, arbitration and game balance. Games like *Anarchy Online*[13] and the already classic

EverQuest allowed player-versus-player actions only in certain areas. Balancing the design of this type of gameplay with the sheer number of players involved in a MMORPG, combined with the experiential ladder that these games present, has led some designers to view player-versus-player gameplay with contempt.[14]

But *World of Warcraft*'s designers chose to enable player-versus-player combat in a different way. In the player-versus-environment and role-playing servers, players can choose to be eligible to engage in player-versus-player gameplay or not. A player of the opposite faction cannot attack a rival who has chosen not to participate in player-versus-player. Nevertheless, Blizzard provided servers where there was no need for consent in order to engage in this kind of gameplay. If any player spotted an opposite faction character, they could attack and then a duel would start. In this way, Blizzard ensured that the dangers that the fictional element of the game suggested for players, this never-ending war, could be matched with the gameplay players could experience.

The possible pitfalls of player-versus-player revolve around how the players will behave with each other. Given the fact that a difference in levels of experience implies differences in powers and abilities, there is always the risk that players with more power will harass players of lesser power—not to mention that players can always group and hunt down lower-level players. But in some way, it seems like the developer conceived that as a part of the fictional level of the game, and thus as a set of behaviors against which policing is superfluous. In fact, in the policies stated by the developers,[15] when harassing is mentioned (in the form of griefing other players), player-versus-player content seems to be beyond these laws of conduct, quite coherently within the game world's fictional basis.

World of Warcraft is, at the moment of writing, not only the most successful MMORPG in the world, but also the design example for other developers to follow. With a very careful balance of classes and races, a fascinating game world, and engaging gameplay that attracts both casual and hardcore players, *World of Warcraft* is an example of excellence in game design. But, how good is it from an ethical point of view? To answer this question, I will describe a design choice, which I will argue demonstrates the ethical affordances and constraints that players of *World of*

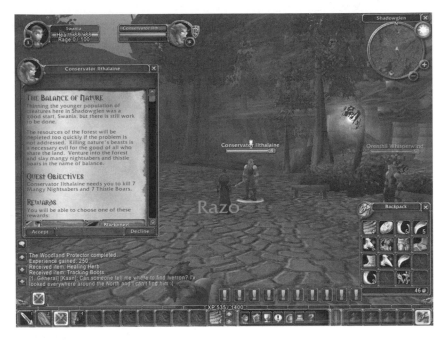

Figure 5.9
World of Warcraft: Quest Structure and a Sense of Story

Warcraft are faced with. This design choice is the honor system, as implemented and modified before the 1.7 patch.

The honor system illustrates the effects of embedded moral values in the design of the ludic system, and how they affect the community. When the game was launched in March 2005, it came almost as a surprise that the designers had implemented a system for player-versus-player combat on certain servers. For the first months of gameplay, there were no rewards for engaging in that activity. Player-versus-player combat was reasonably limited in low-level areas, and quite extensive in zones where only those characters that had already reached the end level of the game could survive. There were large-scale battles, but as a general and not always respected rule of sportsmanship, high-level characters would spare the life of lower, less powerful players.

Everything changed with the introduction of the honor system.[16] In the beginning, the honor system was a reward points system based on the number of "honorable kills" of other players. By "honorable kills," the developers meant those kills that took place in a gap of eight levels, meaning that a level-60 character could slaughter level-52 players and so be rewarded. Those honorable kills were translated into player-versus-player points, which were used to access rewards. The honor system did not contemplate any kind of punishment for any kind of behavior.

As it turned out, the honor system created certain chaos in this game world: the large number of players that had already reached the endgame level saw the system as a way of adding content to their gameplay, engaging in major battles in specific points of the geography of the world, in search of honorable kills and player-versus-player points that could give them the glory of new items and social recognition. This situation created major lags in areas of combat, because the servers were not prepared to support such a large number of players battling others simultaneously, and because end-level players were actually strolling around the world engaging in combat with low-level characters, which spawned a large amount of ganking[17] and other player-versus-player-related behaviors. With these rewards came also a rupture of the sportsmanship that had characterized player-versus-player gameplay—deviant behaviors emerged, exploiting the fact that the honor system rewarded aggressive play styles against other players, with no risk of punishment.

The honor system divided the community of *World of Warcraft* players. There were a number of players who considered it highly unbalanced, shattering the hitherto well-crafted gameplay balance. On the other hand, numerous players found the new player-versus-player system an extra encouragement to continue playing with more people, seeing it as a way of extreme socializing within the gaming environment of *World of Warcraft*. This situation rapidly changed when the honor system was completed with the introduction of "battlegrounds," instanced maps specifically dedicated to multiplayer player-versus-player, outside of the flow of the game world. Battlegrounds introduced specific places for player-versus-player gameplay, as well as unimaginable rewards. Players who just want to engage other players meet at the battlegrounds and do not interfere with the rest of the world, and therefore with the rest of the players. Sportsmanship is valued again; gankers and other kinds of griefers are not so ubiquitous.

If we were to analyze the honor system from a virtue ethics perspective, we could argue that it is unethical, because it encourages and fosters aggression toward other players without putting in place any punishment system. With this system, the possibilities for players to practice and use their moral reasoning are limited, and it creates behaviors that are deemed unethical by the player community, which is at the same time disempowered to react to this embedded ethical affordance. Again, it must be stated that the player is a virtuous being. When immersed in a game situation, players apply their ethical reasoning. In the case of *World of Warcraft* and the honor system, they at first accepted the open, self-regulated player-versus-player gameplay as an exciting element of gameplay mechanics. Some ethical rules and values were created for exploring the possibilities of this kind of gameplay. Even though there were players that enjoyed harassing weaker rivals, or that engaged in grievous actions,[18] players enjoyed the casual duels, self-arranged battles, and the dangers of possible mousetraps. It was a dangerous world, Azeroth, but a world of honor.

When the honor system was first introduced, players reacted, as I have already stated, in very different ways. The game system rewarded player versus player gameplay, and did not punish the potential advantages of engaging in combat with weaker adversaries. Furthermore, the honor system rewarded those players who engaged in player-versus-player, giving them access to items that made them even more powerful, and it did not punish those players who exploited an evident weakness in design: there was no punishment for harassing other players of weaker capacities. The reaction of those players who rejected the honor system shows that players reflect ethically about playing a game and about the consequences of the design affordances. Many players showed their disgust for a system that unbalanced the game, which allowed and encouraged actions that a part of the community saw as contrary to those values that the same community had tacitly agreed upon. Some players that complained threatened to close down their accounts, even though those threats may have been just a verbalization of their disaffection with the game.

What this example shows is players reflect on the values that the game system tries to impose on them. If the community of *World of Warcraft* player-versus-player users had not been split, if it had not disagreed about the effect of the honor system on their gameplay experience, then we would have to think of players as mindless subordinates to the game system. But players, some at least, reacted; they argued against the honor system using reasons that concerned their experience of the game, reasons that were of a moral nature. Players behaved like moral, responsible agents.

This best possible player-subject is not only one who can win the game, or achieve more of the game goals (in the case of games without a clear winning condition). The virtuous player is the one who is capable of adapting her behavior to the situation of the game as well as to the goals and constraints it creates. What kind of player somebody wants to be is not determined by the promise of victory, but by how to win; that is, the virtuous player will try to win by playing virtuously, using her ludic phronesis to assess the strategies and choices made. In this sense, the players who refused to accept the honor system in *World of Warcraft* showed how this reflection process takes place: there are unethical affordances in the new design of the game, and those affordances actually collide with what they consider to be the best way of playing, thus they publicly show their disagreement with that design decision.

If we apply the ludic hermeneutic circle to the case of *World of Warcraft* and the honor system, it can be seen as follows: a player agrees to play on a player-versus-player server, assuming the inherent affordances of the game design. Nevertheless, the player interprets those affordances, giving a certain meaning to the act of playing against another player. It could be deemed as something wrong, or avoidable, to harass other players of inferior powers. This player then participates in the player community by the mere act of playing the game, developing a tacit moral system for the game in player-versus-player mode, created by the players, and run and judged by the players. This behavior seems to be enjoyable, and justifies the monthly fee for the game.

When the honor system is instituted, the player assumes that by killing other players, some of them of inferior powers, she will get rewards and no punishment. But her reflection as a moral player deems that wrong, for reasons that the player feels are important. These values are also those of the player community, or, at least, of that part of the player community who cherishes one type of experience of *World of Warcraft*. The community perceives this change as an immoral affordance in the game design. For some members of that playing community the ethical dilemma reached beneath their player-skin—they found it wrong also in their real-world ethics: paying for a service that provides means for unethical behavior is not to be accepted.

In the case of *World of Warcraft* and the honor system, I argue that the game does not provide a sufficiently strong ethical framework, which led to the problems caused in a part of the community. The implementation of the honor system, the battlegrounds, and the lack of punishment for possible grievous behavior were all done in a top-down manner by the developers. The game design was significantly changed, including ethical affordances that collided with those created by a part of the community. This lack of openness in the ethical experience produced reactions against it by those members of the community who had an ethical investment in the player community. Moral agents complained, and were neither heard nor respected by the game's ethical development.

In the case of the honor system, *World of Warcraft* provides an example of unethical game design: it did not respect the creative and ethical capacities of players and their communities, and it imposed by force an ethical design affordance that caused an unwanted and unnecessary disruption in the game world. The player and the community are partially responsible for the ethical values of a game, together with the possible ethical affordances and constraints that the game may have in its design. Because in the case of computer games access and modification of most of the design is quite difficult, if not impossible, game developers have a share of responsibility for how that design encourages players' values and actions. A player is responsible for her acts in a game, for the way she behaves and for what she makes of a game. The ethical issues that a game may create are the responsibility of the player, to the extent that the game designers have allowed players to create and afford their own values in the game.

Understanding this ethical imbalance in the game, and how the informational relations between the agents and patients of the infosphere shape the ethics of the game, requires using of the concept of levels of abstraction. In *World of Warcraft*, the four relevant levels of abstraction are:

1. the game as a system of rules, mechanics, challenges, and goals; that is, the world of Azeroth as a space for play.

2. the player as an in-game agent; that is, the player that selects a class and plays according to the affordances and constraints of that class, leveling up and completing the quests relative to that class.

3. the player in the world; that is, the player as how she relates to other players by means of the tools, challenges, and methods provided by the game.

4. the player as a *homo poieticus*; that is, the player in the community creating and actively enhancing values on the good play.

It is in the third level of abstraction where we see the ethical implications of the honor system in *World of Warcraft*. The informational charge that the honor system brought to *World of Warcraft* changed the relations and dependences of the beings in the game. By assigning value to a certain part of gameplay, and considering that gameplay could be defined as the exchange of information as required by the game system to achieve ergodic experiences, the designers introduced an element of disruption into the game balance. Now potentially grievous actions such as corpse camping were rewarded, and became, on the game system level, desirable actions. But those actions disrupted the gameplay for a majority of players who complained and found their experience shattered by those players who did not see that the game is more than the system in itself—the game is the system as infosphere, including all the agents and informational beings that comprise the system.

If we contemplate the honor system from the fourth level of abstraction, where the player does adopt a more proactive approach, we could argue that the players of *World of Warcraft* showed their care for the game experience where they are player-subjects. Players of this virtual world, and of every virtual world, effectively present active stewardship in the construction of the values and behaviors of that world, and they can do so from inside the game, if that is possible, or by participating in the game community. Again, the importance of the game community is revealed. In this case, ethics explains the presence of players as active elements of the game world, casting a shadow over the procedures of the *World of Warcraft* developers: if the players are in fact morally capable of reflecting on the harm that a specific design implementation causes, but yet are not heard and their influence is not rewarded in the design of the game, can *World of Warcraft* on player-versus-player servers be then considered an ethically sound game?

From my perspective, the answer would be no. By design, and by the developers' policy, W*orld of Warcraft* is a game in which one party can cause the users ethical harm, whereas the users are not capable of implementing their ethics in the game. Assuming that a player is a *homo poieticus*, voluntarily engaged in this game, then she has to be allowed to intervene in the structure of the game. Only if the player complaints had yielded a reaction from the developers that restored the balance of the game according to those values that the users believed were appropriate— or better, only if the players were able to actually police themselves, and the developers acted only as a guarantee against harmful informational imbalances (cheating or grieving)—only then could *World of Warcraft*, in its implementation of the honor system, be considered an ethical game. But the game is still closed to players' self-policing, and the developers remain the only ones capable of creating policies and enhancing design choices, ever hoping (or expecting) that players will adapt to those choices as they ultimately did adapt to the choices derived from the honor system.

Despite being one of the best-designed and most successful MMORPGs in history, the player-versus-player implementation in *World of Warcraft* (at the time I described the game) made it at least partially unethical. Its structure does not take into consideration, nor respect, the possible influence that design choices with embedded ethical values have on the game experience. Furthermore, players are denied their capacities as moral agents—once there is a formal implementation of unidirectionally appointed player-versus-player rules, the player's voice is not heard, nor are the player's self-created ethical policies, which did actually preserve the informational balance of the game before the honor affordances, respected. In this respect, *World of Warcraft* is an unethical game.

World of Warcraft is a symbol of dominant trends in virtual world game design. Its tremendous success, grounded in an excellent design and compelling environment, will most likely ensure that online worlds will look like it for some years to come, and furthermore that innovation will always look at the essential design mistakes that this game made. One of the elements that could be improved is the ethical balance of the game, especially the capacity for players to create their own values in the game, and live by them.

Managing 10 million players, or even managing some thousands, is a complex task, and by no means do I want to downplay the quality of this game. But the absolute control over the game world and how players experience it that Blizzard showed with the implementation of the honor system is a misstep on the path toward the implementation of ethics in online worlds. The most effective way of creating ethical experiences in games is to balance the network of responsibilities in such a way that players are responsible for behaviors within the game experience, without any interference from the developers, while developers focus on maintaining the game system and dynamically responding to player needs in terms of game world evolution or balancing the economy.

A game like *Eve Online* shows a possible way of understanding the ethics of online worlds: by letting the players manage the values of the game, the developers are contributing to the expansion of and attachment of players to the experience of their game. Because players are reinforced as ethical agents with relative constructive capacities within the game experience, *Eve* is a better example of applying the principle of players as *homo poieticus*, and how that can affect game design.

Online worlds are fascinating environments of almost unlimited potential. The games and the social experiences that players have at their disposal are symptoms, perhaps, of the types of games and worlds we will be inhabiting in the future. But for these worlds to be ethical, they need to be open to our ethical being—they need to respect and reflect the ethical agency of their denizens. The ethics of online worlds are simple to summarize: give players a world, and word in that world, and let them determine the values they are going to play by. Developers have the ethical duty of facilitating that process, and players the moral obligation of inhabiting those worlds not only as denizens, not only as players, but as full, mature, ethical beings.

6   Unethical Game Content and Effect Studies: A Critical Ethical Reading

Having a comprehensive framework for describing the ethics of computer games is not only of importance for the specific analysis of games or game genre: it also needs to be applicable as a critical tool to more general moral problems regarding digital games. It is not enough to describe games and their ethics: it is also necessary to put the theory in relation to other research that focuses on the moral matters of computer games, and explain what the connections are between these other approaches and the framework presented in this book.

For those reasons, I will now focus on two different and relevant ethical issues that regularly come up when thinking about computer games and morality: the ethical implications of unethical game content, and the study of the (moral) effects of computer games on their users. The first one refers to computer games that simulate actions that our culture considers unethical—it is a general way of referring to issues like violence and computer games, for example. The second one is related to the psychological research on the impact these violent games have on physiological and mental behaviors. In this chapter I will provide a brief introduction to each topic from the perspective of the ethical framework analysis.

I started this book by reminding the readers about a common place computer games tend to occupy in our society: the bull's-eye of morality. Violent computer games, which are nowadays ubiquitous, pose interesting ethical challenges because the actions they simulate, actions the player has to do in order to progress in the game, appear to be of a highly unethical nature. But I have argued that computer game ethics are actually a rather complex construct that has to take into consideration, beyond the worlds represented by games, the presence of a moral player who interacts with a designed system of rules, mechanics, and processes. It is my intention here to analyze the nature of these ethical concerns regarding the content and effects of computer games, keeping in mind and applying the findings about the nature of players as moral beings and the ontology of games as ethical designed systems.

6.1 Understanding Unethical Game Content

When creating a simple game regardless of demands for innovation or originality, an approach that often works is to focus on conflict: make two players fight for limited resources, or make players try to temporarily eliminate others from the playing field, rewarding that action with tokens of some value in the game. In our Western audiovisual culture, we are also used to conflict, from Homer to the myth of the Wild West. Conflict is an interesting source for reflection and action, and as such we have used it in media to convey messages and to entertain. The combination of games, which excel at presenting interesting conflicts, and our media landscape often results in games that use, in their representational layer, the metaphors and actions of violence to convey conflict.

This violence is, as I have already mentioned, at the core of some of the ethical concerns raised by computer games: should we have a medium that is so focused on violent conflict? Is there any effect of violence on its users? It is obvious that the obsession of the computer game industry with weapons and blood raises interesting ethical questions—but which are these questions? And, more importantly, how can we answer them? It is time now to put our analytical framework into practice on one of the most relevant matters relating morality and computer games.

But before I start, I would like to get back to *Manhunt,* which I have referred to before as an interesting example of ethical gameplay. This game basically consists of perfecting the murderous skills of our in-game avatar by crafting gruesome executions while starring in a fictional snuff movie. *Manhunt* is well known for its complacence regarding gore and violent simulated actions, and when released it stirred some controversy concerning the relation between computer games and violence. This relation, often picked up by media as an argument against the growing popularity of computer games as a means of adolescent entertainment, is one of many examples of societal concern over the impact of unethical content in computer games. What is the unethical content of *Manhunt*, or of any violent computer game?

By unethical content I am referring to the simulation of actions that outside the simulated game world we deem ethically despicable. Torture, for instance, is generally conceived of as an immoral way of gaining information, since it attacks the very foundations of personality and humanity. Nevertheless, in *24: The Game*,[1] torture becomes a set of gameplay mechanics that the player has to exploit in order to progress. And, as in any computer game, the simulation of torture is designed in a way that makes it interesting to play with. This does raise ethical issues that need to be addressed. But it is not violence per se that is interesting: it is violence as something interesting, and a challenge within the experience of a computer game.

Unethical content is the actions that are designed to simulate what we would consider unethical behavior outside the game, but also simulations that, in themselves, can be considered unethical. For instance, in the game *Soldier of Fortune II*,[2] the developers included a physics simulation that gives the human models thirty-six "gore points" so the player can actually dismember her enemies in "realistic" ways. That degree of carnage, and the possibility for the player to inflict it, presents ethical issues related to the construction of the game world and the possibilities of interacting with it.

The ethical concern about unethical content in computer games has been, needless to say, a long-standing one, a controversy that is almost as old as computer games. A look at computer game history takes us back to two landmarks: *Death Race*[3] and *Custer's Revenge*. These games pushed the ethical boundaries of what computer games could simulate for entertainment: *Death Race* was an arcade game that basically consisted of racing a car over pedestrians—of course, both the "car" and the "pedestrians" were crude pixels that required a player's imagination to actually fulfill the gruesomeness of the gameplay. *Custer's Revenge*, the other game I am indicting here, was an Atari 2600 game in which the player had to navigate from one end of the screen to the other, avoiding arrows. If the player was successful, she was rewarded with the rape of a female Native American tied to a pole, which also gave in-game points, in a terrible act of poor game design. These are two shameful cases in the history of computer games, but the polemic they created is alive and present today, so much so that it has even permeated the political discussion in the Western world: for instance, there is a strong debate in the United States regarding legislation against selling computer games to minors.[4]

Perhaps the best-known contemporary example of this controversy is the *Grand Theft Auto* franchise. These games are pioneers in the use of large 3-D open-ended environments that the player can freely explore. But they are not only about exploration of simulated urban landscapes: in these games players experience a set of narratives that are more than reminiscent of underworld cinematic epics like *Scarface* or *Boyz n the Hood*. In this sense, the *Grand Theft Auto* series is to computer games what *Goodfellas* or *The Sopranos* were to the cinematographic representation of urban American crime.

The *Grand Theft Auto* series has been singled out regularly as one of the most unethical games,[5] perhaps because most of the interactions the players are allowed in the game are in fact simulations of unethical acts, like robbery, murder, blackmail, carjacking, prostitution, and the like. Nevertheless, in the world of *Grand Theft Auto*, crimes have a price: if the player commits a crime close to a police officer, she will start being chased by the police, with differing intensity depending on the nature of the crime. And if the player gets caught, she will lose some money, lose all her weapons, and fail any mission on which she was embarked.

Another example, of a rather different nature, is the game *Killer 7*,[6] in which players commit highly stylized murders in a semi-abstract environment. These murders are full of gameplay-relevant gore, since the blood of their enemies gives players better powers and killing capacities. The game would be considered unethical because engaging and rejoicing in murder and blood, whether or not it is in a stylized fashion, is unethical in itself. Similarly, in the case of *Grand Theft Auto: Vice City*, players can have simulated sex with a prostitute for money, and then beat her up to recover the payment. This gameplay mechanic gives players a bonus in health that is useful for accomplishing more complicated missions, but it is also deemed to be unethical for what it represents.

In general, the controversy surrounding computer games is based on the argument that games marketed to children and adolescents should not be violent or depict unethical actions; and furthermore, computer games, due to their interactive nature, should not simulate these actions, because interacting in immoral ways, even in a game world, is enacting unethical actions and is therefore the wrong thing to do from a moral perspective.

The logic behind considering these game world actions "unethical actions" is based on the fact that games excel as simulating devices. Most computer games are simulations with which the player engages voluntarily, with the intention of creating a ludic experience. In these simulations, the player has to interact with the environments in predetermined ways. In the prostitute sex mechanic from *Grand Theft Auto: Vice City*, the player engages in sex, and then kills the computer-controlled character in order to get the money back. All of these are actions performed in the context of a simulation where they are relevant. The way of interacting with most computer games is through input and output procedures that present a semantic layer with which we, cultural players, can relate and understand. Formally, the sex mechanic is a set of algorithms based on game rules by which players acquire an extra amount of energy after exchanging some in-game tokens. These tokens can be recovered afterward by means of a different input mechanic. To make this information exchange easier to understand, developers use conventions, representations that help players interact with the game world. These conventions are more often than not based on what we would define as unethical actions. And there is where the root of the ethical problem lies: is it appropriate to simulate unethical actions? What are the consequences of simulating these actions, both for the player and for the developers? Is it morally correct to develop these games?

These issues can be understood and partially explained by referring to virtue ethics, due to its cultural impact on and its presence in Western culture. From a virtue ethics perspective, computer games like *Grand Theft Auto*, *Killer 7*, or *Manhunt* are unethical because they reward the practice of unethical actions. To become a good individual who fully develops the values of the good, human beings have to practice these values of the good. Virtuousness is the development of good virtues by means of exercising them, which we do by developing our good moral values and our practical judgment, which will help us make the right choices in the face of ethical dilemmas. Virtue ethics is about practicing the good.

Playing certain computer games, then, would be deemed by a classic virtue ethics approach as an unethical practice. To play *Grand Theft Auto* would mean to actually engage in actions that build the wrong values: theoretically, there is nothing good to be learned from this glorification of urban North American crime. Virtue ethics, in all its different incarnations throughout the history of humanity, from Aristotle to Confucius, determines a number of virtues and values that need to be fostered, and computer games could foster those values by means of their interactive capacities. Games like *PeaceMaker*[7] try to act within this perspective. This game focuses on simulating the Israel-Palestine conflict, and it does so by creating a system in which players, to a large extent, can afford their own ethical values into the processes to solve the simulated conflict. Furthermore, *PeaceMaker* actually rewards the choice of nonviolent conflict resolution, thus building on a classic virtue ethics proposal: good ethical games are those that foster the development of good virtues and knowledge.

On the other hand, and from this perspective, games like *Killer 7*, *Manhunt*, and the *Grand Theft Auto* series are games that enforce wrong habits. By playing these games, the virtuous being engages in actions that are morally wrong, and yet they are both the only actions possible in that simulated world, and the actions rewarded by the game system. Virtue ethics would argue that computer games with unethical content actually reinforce practices and habits that ought not to be present in the virtuous human being, and that to commit an act of unethical meaning within a game world is to practice the wrong habits that will lead to the nonvirtuous life. This reasoning permeates the conventional argument against unethical content in computer games: players of violent games, for instance, are practicing the habit of killing, losing the capacity for attachment to human life and blurring the notions of good and evil.

Even in propaganda games like the U.S. Army's *America's Army*, these ideas about the relation between playing games and developing our moral virtues are present. *America's Army* is intended to be both a training tool and a recruitment advertisement. It can only be so if we consider computer games to act as exercises of moral habits: the game can only be effective if the habits and values contained in the game simulation are directly transferred to the players, who will uncritically accept them.

This is beyond the purely instrumental use of this game as a recruiting tool: the ultimate goal of propaganda games is to spread ideas convincingly to the player population—to serve as interactive brainwashers. There is, to date, no conclusive data that empirically proves this argument— it wouldn't be surprising to actually find this argument true, but there would still be large ethical steps between being persuaded by a game and being morally affected, due to players' ethical capacities for reflection in context.

But let's return to virtue ethics, since this theory makes one point with which I can only agree: computer games could foster good virtues, such as nonviolent conflict-solving skills, by means of their design, their gameplay, and their game worlds. Nevertheless, the approach that links games with unethical content to the development of vices and unethical behaviors lacks an understanding of the inner workings and nature of computer games.

A more classic Aristotelian would argue that computer games with unethical content could be seen as games that foster a kind of player catharsis. This perspective, argued by some followers within the field of game research,[8] is not adequate, in my opinion, with regards to the ethics of computer games. For catharsis to work there must be a unified subject that plays the game and is affected by it, meaning that there is not a player-subject, and the values we play by are the exact values we live by. In this book I have argued that the player is a specific subjectivity that comes into being in the experience of the game, a subjectivity that actually presents specific characteristics derived from the ludic experience of the game as moral object.

The understanding of the unethical content of computer games, then, has to take into consideration that playing games is also the act of creating the player-subject as an operative moral being who interprets her acts within the game from an ethical perspective. The virtue ethics-based analysis that permeates the public understanding of this issue does not consider that players are capable of applying ludic phronesis, or that games not only foster their own virtues, but that they also have ethical values of their own, which have to be understood within the perspective of the game as a moral object.

In other words: a player of *Grand Theft Auto* is seeing the simulation of violent acts within a game world not only with her ethics as a human being outside the game, but also with the ethics of the game player (unless, as I have argued before, the player interprets her actions as contradictory using stronger ethical values from her self outside of the game, in which case the subjectivization process is broken and there is not a player-subject experiencing a game). In any case, it is the player, with player ethics, values, and understanding, that is the subject that affects and is affected by the ethical content of the game. To play a game is to become a player in a ludic experience, which also implies developing the player virtues and the understanding of games as interpretable simulations.

Players engage in unethical actions in computer games because those actions have meaning within the game for the player-subject. Killing the prostitute after having sex with her is the most rational approach: the player gets her energy level topped up, and she recovers the money. From the perspective of the game, it is an action that can be beneficial for the game experience. Furthermore, it is not compulsory—only players who voluntarily explore that possibility will be exposed to it. Similarly, the acts of violence in *Killer 7* are only meaningful to the player of the game, and they are so because they represent the challenges that have to be solved in order to progress in the game. Therefore, it is necessary to understand that the unethical content of a game does not affect the virtuous being outside the game world, unless in her process of interpretation of the game experience her external ethical values play a role, by means of encountering a taboo of some sort. It is the player as moral being who encounters and experiences this unethical content. Could there be a transfer of values? In the mature, ethical being, both as a player and outside the game, that would not happen—the process of ludic phronesis and its evaluation by the external subject avoid in principle the transfer of values, within the given condition of moral maturity.

This is a process in which ludic practical judgment plays a role, introducing a relevant caveat to this perspective: if the player-subject has developed ludic practical judgment and player virtues, does it become impossible for a game's unethical content to have an effect on the self outside of the game? The player has to have the ludic maturity to understand the reasons behind the simulation and the fact that she is interacting with a game world specifically designed to produce a ludic experience.

This implies that games with unethical content should only be experienced by users who have developed the ludic maturity to understand the experience of playing a game. Therefore, age regulation codes and the moral education of game consumers and developers have a crucial role in the ethical configuration of computer games as objects and experiences. Virtue ethics can be right when analyzing the unethical content of computer games in the case of immature users: interacting with computer games that present unethical simulations may cause trouble for those who have not developed the interpretational tools that are used when developing the player's virtues. This trouble has to do with the necessity of developing the moral understanding of the player-subject, and how it relates to the larger subject outside the game.

Games with unethical content should only be marketed to and consumed by virtuous players, those player-subjects who have actually developed their ethical reasoning. Let's take, for instance, *Grand Theft Auto: Vice City*. A player of this game ought to understand that what she is interacting with is a simulated urban American environment, heavily inspired by cinema clichés, where violence is the main means of interacting with the world and progressing in the game. Furthermore, the virtuous player of *Grand Theft Auto: Vice City*, when performing the prostitute game mechanic, should be aware that she is actually increasing her chances of passing a challenge by means of exchanging game tokens in the most efficient way. All of this is wrapped in a provoking simulation that the player understands is only meaningful within the game, because the meaning is related to the game system.

This kind of ludic phronesis, as I have said, takes time to develop. To become players is not only a synchronic process of subjectivization that takes place when experiencing a game, but is also a diachronic process by which players create their history and culture in the time spent playing games. Player-subjectivity is who we are and how we morally relate to things when experiencing a game, but it is also who we have been in our ludic experience history. The unethical content of games has to be related to the moral maturity of the player as an interpreter of her actions within the game experience.

What are, then, the ethical implications of unethical game content? If the player is a fully mature player body-subject, the implication may be a paradox: for those players the use of computer games as a means of expressing interesting events and ideas must be obvious. The game designer of the *Super Columbine Massacre RPG!*, in the forums he set up for discussing his game, is appealing to these mature users of computer games. He believes that his game has to be understood as a mature game for mature players, a game that fosters discussion. And this is only possible if players are mature moral subjects who understand and develop the ethics of being a player-subject.

This implies that those players who are still developing this moral understanding should be prevented from accessing that game, or should only do so in controlled situations—for instance, in an educational environment. Understanding World War II using a game like *Battlefield 1942* could be possible in the right setting, provided that players are mature enough to understand the implications of this game. This perspective puts the responsibility on the players, who ought to develop an ethical understanding of games and their interpretational capacities within the game experience.

Nevertheless, game developers and designers also play a role, due to their duties in the distributed responsibility network. That role is dependent on how they design and market this unethical content. Games should be allowed to include the possibility to interact with environments in an unethical fashion. *Grand Theft Auto* and *Manhunt* are games in which violence is also showing some aspects of our cultural zeitgeist, but these games should not be marketed to the wrong audiences.

This is not the only responsibility game developers ought to consider. Violence, or any other unethical content, has to be included in the game not as a glorification of technology or because of the fascination for guns and fast action that the main segment of computer game consumers feel. Unethical content has to be meaningful—it has to play a role in the process of experiencing the game, and that role has to take into consideration the fact that playing a game is also interpreting a game experience from an ethical perspective. The use of unethical content has to be justifiable within the ethical nature of the game experience, either as a way of creating meaningful challenges, or as a tool for conveying an agenda.

Players are moral beings capable of ethical reasoning, and games are experiences that have a relatively encapsulated existence. But that does not mean that games do not affect the players' ethical being, or that games bear no importance of effect outside their experience. Games are powerful simulation tools that convey worldviews, messages, and values. Emptying games of ethical reflection in their design and using unethical content for its shock value as a marketing resource means not only devaluing the possibilities of games as a means of expression, but also making products that are unethical objects.

Computer games should by design take into account the ethics of their users. And that includes reflecting on how their ethical content is going to be implemented, and in which ways players will understand and reflect upon it. There is nothing essentially wrong in games with unethical content: they do not foster the wrong values in human beings, because player-subjects with ethical capacities experience them. But this does not mean that computer games can use unethical content and expect their users not to be affected. Computer game designers and users have a great deal of responsibility when it comes to this content and the ways it is experienced. To play and design computer games are both acts that require ethical maturity, but which also bring forth interesting ethical dilemmas. Computer games can and ought to use their language and simulation capacities to create interesting experiences that make their users reflect upon their being, culture, and society. But games will only be able to do so when their use of unethical content is dictated by a creative, reflective drive, and not by the pressures of marketing or the idea that computer games are *just* children's entertainment.

6.2 Effect Studies and the Ethics of Computer Games

These violent computer games I have just written about pose an interesting question: do the actions performed in the game world affect our moral fabric, and our body and psyche? The focus on violent computer games is mostly concerned with the values of the game objects, and not as much with the effects of the games on the users. For answering that other question, there is a relevant and oft-cited body of research focused on analyzing the effects of violent games on their users. This research has been used as a spearhead by the media and policy makers when it comes to defining the morality of games in a larger, cultural perspective. By effect studies I am referring to psychological empirical studies that argue for a causal link between the game's ethical content and the player's behavioral patterns.[9] In what follows I will formulate a criticism of this effect studies research from the analytical framework of computer game ethics that I have argued for.

The research on the effects of computer games on the behavior of their users is a reasonably well-consolidated field of research in psychology; a field that, much like many similar studies done with other media as targets, has yet to provide conclusive data on the correlation between violent or sexual content and what I will here call "unethical" behavior. Nevertheless, there is some evidence that may point to a certain relationship between the violent content of a game and the unethical behavior of players. This connection is of extreme interest for understanding the ethical footprint of computer games in our culture.

It is not my intention to delve deep into a methodological discussion about these studies, as our methods are not compatible.[10] Furthermore, the goals we are seeking to achieve are not similar: while effect studies tries to connect unethical content with unethical behavior, I have tried to define what constitutes the ethics of computer games, and how we can analyze them. Nevertheless, there is an obvious connection between the field of effect studies and the interest in the ethics of games. In the intersection of these two areas I find some substantial flaws concerning the ethical discourse and rhetoric that informs many effect studies. I shall present arguments against the use of these effect studies as a tool for analyzing computer game ethics.

Effect studies focus considerably on the content of the computer game. Most of this research takes as a starting point how the game world looks— the audiovisual representation of the player's actions in computer games. This is their main ethical flaw: these studies can say much about the relations between the graphical representation of the players' actions and the effects on their out-of-the-game behavior, yet they are leaving out the complex network of elements that also make playing computer games a moral experience. While their results concerning physical reactions are interesting, pointing at some correlation between actions in the game and the reactions of our bodies when playing, these studies seem to deny the fact that players are moral beings, and that we are not slaves to our corporal, primordial reactions.

The content of computer games, their fictional element, is relevant for their ethical construction of meaning, and thus these effect studies do make a valid point. I am not advocating here a total disregard of content when it comes to considering the effects of computer games on their users. Nevertheless, in this book I am arguing for a networked ethical system that explains the moral nature and structure of computer games beyond their fictional content, which, though relevant, is not alone in the configuration of the experience of a computer game, and thus it should not be considered as the only source of behavioral conditioning.

Effect studies tend to fall into a guilty/victim user conception: players are victims of a game system that "forces" them to behave violently, both in the game and outside the game by "direct" correlation of the game content and the actions outside the game experience; but players are also guilty of engaging in those activities, both the violence and the act of playing a game. Effect studies tend to consider players moral zombies, unable to critically reflect on what they do inside or outside the game. This consideration is in itself an unethical statement, since it is treating ethical agents as mere input providers who cannot reason on their own. As I have repeatedly argued throughout this book, players are ethical beings capable of deep and complex ethical reflection about their acts in the game.

There are recent claims, both from computer game critics and from other social institutions, about computer game training disinhibiting users, making them less sensitive to committing violent actions. Again, this reveals a discourse that is damaging for computer game culture: the player as a passive puppet in the hands of mischievous game designers.

But before I present my criticism of this perspective, I believe it is necessary to state clearly once again that there is a certain truth to the importance given to the game content and to the relatively passive role of the player, though these perspectives are often misguided. Players need to be morally mature to understand the ethical values of the game they are playing and the moral nature of their actions. This moral maturity is achieved through time, by means of playing games and reflecting upon them—it is a knowledge that we as players have to acquire. This ludic moral maturity implies that players can engage critically in the gameplay experience, using their own game culture, their self-perception as players, and their ethical being outside the game as evaluation tools for the morality of their acts.

If we don't have the moral maturity to understand the ethical implications of a computer game—of its content, design, or culture—then we are actually being nonvirtuous beings, and games can be considered a source of harm. Hence the importance of age regulation codes, game education, and other social and cultural institutions. For now, suffice it to say that the content of computer games does play a role in the ethical construction of meaning and in the effects of the game, but its true importance has to be seen from a wider, more inclusive perspective.

What effect studies have consistently left out of their research are two elements of fundamental importance for the ethics of games: the game as designed object/experience, and the moral presence of the player. To leave out the importance of game design and the ethical affordances that it may have means not addressing a very important issue: how the content of the game is designed to be interacted with, and how the game system encourages and rewards the player's participation. The design of the game is a fundamental element in the ethical construction of meaning in computer games, as it is also highly relevant for the perception and interpretation that players have of those ethical values. Furthermore, because it is the game as object, and thus the game design, that initially creates the subjectivity of the player, and because it is also the underlying structure that makes the game world playable, the game design has to be taken into consideration when it comes to evaluating the effects of computer games.

When playing a game that is poorly balanced, frustration may arise and, in some personalities, anger through frustration. For example, as a thought experiment, playing a platform game in which there are no saves and in which the jumps have to be extremely well calculated or the level will restart, wasting all the progress achieved during gameplay, might foster in the players a state of frustration that could make them angry. This game can have colorful, bright, innocuous content, like a clone of the Mario games, and yet it can produce an unwanted physical effect. As I have argued before, the design of the game is partially responsible for the ethical configuration of the player-subject in her relation with the game world and her interactions with other agents using the afforded game system mechanics.

The design of computer games is not neutral. Game designers elaborate complex challenge systems that pretend to engage us in a ludic activity. As I have argued before, part of our player-subjectivity is determined by the game system and its affordances. A game design in which cheating and harassing the opponents is encouraged, helping those who are ruthless, is unethical. A game like *Burnout 3*, in which players race against each other trying to crash their opponents' cars, would be unethical if the game design was not balanced, since some players could harass others without being punished. Balancing the game, in this case, is creating an appropriate equilibrium between the actions the player can do against other agents and the negative consequences of those actions. Another case of unethical design due to balancing issues is *Age of Empires 2: The Age of Kings*.[11] When played in difficult single-player mode, this game's computer-controlled civilizations receive an advantage in the number of resources they are given and the speed with which they can harvest them. Finally, the example of the privileged strategies in *Warcraft* (which I mentioned in the chapter dedicated to game design) illustrates other possibilities of unethical design that ought to be considered because they affect and harm players and their ludic experience, since they systemically allow for some players to defeat others by virtue of a failed game design.

A proper expansion of effect studies' methods would be to incorporate an evaluation of the game design and questions directed to the players as a part of their empirical method. By relating the content of the game to the way it is designed, researchers should be able to point out those ethical affordances that might be of relevance for their study on the effects of a computer game. Then the result of the research would take into account how the actions that players can perform in computer games are partially determined by a game design that has the goal of limiting player behavior and encouraging certain actions.

Nevertheless, taking into account the game design is not enough to validate the ethical relevance of effect studies. It is essential to overcome the discourse of the guilty victim and to define the player as a moral being who has responsibility and reflective capacities when it comes to playing games. Effect studies cannot disregard the moral capacities of players; they should not be treated as moral zombies, for they do actually behave ethically in the context of playing computer games.

Effect studies in general do not ask the players about their reflections on the game itself, but they ask them to correlate the act of playing the game with their feelings and actions immediately after playing the game, and a while after doing so. Therefore, there are no insights about how the player perceives the act of playing a violent computer game, and there is no depth in the understanding of what players feel and think when engaging in a violent computer game. Players are not entitled to reflect upon the morality or even the nature of their acts—their status as moral beings is disdained, thus leaving out most of what makes computer games ethical experiences. Effect studies discard players as moral agents, and thus their work has to be taken as just a partial view of how some content of some games may influence some actions, but not the moral fabric of a player or a community.

Only by reassuring us that researchers acknowledge the ethical being of computer game players can effect studies yield relevant information about how computer games affect their users' behavior. Effect studies can be a very valuable tool for understanding how players relate to the game experience and how the game experience carries ethical values from inside the game to outside the game, and the other way around. The relations between the game and the player need to be charted if we want to understand how some design choices affect the player's ethical reflections and her behavior, and how those changes may affect the way she relates to the game. Serious effect studies should take into consideration the ethical construction of games as experiences; only then would we be able to answer some of the most interesting questions regarding the actual effects of computer games in our moral universe.

In this chapter I have approached two of the most interesting ethical issues that computer games create: their violent content and the possible effects that this content has on game players. Throughout my reflections on these two closely intertwined topics, I have insisted on the importance of understanding this ethical agency not as a quality that is always fully developed, but that we, as cultural beings, develop and learn through our experiences as players. To be a player is a learning process that takes years—and to be a good player from a moral perspective, to be aware of the ethical choices and dilemmas that computer games pose, to be able to act according to our moral fabric, is a lifelong process—one that also has the promise, for game development, of future players who are also interested in ludic experiences of heavy moral load.

Some readers may be now wondering: "Is it ethically correct to play computer games with unethical content?" To those who ask this question, I can only answer: think about who plays. Is the player mature enough? Does he or she understand the meaning of the rules, of the gameplay, of the game world? Is the player aware of her ethical agency, of her ethical being? Is the game respectful of that ethical agency? Players are ethical beings: we can reflect about our actions in games, and we have the moral tools to distinguish between the values in a game and the values we live by. But we, players, developers, parents, citizens, politicians, have the duty to foster this culture of game ethics. We have to foster the development of ethical players and the maturing of computer games as expressive media. This duty is a fundamental part of our ethical being and obligations toward others and society.

Computer games pose ethical problems for their moral content and the way they affect us. But I insist: as players, our ethical capacities allow us to experience those problems not only as challenges, but also, and more importantly, as opportunities for experiencing morals, for testing and applying our virtues, and for building, within the game, a successful ethical experience.

7   The Ethics of Game Design

Designing computer games is a complicated task—there are considerations to be made concerning the player, the balance of the system, and how to create fun or engagement in an activity that will generate the intended ludic experience. To these complexities, I would like to add one more: if game design is a moral activity, since the object created is ethically relevant, and if the goal of game design is, generally speaking, to create compelling gameplay—how can we create interesting ethical gameplay?

In this chapter I will not directly answer this question. What I will do is approach the question of ethical gameplay from an analytical perspective: I am not trying to provide specific tools for a game designer to appropriate, apply, and instantly generate ethically interesting gameplay. My goal in this chapter is to think about ethical gameplay, to understand what this means, and to provide a framework that can inspire and challenge game developers.

Before presenting such a framework, I am going to briefly analyze some recent computer games that have allegedly included ethical gameplay as a significant part of their experience. I will argue that those games are noble but failed attempts at embedding ethics into computer game experience because they have not taken into consideration the different actors in the network of ethics that every game experience creates. This also means that they have neglected the understanding of the player as a moral being. With those games I shall start my reflections on designing ethical gameplay.

7.1   Failed Attempts: Ethics as Statistics

Two of the most successful single-player role-playing games of recent years, Bioware's *Knights of the Old Republic* and Lionhead's *Fable*, use the enticement of gameplay-relevant moral choice as a unique selling point. Both games promise a world of adventures and excitement in which the players' actions and decisions in ethically compromising situations have an effect on the evolution of the character, the physical appearance of the avatar, and the player's relations with the environment and the computer-controlled characters populating these single-player game worlds. Moral choice is allegedly integrated into gameplay as a mechanism for enhancing the game experience—the player can explore the consequences of unethical actions in the game, and those consequences will have relevance in the way the game experience unfolds.

Yet these two games represent failed attempts at including effective computer game ethics in the experience of the game by a moral agent, due to a misunderstanding of the nature of computer game ethics and their creative possibilities. Some gameplay elements in *Fable* and *Knights of the Old Republic* are similar: the player controls an avatar or, in the case of the *Star Wars*-based game, a number of avatars that have to navigate a relatively open game world, completing quests in order to finish a main story line. There are also side quests that allow the player to explore the world, acquire new items, and gain reputation with the nonplayer characters. These two games include moral evaluation as an important part of the gameplay. The choices the player makes in the side quests, and in some of the main quests, are rewarded with "good" or "evil" points, which decide the player character's ethical alignment in the world. In the case of *Fable*, the players can become evil heroes, feared by the population of the game world; in *Knights of the Old Republic*, the choice is between becoming a Jedi knight or a Sith lord, following the mythology of the *Star Wars* cinematographic saga.

Moral choice, then, becomes a rewarded element of gameplay, giving alleged ethical depth to the ludic experience. For instance, right at the beginning of *Fable* the player has to choose between lying to a woman whose husband is cheating on her, or telling the truth. The choice will affect the future development of her relations with these characters, and incidentally the ways the rest of the computer-controlled characters will treat the player. In *Knights of the Old Republic*, players will be faced with nonplayer characters who initially will not give away the information needed for proceeding in the adventure. The player will have to choose between using her powers to forcefully get the information or a more nonviolent approach. The outcome of these choices affects gameplay and the way the main narrative evolves, ending in very different storylines depending on which side of the Force the player has decided to play.

Both titles are interesting because of the stress on ethical choice within the game world and its effects on the world and the gameplay experience. Depending on which alignment players choose, they have access to different powers and items, which varies to a certain degree the ways the player has of interacting with the world. But does the inclusion of ethics as a gameplay option make them "good" games; that is, games in which the ethics of computer games as experiences are relevant?

The answer is no.

Both *Fable* and *Knights of the Old Republic* are examples of how not to design games as ethical experiences, precisely because of the way the ethical system has been included as a part of the gameplay.

In *Fable*, there is a gameplay system that allows the player to change the avatar's ethical alignment. There are two places in the game where, after paying a certain amount of money, the alignment returns to the blank state in which the game started, so the player's previous actions and their ethical evaluation by the system are no longer taken into consideration. This is obviously a game mechanic focused on encouraging the player to experiment further with the game world, and it is an interesting design choice when it comes to increasing the life of the game in terms of hours of gameplay. Yet it compromises the possible ethical interest in this game, as it does not give true moral depth to the decisions the player made up to that moment in the game. By trivializing those decisions and making them reversible by means of collecting and exchanging game tokens, the game designers emptied *Fable*'s moral system of any depth.[1]

In *Knights of the Old Republic* the situation is different. It is not possible to change the alignment of the avatar at any moment. The real issue behind the failed attempt at creating a relevant ethical game experience is related to how shallow the options are. For instance, players can choose to use violence to convince a nonplayer character to give away information, or they can try to get that information by more subtle means. This dichotomy, the player knows, will be evaluated by the system, which will give "dark side points" to the use of violence, and "light points" to the use of persuasion. The choice is not ethical, but merely statistical. The player

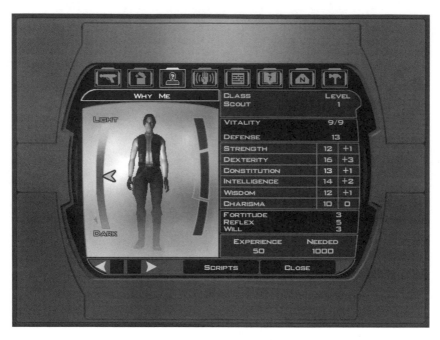

Figure 7.1
Knights of the Old Republic: The Moral-O-Meter

is not facing a moral choice, but a mere bifurcation of paths leading to different gameplay possibilities. There is no ethical reflection in *Knights of the Old Republic*, but a statistical analysis of choices and outcomes.

Neither *Fable* nor *Knights of the Old Republic* are ethically deep games, nor are they good games from an ethical perspective. The problem is their game design, which tried to provide players with a moral layer of experience, including ethical decision making as a gameplay element that should be taken into account because it affected the progression, appearance, and final outcome of the virtual world. They did so by including an in-game evaluation system that classifies actions into ethical schemas, triggering the world and the computer-controlled characters to act in certain ways. In other words, the state machine underlying the fictional world changes state when a player performs an action, and it does so toward one or another different states depending on the conditions ascribed to the player input. The player is enticed, with different success, to consider these conditions as moral choice; for the game system it is just two different input signals that lead to different states. Thus, ethics is computable in these games, as it is directly related to the game as state machine.

In their dimension as ethical games it is this mechanization of the ethical choice that constitutes the failure of *Knights of the Old Republic*, *Fable*, and games presenting a similar game design. I have argued that players interact with a game system that may have a fictional game world. While the game world does have importance in the ethical configuration of the game, it only does so when it can be related to the ethics of game design; that is, the ethics of the game as object are the ethics of the design as projected in the game world. Players perceive these game worlds, but they interact with them by means of interacting with the game as system, a process in which they use their own moral reasoning to articulate the ethics of the game experience.

In the case of these games, players are deprived of the privilege of ethically reflecting on the game experience by implementing ethical choice as a part of the game design. Because the choices they make are going to be measured and evaluated by the game system, moral choice no longer implies a reflection upon their actions, but rather a strategy, another token in the world of the game. In any other computer game, moral reasoning is not embedded in the game, and thus it is up to the player to be empowered as a moral agent, to create the values she wants that experience to have. By implementing moral choice as a gameplay token, players are less free to pursue the practical use of their moral reasoning, for it is the game that tells them what is good and what is bad. Ethical decision making becomes another algorithm for the state machine to take into account, disempowering the player as an ethical agent with the capacity for self-evaluating her actions. These types of design make explicit, embed, and trivialize the ludic ethical interpretation of the player, thus creating a distance between the morality of the player, her phronesis, and the act of playing a game.

It could be argued that precisely by implementing ethics in the game design the way these games do, players are faced with the consequences of their actions and they are in this way experiencing a world that changes according to their ethical reasoning. This is without doubt the goal the game designers envisioned when creating these systems. It is correct to believe that a game with a world that evolves according to the moral actions of the player is an interesting game world because it makes ethics a relevant part of the fabric of the game. The problem arises when the player is bereft of her creative capacities, leaving a system that evaluates and labels her actions according to moral standards that are external to those the player has created.

As I have insisted throughout this book, players' values and choices make them ethical agents in the game experience—and, by extension, this makes the game experience a moral one. By embedding the morality of the players' actions in the game design and systemically evaluating them as "good" or "bad" actions, these games are taking away the player's moral responsibility, making the process of self-evaluation just another element in the game system and not a part of the moral interpretation of the game experienced by the player. The main ethical concern is that the game system extends its influence to the sphere of the player, to the particular realm of the player as moral agent. By creating a system that gives an explicit moral value to actions, a value that can be numerically calculated by the game system, the player's creative stewardship in the moral construction of the game experience is limited to that of a mere input provider who does not need to evaluate her own actions, but only make choices that will be evaluated by the system. The root of that choice may be moral, but its interpretation and its affection in the game experience are no longer a matter of the morality of the agent, thus trivializing the experience of the game.

These games are examples of poor ethical design. It could even be argued that they are in fact unethical games, as they mechanize the player's morality, trivializing her role in the moral construction of the game experience. It is because players are moral agents who reflect upon the ludic experience of the game that we can actually describe the ethics of computer games. Furthermore, we have to consider players as ethical beings so we can think about games that actually reflect on serious ethical concerns with aesthetic and cultural importance. Serious games, without an ethical player, could not exist. But how can we have ethical gameplay?

7.2   Ethical Design: The Open and the Closed

I have argued that some games that have included as a part of their game systems some kind of ethical simulation evaluating the players' actions are failed attempts at implementing ethical gameplay. They are so because they alienate the ethical capacities of players, but also because they turn gameplay into a statistical contest between causal chains. Ethical gameplay is more complex than that, but by no means impossible to design for.

This is my basic hypothesis: the ethical game is not that which evaluates the players' actions according to predetermined moral systems embedded in the game, but that in which the ethics of the game experience and all its elements are reflected on and visible in the game design, in the game experience, and in the game community. A good game has been designed keeping in mind that creating computer games as objects is a moral act, that the design of the game can have ethical affordances, and that the game is going to be experienced by a moral agent. This moral agent has to perceive the game as an experience where she can exert her moral judgment as a player, where she can create the values that will guide her gameplay, and where her ethical virtues are respected. The resulting game experience has to be communicable to other players who will understand, share, and/or contribute to creating the values of that game in the community.

These are, of course, very general approximations of what ethical computer games can be, and how to design them. Again, it is not my intention to provide a toolset that can be directly applied, as a program, to any game design in order to create ethical gameplay. What I am suggesting here is a theoretical framework of analysis that, given the right circumstances, can provide an interesting source of inspiration and challenge to game designers. For doing so, I will suggest an analytical model for ethical gameplay, exemplified by commercial computer games. These categories are not absolute, but analytical patterns that emerge when considering the different roles and importance given to the player by the game design. It is possible to find games that present aspects of all the methods, but there will always be one of these patterns that is dominant when we analyze the ethical design of a game.

There are two types of ethical game design: open ethical design and closed ethical design. This presents two not mutually exclusive modalities: closed subtracting ethics and closed mirroring ethics.

An open ethical game design is a game in which the values of the player and the player community can be implemented in the game world or are reflected dynamically by it. This results in either new content or community-driven practices, or an adaptation of the game world to the ethical choices of the player. Massively multiplayer online games of any kind should fall into this category, as well as other multiplayer games, including those that are asynchronous;[2] that is, those that are played by many players, only not necessarily at the same time.

But this is not a category exclusive to multiplayer games: single-player titles like *Civilization, Balance of Power,* or *The Sims* are games in which the player can effectively experience the game in different ways depending on her ethical judgment. For instance, a player can choose to be abusive toward her Sims, or to create a pacifistic civilization that will expand by means of science and commerce. These choices have a weight in the ethical configuration of the game experience. Single-player ethical games are often based on the development of the storyline by player input: *Deus Ex* is the classic example of open ethical design. Other single-player open ethical game designs would be *Fable* and *Fahrenheit.*

Open ethical games are those in which the players' values can be used in developing a relation with the game world, and in which the game world accepts and encourages this player-driven ethical affordance, and on occasion reacts accordingly. That relation can be a strategy to win the game, but also possibilities to modify the game world, or to create new content. The player will use her moral reasoning and her values, both as player but also potentially as a human being, in her relation with the game world, and the game world will be open to the results of that reflection. An open ethical game experience is based on production, participation, and creation.

In a closed ethical game design, the game creates an ethical experience in which the player cannot implement her values beyond the constraints of the game. The game is designed to create a set of possible actions with different moral weights, and the player will create her values as a player according to the game's values, without the possibility of contributing her values to the game itself. The game is designed with a moral agent in mind, trying to give her ethical choices that are ultimately limited and determined by the game design. Most single-player games fall into this category, especially character-driven adventure and role-playing games, like *Tomb Raider*[3] or *Planescape: Torment.*[4] It is possible to find closed design in multiplayer games: for instance, the multiplayer cooperative version of *Halo 3* presents a rather closed structure in which players can afford strategies but not values to the gameplay experience.

In closed ethical games, designing a ludic experience is the goal of the development process. From a distributed responsibility perspective, the developers are the most important elements in these kinds of games. *Knights of the Old Republic* and *Bioshock* intend to be open ethical games, since they aim to create a game experience in which ethics play a role in the relation to a responsive game world. They do not succeed because the developers overemphasized the closedness of the game experience, not allowing the player to reflect on and experience the game as a moral agent. Other games like *Shadow of the Colossus* or *Manhunt* are more successful in being closed ethical experiences. They are so because the act of playing, and thus of experiencing the game, involves making moral choices or suffering ethical dilemmas, yet the game system does not evaluate the players' actions, thus respecting and encouraging players' ethical agency.

A closed ethical game provides the player with the values she is going to live by in the game world. Closed ethical games force players to experience the otherness of the ethical values: if they want to play the game, they will have to adapt to these values, insofar as they don't break the subjectivization process. This creates an ethical experience of both disempowerment, since the player cannot exert direct moral action on the game world, and reflection, since players have to reflect on the values they are playing by. Players' ethical fabric is respected and encouraged here not by appealing to their creative capacities, but to their ludic phronesis, to their understanding of the game and the experience from a moral perspective.

The successful closed ethical game operates with two distinct design procedures, which I shall call "subtracting ethics" and "mirroring ethics." The term "subtracting ethics" is heavily inspired by the subtracting design principles developed by Fumitu Ueda,[5] but it is here adapted to focus on the process of creating ethical experiences.

Subtracting ethics is the process of creating a game that has ethical choices made by an ethical agent at the core of its fictional universe by means of gameplay mechanics. Subtracting ethics creates a moral experience, but leaves the ethical reasoning to the players, thus respecting their presence as moral agents in the networked ethical system of computer games. In *Shadow of the Colossus*, for example, players might wonder if killing the colossi, which are not aggressive until attacked, is the right thing to do, despite the fact that this the only goal of the game. In this game the very vague introduction is followed by the slaying of the first colossus, and the whole sequence is designed to provoke a certain range of emotions and ethical reflection in the player: the way the colossi die and the lack of immediate reward force the player to think about her actions and their values. *Shadow of the Colossus* is interesting because, in more conventional games, effectively overcoming challenges yields better tools for agency: powers, leveling up, and such. But in this title, after each success, the player is absolutely deprived of agency and thrown into a cut scene that could be interpreted as defeat. The game is forcing the player to interpret her actions by means of manipulating the conventional rules and mechanics of games, in an example of good closed subtracting design.

Another example of subtracting closed ethics is *September 12th*. When playing this game, we initially create a set of values based on what the design and other elements such as the instructions suggest to us. We are in control of a weapon, there are terrorists, and we act: we shoot, there are victims, innocents are mourned, and mourners turn into terrorists in an endless cycle. The game never evaluates the morals of our actions, but it appeals to our ethical values to understand that the only ethical gameplay is not playing, suspending our agency in the game world.

In subtracting closed design, players create their values according to what the game suggests, in the first step of the ludic hermeneutic circle. The game experience will not take those values into consideration—it will subtract them from the direct interaction with the game world. Yet the actions in the game are oriented to create ethical reflection and awareness, and as such they generate a moral experience.

Closed mirroring design also takes into consideration the player as a moral being, but forces her into an ethical position that can be uncomfortable. In *Manhunt*, the player has to commit gruesome acts of cruelty in order to progress; it is a game designed to encourage these unethical acts. But this game also uses its fictional element, forcing the avatar to star in snuff films if he wants to survive, to project an ethical experience to the player. Players tend to identify with their characters in games, and in this case, this identification implies an exploration of the moral boundaries of the player. Furthermore, there is a mechanic in *Manhunt* that encourages players to commit even more gruesome acts of violence by rewarding them for their cruelty: players don't have to commit these executions, but that means not achieving the maximum score. In this tension between the values of the player and the values of the subject external to the game, by means of game mechanics, we find the application of mirroring ethical design.

In the case of *Bioshock*, and the moment of revelation of the mind-control mechanic, the use of a mirroring ethical design technique involves players as ethical agents both during the actions where they have no direct agency while killing Andrew Ryan, and in the reflection about the consequences of actions past, where what seemed like a subtracting method turned out to be a disguised mirrored structure. The subtle use of these two modalities of ethical design shows how it is possible to combine them in creative, productive ways.

A mirror ethical design narrows the ethical options of the player in the game, forcing her to experience what the designers wanted her to experience in terms of her ethics as an agent in the game. The game world and occasionally the gameplay act as a mirror of the ethical experience the player has to go through in order to play the game. Designing with mirror ethics means forcing the player to go through an ethical experience similar to the one the game object encourages. It takes into account the player's ethical being, but it limits it with creative goals. These games become an exploration of the ethical boundaries and capabilities for expression of the players. In mirroring ethical design the game is aware of its own value system and builds gameplay around this awareness, without players being able to do anything but play these external ethics.

Closed game designs, then, have two different modalities that can be used to achieve different creative and ethical goals: subtracting ethics patterns leave players the task of understanding the values they are playing by, and reflecting on them; mirror ethical patterns are more direct experiences of predetermined ethical situations, a much harsher kind of experience that can also yield intense reflection when we are not players. And of course the combination of both techniques can yield rich game experiences in which ethics play a fundamental role.

The most important conclusion derived from these analytical tools is that during the design process, the developers must take into account that players are moral beings who will evaluate the act of playing the game using not only gameplay strategies, but also sets of values derived from their experience as players and their belonging to a community. Players form communities in multiplayer games not only based on social needs, but also on ethical principles. By letting players interact with a game, developers are letting them create the values that will organize their experience of the game. Communities are also effective moral agents in the game, creating policies of behavior and codes of conduct that they will extract from the game, adapt, and then apply in their gameplay. Players not only create content and communities, they also create values.

An open ethical game design acknowledges the presence of these moral communities, and lets them reinforce their values in the game. Player-created content is a usual topic in massively multiplayer online games literature,[6] and one that usually brings forth issues of creative control, ownership, and community management. Allowing players to create persistent content for a massively multiplayer online game is a complicated technical issue that requires a strong balance in the game design and in the game tools, as the world could easily be swarmed by subpar player-generated content. Also, content created by players in a world strongly regulated by binding end user license agreements in terms of copyright and ownership laws might raise severe problems of regulation and control. In this perspective, companies tend not to allow players to create content in massively multiplayer online games.

Allowing players to afford their values in the game system is not, however, a matter of player-created content, but of balancing the distributed relations of ethical responsibility in the game to a more favorable position for players. Players have to be able to reinforce the values they want to live by in their gameplay, and the developers should limit themselves to being mere conflict arbitrators. In current massively multiplayer online games, due to the confusion between ownership and players' empowerment, companies tend to act as tyrants who direct players as to how they want the game to be played, and do not respect the presence and power of the community when it comes to value-based gameplay. An interesting game that allows its player communities to create their values as they want in a *laissez faire, laissez passer* moral style is *Eve Online*, which is perhaps the massively multiplayer online game closest to the goal of ethical soundness.

Because players are moral beings, they have to be allowed and encouraged to afford their ethical values in the game. Players need to see that their discussions about the values of the game are heard, respected, and the possible conclusions implemented; game developers should be present in the game and in the community spaces as arbitrators who know the community values as well as the original game values. Creating a multiplayer game is creating a place where people play together, a place where their rules are also significant. Open ethical games are those in which the ethical reflection of the player goes back into the game system, where the ethical process of development does not stop in the designers' computers but goes further into the player community. In this way, multiplayer computer games will actually become ethical objects and experiences, living and breathing worlds.

Open ethical design in online games requires a high degree of involvement from players' communities, which also means that developers should have the possibility and the responsibility of resisting certain community or group-based ethical implementations in the games. Open design requires developers and the community to engage in a relationship in which the ethical boundaries between them are respected.

This is a theoretical reflection on open ethical games, but how would the design of such a game look, as a thought experiment? First, the developers would have to establish a set of minimal rules determining what conducts and practices are directly considered undesirable and subject to expulsion from the game. This set of ethical rules should be minimal, and comprise more or less commonsense features concerning data and privacy protection, as well as foul or offensive language, and some variations of cheating and griefing. Then, a body of referees in charge of refereeing situations inside the game and in the community forums would be trained to read, understand, and act upon the values of the game, as they are intended to be in that foundational set of principles, and as they are interpreted and created by the community. The developers have to have direct, constant, and persistent insights into the development of the values enforced by the community.

This hypothetical game has to be designed in a way in which the players can create their own sets of values, within the boundaries suggested by the developers, and those values can be implemented in the game as codes of practice. There are two ways of doing so: first, by not imposing on the players any limitations on design when it comes to their value experience of the game, including changes that may affect that value system; second, by giving the players a system by which members of the community can be chosen to have actual policing capacities in the game. The MMORPG *A Tale in the Desert* is an experimental title in which there are no combat mechanics, and everything is focused on the development of the community and the in-game economy. In this game there is a hierarchical structure in which the Pharaoh (who is actually the lead game developer) and a group of game moderators are the supreme legislators of the game (mainly because they have access to the source code). Interestingly, though, the game has a built-in system by which players can create their own laws.[7] The community then votes on these laws, which are passed on to the Pharaoh for consideration and implementation in the game. *A Tale in the Desert*, then, can be considered an open game in which player ethics actually have a strong influence on the development of the game experience. In other words, this game, owing to the importance given to the community and the tools provided for their expression, is an ethical game.

Implementing open ethical designs means taking daring steps in creating multiplayer experiences. It implies an effective release of their powers by the developers, and an approach that considers the common game experience as a shared environment in which the power, as the responsibility, is distributed. I am aware that at the moment of writing these lines, the kind of massively multiplayer online games that are being developed will follow the popular and highly authoritarian model of *World of Warcraft*. Even so, what I am advocating for here is an ethical design for ethical beings, and eventually that need, that presence of ethical players, will call for a more open design of shared ethical ludic experiences.

In this chapter I have introduced some design notions that can be inferred from the framework on computer game ethics that I have presented. I have outlined some categories and methods of design that may be of use for those designers who may be interested in using the complex ethical experiences that can take place while being a player.

Games that take ethics into account beginning with their design need not be good ethical games. A Gandhi simulator could be the most unethical game experience ever made, depending on the design choices that the developers make, and how the players and their communities interact with the system. A game in which there is no conflict, or there are no interesting ways of resolving conflicts, may seem an ethical game, but such a game will eventually fail because games are essentially about resolving conflicts of one kind or another. Games are experiences, and game designers and players are responsible for making these experiences satisfactory not only from a ludic perspective, but also from an ethical point of view. Ultimately, the ethics of computer games depend on how these games are played. It is in the act of experiencing a game that we find its ethical relevance, and it is the craft of creating these experiences that we call game design.

8 Conclusions

I started this book by claiming that the understanding of the ethics of computer games in the Western world, and the answers to the subsequent moral issues, lacked a coherent, comprehensive theoretical framework that could be used to claim that games are a significant cultural product of our times. In this book I have suggested such a framework, analyzing what makes computer games ethically relevant, and describing how we can understand the ethics of computer games. The research behind this book was initiated in response to what seemed a certain zeitgeist, a moment in time at which it started to become appropriate and possible to think about computer games not only as one of the largest entertainment industries in the world, but also as a powerful means for expression and communication, a pervasive tool for twenty-first-century creativity.

As I have already stated in the introduction, this is not always an easy book to read, but at the time of writing I felt that to redefine what we understand as the ethics of computer games would require a serious, academic reflection on the nature of games and of those who play. Again, this is not a textbook, nor a self-help book: this book is a philosophical approach to computer games and the ethics that inform them, with no intention of being immediately applicable to design or game production.

I have argued that computer games have to be considered designed objects with embedded ethical values that affect the ways players can interact with them. I have also argued that players are moral beings who care for the well-being of the ludic experience. Finally, I have argued that to understand the ethics of computer games we have to take into consideration the ways in which moral agents interact with designed systems that have embedded ethical values. Therefore, in order to determine the responsibilities of the ethical implications of computer games, it is necessary to develop a distributed responsibility network of agents involved in the formulation of the ethics of any computer game. I will now revisit each of these notions, adding some closing remarks and reflections.

8.1 Computer Games as Moral Objects

In order to place computer games in the perspective of ethical research, I have suggested that computer games should be described as objects and as experiences, and that in both cases there are interesting elements that should be taken into account. This distinction between computer games as objects and computer games as experiences is based on an interpretation of the Aristotelian division between potentiality and actuality: games played are the actuality of the game, in that sense their most complete being, but games as designed objects need to be taken into account because the experience of the game is largely dependent on how that game is designed, and how that design influences the ethical being of the player.

Computer games as objects are designed systems of rules that project a game world in which meaningful ludic interaction takes place. The importance of considering games as designed systems that pattern player behavior is that designed systems (and objects) can have values embedded in their very design, an idea that is frequently argued for in science and technology studies, in postphenomenology, and in some branches of computer ethics.

Though the research on the ethics of computer game design is interesting, it is far from the only approach to the understanding of ethics and computer games. It is not possible to describe games from a moral perspective if we only focus on their nature as objects. Their design, and how that design influences the actions of the player in the game world and even the constitution of the game world in itself, is relevant, but only as a part of the game experience. A thorough description of the game design, pointing at the ethical affordances and constraints, may provide useful knowledge about a game's ethics, but only if it is put in the perspective of an actual game experience, of players interacting within its game world under the boundaries of its formal rule system.

It has been my intention to suggest the importance of design for the analysis of computer game ethics, which in turn implies a strong degree of ethical importance and engagement on the part of game designers and developers.

8.2   The Player as Moral Being

Perhaps the strongest claim I would like to make in this book is for considering players moral beings who are responsible for their experience of a game, and ultimately for the ethics of computer games, as opposed to mere passive victims of unethical games. I have argued that players are subjects that exist in a game experience. By subjects, I refer to specific modes of subjectivity, or ways of saying "I."

The core of the player-subject is found in the game system, but is not limited to it. Players are not passive subjects: players reflect on their actions and their presence in the game world. Again, players are moral beings using their ethical thinking to make meaningful choices in the context of the game experience. These ethical capacities of players have a fundamental quality: if the player is confronted with a game in which her ethical player boundaries, defined by her culture and her history as player, are broken, then the subjectivization process will stop and the ethics of the human being outside the game experience will enter into effect. This explains that the representation of violence in computer games is an ethical concern of secondary order, because the interesting and more potentially harmful ethical issues that arise in computer gaming are mostly related to the design and experience of game worlds by ethical agents: playing systems is dominant to perceiving them as representational.

By introducing a strong description of the player as moral agent, I am pursuing a twofold goal: on one hand, to give the player as moral agent her due importance in the aforementioned representation of unethical actions in computer games; and on the other hand empowering the player as a virtuous being capable of reflection on her own actions. This means not only that players are responsible when playing a game for the actions they take, but that they also have the capacity to morally choose which games to play.

Becoming this moral player is a process: we learn to become ethical players. We mature in a process of acquiring the ethical understanding that allows us to participate in a meaningful way within game worlds, with other players. Becoming an ethical player is the development of an ethical capacity that, as moral human beings, we have, but that we need to develop further. Thus, the importance of age regulation codes and education of computer game players, beyond the marketing impositions of contemporary consumer computer game culture.

I am advocating a perspective on what it means to be a computer game player that empowers players by giving them great ethical responsibility. As I have mentioned before, players tend to be perceived as the victims of computer games—nonreflective, unethical beings that just follow the rules. And players are much more than that: players are moral creators of values and experiences, and as such they should be respected, both by research and by game design. They should also be required to behave as such, becoming ethical co-creators of the ludic experience of computer games.

8.3   The Ethics of Computer Games

Simply put, the ethics of computer games are the ethics of the game as a system of rules that creates a game world, which is experienced by a moral agent with creative and participatory capacities, and who develops through time the capacity to apply a set of player virtues.

Of course, to reach such a condensed phrasing, I went through a number of reflective steps. Using information ethics, I argued that computer games are an infosphere, an environment where agents and patients exchange information—an environment in which there is a need for balance and equilibrium, as opposed to any action that unbalances the system, creating harm to any agent or patient, be these humans or the computer-created game world.

Information ethics also provides a framework that gives consistency to the two central claims regarding the ethics of computer games: designers and developers are ethically responsible for the information systems they create. A game designer, and a game developing company, ought to develop ethical environments, which are not necessarily representationally ethical, but informationally ethical: the well-being of all agents in the system has to be respected, preserved, and encouraged to flourish.

This leads to the second claim of this book, as interpreted from an information ethics perspective: players and other agents in the game world ought to act and interact in ways that preserve the informational balance of the system, but they also have to contribute to the flourishing of the game as such. This is defined as the creative stewardship that ought to inform agents' actions in the infosphere, and in computer games it can be related to the fact that players create, by means of playing games, a whole culture and set of practices that are of great importance for the success of the game, and not only for its ethical foundations.

The concept of creative stewardship can be complemented by Aristotelian virtue ethics: how should agents express their creative stewardship? By means of developing a number of virtues, players exert their creative stewardship, as well as develop the moral reasoning that leads them to make the ethical choices that are appropriate not only for preserving the game balance and informational integrity, but also for further developing their own individual culture as players. Virtue ethics provides the concepts of ludic phronesis and player virtues as fundamental tools for understanding computer game ethics—two concepts that offer an explanatory framework for those decision-making processes players engage in, and that constitute the core of the understanding of players as ethical beings.

This approach to the ethics of computer games puts both players and game designers in positions of great ethical responsibility, but it also provides them with ways of understanding, explaining, and enhancing their ethical properties and capacities within the production and consumption of computer games. I am also suggesting that, to understand the ethics of computer games, we need to take into account the network of agents that, to differing degrees, provide values and practices for computer game culture. With this book I have provided not only a framework for the analysis of computer game ethics, but also a set of descriptive procedures that can contribute to identifying the moral stakeholders in a game experience, and their degree of ethical responsibility.

8.4 Challenges and Future Research

Any definitional program leaves behind a number of gray areas that need further coverage, more thorough research, or even a refurbishing of the whole theory. I believe that a future line of research, as initiated by this work, could provide a more thorough application of both virtue ethics and information ethics to the field of computer games. More specifically, it would be of great relevance to identify and define the concepts of "players' virtues" and "infosphere," which I have only superficially introduced, and which by all means need closer attention.

Besides the always-present process of re-elaborating essential notions, there are a number of other possible lines of research. A closer look at the issues of violent computer games and their possible effects on players' ethical beings is an obvious candidate for further development. And the ethical design principles that can inform the process of developing a game ought to be the subject of a more elaborated consideration targeted at the practitioners of computer game design. Both research lines could become central elements in future developments, as well as key arguments in challenging some of the perspectives I have proposed.

There is also a missing topic that may require some attention: game censorship, or the fact that some games are forbidden in certain countries. While this is a topic of extreme social relevance, I believe it is somewhat secondary to the objectives of this book. Censorship would mean involving in the ethical discussion notions of freedom of speech, social responsibility, and politics, none of which have been clearly presented in this book. So the application of this theoretical framework to the censorship of computer games is left to the reader as an exercise of their moral reason.

There are, nevertheless, two large-scale projects I believe deserve closer attention, which I think could bring interesting benchmark results to the study of computer game ethics. One of them is what I would call the ethical map of player experiences—that is, the mapping of the ethical practices and moral boundaries that players present across cultures and worlds. Players are moral agents, but the ways they express their morality and the kind of play that is accepted as a part of that morality is through-and-through different across cultures. For instance, Japanese pornographic games could scandalize any given European culture, while Western role-playing games are often deemed uninteresting in Japan.[1] The task of mapping these boundaries, keeping always present the morality of the player, seems to me a rather attractive, albeit slightly utopian, lifetime research project.

The second project is related to the practical application of these principles in the form of games that play a role in the public sphere, tackling and defining issues that concern the public. Computer games have the rhetorical and ethical power to address complex societal discussions, providing insights thanks to their rather unique interactive and simulative architecture. Those potential public service games—defined as the ludic products that simulate the political implications of a certain public concern—are, by definition, ethical games, in which the reflection of their designers and players needs to live up to the participation in the public sphere.

There are many lines of research concerning ethics and computer games that are yet to be explored. Some of them require empirical studies to be completed, and the results to be confirmed or discarded and re-elaborated. I have taken the first step for a much-needed serious take on the ethics of computer games. As such, it is full of blank spaces that call for discussion and further research in the near future.

8.5 Final Considerations

Without any empirical data, just my moral intuition, I tend to believe that most of the computer game industry does not care at all about the ethics of the products it develops, and it is only marginally interested in reflecting ethically on the consequences of its design choices. And I need to say, I hope I am wrong. Game developers tolerate outrageous working hours while they produce products that more often than not do not contribute at all to the advancement of the medium they are using for expression. Even from a technological perspective, there are many things that are ethically questionable in the realm of computer game development: no other kind of programs, except perhaps major operating system upgrades, demand the constant renovation of hardware and software that the computer game industry forces on their loyal consumers, on the hardcore players who fuel the economy of this business. And, to the extent of my knowledge, there is not even a draft of a deontological code that could regulate computer game design and development practices.

There is also a lack of ethical concern in computer game marketing and mass media, which insists on considering players monomaniacs obsessed with graphic detail, physics simulations (of female bodies preferably), and guns. Paradoxically, both pro-video game marketing media and their detractors, politicians included, agree on this point: their misdemeanor, which approaches insult, against players. Players are thought to be moral zombies trapped in perpetual adolescence. Disempowering computer game users means striking a first blow to the complex ethical architecture of computer games.

And of course we academes are not free of guilt, pretending we have the solution for all the industries' maladies while making educational programs that seem to require the seal of approval of the same industry I claim tends to be unethical. Not to mention the claim that we can effectively contribute, with our methods and ideas, to creating better games.

All nodes in the network are guilty of something—of a cultural moment in which we have allowed computer games, by nature an exciting, innovative medium, to replicate the vices and not all the virtues of other entertainment industries.

But there are also good things: the game industry is full of enormously talented and visionary individuals; the press and marketing departments are starting to pay attention to games that take the medium beyond conventions; and we game academics are trying to discuss and learn, and offer some insights. I believe this book provides some of those insights for all of us who have stakes in the culture of computer games.

This book is about design and about players, about the games we play and how we play them. This book praises our capacity to create enormously compelling experiences with rules, a computer, and the willing souls that agree to play with us. This book also praises how we can play, and the games we could make. Understanding the ethics proves that computer games are a promising tool for expression, for reflection, and for contributing to society. These promises are our challenges, as players, developers, academics, and responsible citizens. I have given a frame of analysis, a frame for actions. It is our game now.

In these final remarks, I don't want to forget players, the central topic of my argument: players who are moral beings, players who think ethically about what it means to play a game as they build complex player cultures that surround their favorite experiences and that can transcend the preprogrammed values of a game. At the center of the whole discussion on the ethics of computer games, beyond developers and publishers and academes, we should find the players—not as inane input providers, target groups, or research subjects, but as complex moral beings who will think, reason, and argue about the ethical implications and values of their actions within the game world. It is our moral duty to encourage players to behave ethically and to develop their moral strengths while better ethical games are produced, and we should encourage ourselves to dare to play ethically. Because nothing is "just a game" anymore.

Notes

1 Introduction

1. Ion Storm Inc. 2000.

2. Rockstar North 2003.

3. Bioware 2003.

4. For a description of the field of game studies, see Aarseth 2001 and Eskelinen 2001.

5. Provenzo 1991.

6. Ihde 1990.

7. "It could be argued that in a game like *Bad Dudes*, *RoboCop*, or *Super Mario Bros 2*, the child is able to experiment with moral identities and work through fantasies and aggressive behavior as part of a process of symbolic play. A critical element is missing, however, which is *the child's ability to define and control the conditions of play for herself*. The struggle between the forces of good and evil defined in the context of video games is narrow and circumscribed, and—what is even more important for the child—it is defined by the game developer and manufacturer instead of the child" (Provenzo 1991, p. 90).

8. Turkle 1984.

9. Ibid., p. 81.

10. Ibid., p. 84.

11. "In circles where people are trying to invent the future of interactive media there seems to be a great divide. Will the player of the games of the future be in a more complex world than is offered by today's games, but still in a world that is created by someone else? Or will the player be the designer of his or her own game? In other words, will players continue to be 'users' of someone else's program, or will they be programmers in their own right? Will they be able to create new characters

and change the rules of the game? Both strategies are being pursued, and surely both will bear fruit. One leads to an image of an interactive *Gone with the Wind*, the other to children building computer worlds as today's children build Ferris wheels with Tinkertoys" (Ibid., p. 77).

12. Reynolds 2002.

13. "I want to sketch out the ways that we would determine whether a particular game is or not unethical" (Reynolds 2002).

14. See, for example, Feezell 2004.

15. McCormick 2001.

16. "It does not appear that the utilitarian can or will have any substantial grounds on which to morally criticize playing violent video games. They are faced by two substantial hurdles. First, the utilitarian needs to demonstrate that violent video games are risk increasing activities . . . second . . . they need to *also* argue that the overall increased likelihood to do harm outweighs the benefits derived from the activity" (McCormick 2001, p. 281).

17. Ibid., p. 283.

18. Ibid., p. 284.

19. Ibid., p. 285.

20. http://www.i-r-i-e.net/issue4.htm (accessed March 14, 2008).

21. "The actions and choices made and offered by game developers, game publishers, marketers, game players, and the choices coded into the game itself can all be investigated" (Consalvo 2005, p. 9).

22. Dodig-Crnkovic and Larsson 2005, p. 20.

23. Ibid., p. 22.

24. Juul 2005, p. 1. Nevertheless, a video display is not always needed—audio games would be a perfect example. Therefore, it may be more precise to say that computer games are games played using computing power; or, more precisely, games played in virtual environments simulated by means of computer power.

25. Neither do mechanical games like Pinball, which Turkle (1984) points out as the ancestors of computer games.

26. Konami 2004a.

27. Sony 2006b.

28. Nintendo 2004.

29. See Aarseth 2005.

30. See Johnson 2004, p. 65.

31. See Brey 2000a and 2000b.

32. Brey 2000b, p. 57.

2 Computer Games as Designed Ethical Systems

1. Ubisoft 2003.

2. See, for example, Salen and Zimmerman 2005, Suits 1978, or Juul 2005.

3. Huizinga 1950.

4. Caillois 1958.

5. Sutton-Smith 1997.

6. Juul 2005, p. 36.

7. Ibid., p. viii.

8. Salen and Zimmerman 2005, pages 84–92.

9. Ibid., p. 87.

10. Konami 2002.

11. Blizzard Entertainment 2005.

12. While in computer game development a game engine is considered the software tool that provides the visual technologies that create the game world (from 3-D graphics rendering to physics simulation or collision detection), I am using game engine here in a more generic way: a game engine is a system with rules and meta-rules that creates the game experience. The D20 system is an example of a nondigital game engine.

13. See Juul 2005, pp. 64–67.

14. Blizzard Entertainment 1994.

15. Rollings and Adams 2003, p. 247.

16. Salen and Zimmerman 2005, p. 88.

17. Ibid., p. 125.

18. Ibid, pp. 129–134.

19. Aarseth 2003.

20. Valve Corporation 2004b.

21. See Aarseth 1997, p. 179.

22. See Turing 1936 and 1950.

23. See Juul 2005 pp. 59–62.

24. Criterion Games 2004.

25. See Juul 2005, pp. 130–132.

26. Rockstar North 2004.

27. See Juul 2005, pp. 199–202.

28. For an introductory discussion on what is fiction applied to games, see Juul 2005, pp. 109–110.

29. Juul 2005, p. 111.

30. Valve Corporation 2004a.

31. For the distinction between simulation and fiction, see Aarseth 2005.

32. Juul 2005, pp. 139–141.

33. id Software 1999.

34. Retaux and Rouchier 2002.

35. Salen and Zimmerman 2005, p. 60.

36. More specifically, it is not only rules but the way the rules relate to the game world and constrain the players' actions that has an ethical dimension. In other words, it is how the rules of a game allow us to interact with a world, and how they contribute to the shaping of that world that makes them ethically relevant.

37. See Reynolds 2007 for an ethical description of these types of acts in persistent online worlds.

38. Newsgaming 2003.

39. Crawford 2003, p. 8.

40. Quoted in Crawford 2003, p. 9.

41. Maxis 2000.

42. See Rouse 2000, pp. 382–392.

43. See Rouse 2000, pp. 10–11, 70–71, 463; and Rollings and Adams 2003, chapters 1, 7, and 8.

44. Koster 2005, p. 76.

45. See Rollings and Adams 2003, pp. 41–42, 148–149 and Byrne 2005, pp. 57, 62–65.

46. Winner 1986.

47. Norman 2002, p. 9.

48. For more on the morality of artifacts, see Verbeek 2005.

49. Strangely enough, there is not a professional ethical code for game designers or game programmers; strangely because software engineers, computer scientists, and other related activities have a tradition of writing down their ethical codes of practice. I believe that this kind of deontological code, by which designers and developers could reflect and evaluate their designs in terms of the actions and meaning afforded to the player, could be a significant contribution to the social recognition of games and game design as an important cultural industry.

50. http://www.opensorcery.net/velvet-strike/ (accessed March 15, 2008).

51. Quoted in Rollings and Adams 2003, p. 200.

52. Rollings and Adams 2003, p. 201.

53. LucasArts 1998.

54. Quantic Dream 2005.

55. Or Boalian, as Frasca would most likely refer to the game. See Frasca 2003 and 2004 and Bogost 2007 for more on political games' rhetorics.

56. Crawford 2003, p. 32.

57. Ibid., p. 33.

58. See Anderson and Bushman 2001.

59. See Juul 2004, p. 54.

60. Rollings and Adams 2003, p. 77.

61. See Rollings and Adams 2003, pp. 221–224.

62. Koster 2005, p. 162.

63. Ibid., p. 168.

64. Ibid., p. 84.

65. By semantic quality I refer to the fact that Koster believes that games can have an ethical discourse, but he does not seem to acknowledge that playing a game (and designing it) can also be a moral action, even if there are no "obvious" ethical choices in the game.

66. Alexey Pajitnov 1985.

67. Taito Corporation 1978.

68. Stainless Games 1997.

69. As defined by Juul 2005, pp. 130–131.

70. Murray 1998.

71. Nekogames 2008. This game can be found at http://www.nekogames.jp/mt/2008/01/cursor10.html (accessed March 15, 2008).

72. Already presented, in a rather different way, by Juul 2005, pp. 43–45.

73. These concepts are presented in Aristotle's *Metaphysics*, Book IX.

74. The issues related to the semantics of simulation and the representational capacities of rule-based simulation systems are deep and complex. I have approached them with a focus on pragmatism. Nevertheless, articles of interest have been produced and partially inform my claims: see Järvinen 2003a and 2003b, and Frasca 2003.

75. Rockstar North 2002.

76. //////////fur//// 2003.

3 Players as Moral Beings

1. RockStar North 2008.

2. I use the term "subject" following Foucault: "There are two meanings of the word 'subject': subject to someone else by control and dependence, and tied to his own identity by a conscience or self-knowledge" (Foucault 2000, p. 331).

3. Foucault 1980 and 2000.

4. Badiou 1988 and 2003.

5. See Bogost 2006 for a more extensive use of Alain Badiou's philosophy applied to computer games.

6. I use the term "moral being" in an Aristotelian sense; that is, the human being that has the capacity to develop the virtues that will lead to the desired good life. In other words, I use the concept of moral being not as an essentialist category, but a procedural one: a moral being is one who acts with virtue trying to be a better being.

7. United Game Artists 2002.

8. By linear computer game I am referring to those games in which there is only one path the player can explore, and there is a very limited subset of interactions with the world. The aforementioned *Space Invaders* would be an example of a linear game. The opposite of a linear game would be a "sandbox" game or open-ended game, like *The Sims*. This is somewhat similar to Juul's games of progression; see Juul 2005, pp. 71–73.

9. Sony Online Entertainment 1999.

10. CyberConnect2 2002–2003. This series comprises four single-player games in which the player is introduced in a narrative that takes place partially in the world of a simulated massively multiplayer online role-playing game called "The World." Thus, its relevance as an example: it is a simulation of a simulated massively multiplayer online role-playing game.

11. "In games I obey the rules just because such obedience is a necessary condition for my engaging in the activity such obedience makes possible" (Suits 1978, p. 45).

12. eGenesis 2003.

13. "Repertoire" is a term coined by Iser and defined for computer games by Juul (2005, pp. 97–102).

14. This will also link the player repertoire with my use of the hermeneutics of Gadamer: "the reader's communication with the text is a dynamic process of self-correction, as he formulates signifiers which he must then continually modify. It is cybernetic in nature as it involves a feedback of effects and information throughout a sequence of changing situational frames" (Iser 1978, p. 67).

15. Suits 1978, pp. 57–61.

16. Ibid., pp. 45–55.

17. In the late works of Foucault (see Foucault 1997, 2000), the influence of classical Greek philosophy makes him focus more on issues concerning the proper life and the concept of taking care of oneself. It would be possible to argue that Foucault was making a turn toward a more virtue/praxis view on the subject and the ethics of the body.

18. Foucault 2000, p. 340.

19. Foucault 1980, p. 59.

20. See Honderich 1995, pp. 708–709, and Audi 1999, p. 727 for an overview of the concept of power and the approach conflict theorists take.

21. Foucault 1980, p. 119.

22. Foucault 1997, p. 292.

23. Foucault 1980, pp. 74, 98.

24. Developers oftentimes act when it is a case of infringement of the end user license agreement, which seems to be, to the eyes of the game companies, a matter of high importance that is not possible to leave in the hands of their players.

25. See Foucault 1997.

26. Badiou 2000.

27. Alain Badiou's theory of the subject, developed in *L'être et L'événement* (Badiou 1988), is highly complex due to its usage of mathematical set theory. I have chosen to focus on a somewhat more accessible text (Badiou 2000) for this chapter for two reasons: it serves as a better introduction for the overall complexity of Badiou's philosophy of the subject due to its approachability, and it focuses the question of the subject on the ethics that come into being when the subject arises.

28. Maxis 1989.

29. It is worth mentioning, because it may have importance, that *Sim City* was designed, developed, and launched in the last years of the 1980s. The political and economic situation in the world may have played a role in the creation of the simulation model.

30. NanaOn-Sha 1999.

31. Following Oliver Feltham and Justin Clemens, translators of Badiou 2003, and Peter Hallward, translator of Badiou 2000.

32. Badiou 2003, p. 187. The more detailed and more complex explanation of the event can be found in chapter IV of *L'être et L'événement* (Badiou 1988).

33. Faithful in the sense of Badiou's theory of the subject: "Let us say that a subject . . . needs something to have happened, something that cannot be reduced to its ordinary inscription in 'what there is.' Let us call this supplement an event, and let us distinguish multiple-being, where it is not a matter of truth (but only of opinions), from the event, which compels us to decide a new way of being . . . from which 'decision', then, stems the process of truth? From the decision to relate henceforth to the situation from the perspective of its eventual [événementiel] supplement. Let us call this a fidelity. To be faithful to an event is to move within the situation that this event has supplemented, by thinking . . . the situation 'according to' the event" (Badiou 2000, p. 41).

34. CCP Games 2003.

35. See Suits 1978, p. 60, as well as Feezell 2004.

36. Badiou 2000, p. 43.

37. id Software 1996.

38. The combined use of rules that generates emergent behaviors like "rocket jumping" does not contradict any rule, while cheating, for instance, does contradict at least one rule.

39. Badiou 2000, pp. 10–60.

40. Rare 2000.

41. Mystique 1982.

42. Danny Ledone 2005.

43. The case of *Super Columbine Massacre RPG* is of particular interest and it will be brought back in later chapters of this book. The forums can be found at http://www .columbinegame.com/discuss/ (accessed March 15, 2008).

44. Becker 2000 and 2003.

45. Becker 2000, p. 363.

46. Ibid.

47. Ibid.

48. Ibid., p. 364.

49. Ibid.

50. Cryptic Studios 2004.

51. Sony Online Entertainment 2004.

52. Maxis 2004.

53. Bethesda Game Studios 2006.

54. It is not the goal of this book to discuss the questions of the avatar. For a relevant introduction to issues related with embodiment, avatars, and online worlds, see Taylor 2006.

55. Similarly, the interaction with some elements of the fictional world, like doors, depends on the input of the player: a door can be opened slowly or more harshly depending on the pressure the player applies to the controller, which works effectively as an extension of the body presence of the player. And, of course, the Nintendo Wii sports a controller that allows the player to direct input via the motion of the controller, potentially overriding the problematic mapping of actions to buttons in conventional controllers, even though there is not a game for that console that successfully does so.

56. For example, watching sports in a bar calls forth the body-subject of the player, which also acts as the borders of the game situation: at any moment we can step out of the subjectivity and realize that we are screaming, or that it is only a game and thus not worth engaging in a discussion with another player-spectator.

57. Jason Rohrer 2007.

58. Harmonix Music Systems 2005.

59. Namco 2004.

60. Gadamer 2005, p. 103.

61. See Heidegger 1988 and Gadamer 2005.

62. "Play fulfills its purpose only if the player loses himself in play" (Gadamer 2005, p. 105).

63. "[P]lay itself is a transformation of such kind that the identity of the player does not continue to exist for anybody. Everybody asks instead what is supposed to be represented, what is 'meant.' The player (or playwright) no longer exists, only what they are playing" (Gadamer 2005, p. 111). This quote may be understood as a reinforcement of a more atomistic vision of the player-subject detached from the out-of-the-game being. Nevertheless, there is no contradiction, for Gadamer states that, for an external observer, there is a dominance of the player-subject, which is not in contradiction with my ontological claim that the player is actually connected with the cultural, embodied being outside the game.

64. "The structure of play absorbs the player into itself, and thus frees him from the burden of taking the initiative, which constitutes the actual strain of existence. This is also seen in the spontaneous tendency to repetition that emerges in the player and in the constant self-renewal of play, which affects its form" (Gadamer 2005, p. 105).

65. Gadamer 2005, pp. 293–294.

66. "Play contains its own, sacred seriousness" (Gadamer 2005, p. 102).

67. See Gadamer 2005, pp. 317–319, 535–536.

68. Lionhead Studios 2001.

69. Bullfrog 1989.

70. MicroProse 1991.

71. Hacker ethics can explain why some player collectives believe in cheating as a desirable practice.

72. Lionhead Studios 2004.

73. Braben and Bell 1984.

74. Aristotle 1998, Book II, page 27.

75. Courage and temperance, for example, are described in some detail in Book III (Aristotle 1998, pp. 34–55), while other virtues are described in Book IV (ibid., pp. 56–75).

76. The Doctrine of the Mean is described in Book II: "Now by the mean of the thing, i.e. absolute mean, I denote that which is equidistant from either extreme . . . and by the mean relatively to ourselves, that which is neither too much nor too

little for the particular individual. . . . Now Virtue is concerned with feelings and actions, in which the excess is wrong and the defect is blamed but the mean is praised and goes right; and both these circumstances belong to Virtue. Virtue then is in a sense a mean state, since it certainly has aptitude for aiming at the mean" (ibid., pp. 26, 27)

77. See Bartle 1996 and 2004.

78. Origin Systems 1997.

79. Linden Research 2003.

80. Bungie Studios 2007.

81. Bartle 1996.

82. Bartle has extended this typology in 2004, adding new dynamics and a complex three-dimensional model that explains the types and motivations of players' inter-actions. That more complex model does not add any relevant information for the application of Bartle's work on the ethics of players, and thus will not be directly addressed.

83. Bizarre Creations 2003.

84. There are even dedicated websites: http://www.theinsanedomain.com/ KillingSimms/waysto.htm (accessed March 15, 2008).

85. Unless the player cheats, modifying a house requires money that can only be earned by working, which can only be done by actually playing this game.

86. Even the Wikipedia entry for this game is an example of how players try to complete the game's fragmentary story: http://en.wikipedia.org/wiki/Shadow_of _the_Colossus (accessed March 15, 2008).

87. In the case of the community "The Cloudmakers," created around the alternate reality game *The Beast*, Jane McGonigal reported how this community tried and failed to "solve" the 9/11 attacks using the same skill set and network thinking they used to solve the alternate reality game. Their sense of community extended from the community of players of a game to a larger community of players.

88. Bartle uses killers as a term to define the griefers; I am here adapting Bartle's original terms, and by no means I am referring exclusively to those players who harass other players.

89. Rollings and Adams 2003, p. 240.

90. 2K Boston/2K Australia 2007.

91. See Feezell 2004, D'Agostino 1995, Keating 1995, and Morgan and Meier 1995.

92. Even though these authors refer to sports, I will here use sports and games as operational synonyms: unless specifically stated, what applies to sports can also apply to computer games. The differences between sports and computer games are not relevant for this context, and thus will not be discussed unless pertinent to our use of the concept of sportsmanship.

93. Keating 1995, p. 147.

94. Feezell 2004, p. 95.

95. Blizzard North 2000.

96. Incidentally, in *Grand Theft Auto: Vice City* that would be taken into account by the system, for that specific challenge is used to complete a number of motor-bike jumps the player needs to make in order to achieve a 100 percent completion of the game. Much like in the aforementioned example of cheating, *Grand Theft Auto: Vice City* is an example of evaluation of the ethical capacities of its players.

97. Aristotle 1998, Book II, chapter 6.

98. Book VI, p. 102.

99. It is worth mentioning here that Norbert Wiener (1965) argued that computers should contribute to human flourishing.

100. Gadamer also used the concept of phronesis extensively in his work, pointing out how "phronesis is another kind of knowledge. Primarily, this means that it is directed toward the concrete situation. Thus it must grasp the 'circumstances' in their infinite variety" (Gadamer 2005, p. 19).

101. Digital Illusions CE 2002.

102. Also if the player is playing a single-player game alone: "The community of play does not necessarily require real persons present. It is enough for a real player to have a real game and not an imagined one" (Fink 1995, p. 105).

103. "In general, rules function in three ways: First, rules contain positive pre-scriptions for what participants must do and what they are allowed to do . . . such prescriptive rules may be labeled the positively prescribed skills and tactics of the contest. Second, rules function to identify the within-the-contest goal toward which the performance of the positively prescribed skills and tactics is aimed . . . rules prescribe both a pre-lusory goal and the lusory means by which that goal may be pursued . . . third, rules function to proscribe certain illegal action. This function is performed by rules statements which identify prohibited actions" (Frahleigh 1995, p. 185).

104. See Aristotle 1998, Books I, II, and VI.

4   The Ethics of Computer Games

1. Konami 2004b.

2. This approach is deeply inspired by Philip Brey's disclosive computer ethics. See Brey 2000b.

3. A more nuanced and complete history of virtue ethics can be found in Honderich 1995, pp. 900–901 and Audi 1999, pp. 960–961.

4. Ensemble Studios 1997.

5. Even though it usually spawns violence, for other players will try to destroy the marvel to avoid that victory condition. Nevertheless, it is possible, though infrequent, that *Age of Empires* game sessions are won by nonviolent means.

6. "How do we prevent a player from getting bored in a level? We drive him ahead, like a sheepdog herds a sheep . . . many times a level designer must lead the players through the environment or push them in a direction, but at all times the players must be driven or the game will become stagnant . . . " Byrne 2005, page 65. See also Rouse 2000, chapters 1, 7, and 23.

7   See Rouse 2000, p. 127.

8. It is possible to engage in rewarded actions in the game, such as stunt driving, without committing any simulated act of violence or any simulated crime.

9. I am using the concept of fusion of horizons with a slight adaptation from Gadamer's use, for it does argue in favor of a consideration of the player-subject as a part of a larger self: "we must always have a horizon in order to transpose ourselves into a situation. For what do we mean by 'transposing ourselves?' Certainly not just disregarding ourselves. This is necessary, of course, insofar as we must imagine the other situation. But into this other situation we must bring, precisely, ourselves. Only this is the full meaning of 'transposing ourselves.' " (Gadamer 2005, pp. 303–304; see also Part II, 4.2.).

10. For instance, I can relate to the reflections that players have concerning the ethical structure of *Deus Ex*, and while it is a single player game, my experience of it is somehow related to that of all those other single players. In other words, because players of *Deus Ex* can talk together meaningfully about the game, there is a community of players that could play a role in the ethical construction of the ludic experience.

11. See http://en.wikipedia.org/wiki/Catenaccio (accessed March 21, 2008).

12. This information ethics approach is based on the work of Luciano Floridi, Jeff Sanders, the information ethics Group at the University of Oxford (http://web2

.comlab.ox.ac.uk/oucl/research/areas/ieg), and the Research Group in Philosophy of Information at the University of Hertfordshire (http://philosophyofinformation. net/centre/gpi). This chapter is based on Floridi 1999 and 2003b and Floridi and Sanders 1999 and 2004.

13. Floridi and Sanders 2004, p. 3.

14. See Floridi 2003a and Floridi and Sanders 1999.

15. Floridi 2003a, p. 8.

16. See Floridi and Sanders 2004.

17. Floridi and Sanders 2004, p. 11.

18. Ibid., p. 14.

19. A more accurate description of the object-oriented approach of informa- tion ethics can be found in Floridi 2003a: "Consider a pawn in a chess game. Its identity is not determined by its contigent properties as a physical body, includ- ing its shape and colour. Rather, a pawn is a set of data (properties like white or black and its strategic position on the board) and three behavioral rules . . . for a good player, the actual piece is only a placeholder. The real pawn is an 'information object.'"

20. Agency and being are defined in terms that resemble the way object-oriented computer languages describe objects and methods: "The agent and the patient are discrete, self-contained, encapsulated packages containing: the appropriate data structures, which constitute the nature of the entity in question . . . a collection of operations, functions or procedures (methods) which are activated (invoked) by various interactions or stimuli, namely messages . . . received from other agents (message passing) or changes within itself, and correspondingly define (implement) how the objects behaves or reacts to them."

21. "Homo poieticus is to be distinguished from homo faber, user and 'exploita- tor' of natural resources, from homo oeconomicus, producer, distributor, and con- sumer of wealth, and from homo ludens, who embodies a leisurely playfulness devoid of the ethical care and responsibility characterizing the constructionist attitude. Homo poieticus concentrates not merely on the final result, but on the dynamic, on-going process through which the result is achieved" (Floridi and Sanders 2005).

22. I am using state machine here more as a metaphor than as an actual application of the original Turing term, as applied in computer science.

23. U.S. Army 2002.

24. This concept is my adaptation of Floridi and Sanders's "distributed morality," in Floridi and Sanders 2004.

25. Nonplayers ought to be taken into consideration to avoid creating a game-centric version of the digital divide. By nonplayers, I am referring to those who are participants in the game infosphere but are not player-subjects; for instance, legislators and distributors, or family. Game developers are actually not player-subjects, but they do have a specific position in the infosphere due to the fact that they are the originators of the game object.

26. See Floridi and Sanders 2001.

27. It only tends to because virtue ethics states that a game that encourages the fostering of the ludic virtues by design is also a virtuous game. Nevertheless, it seems to be so in a second-degree order—because if the agent can develop virtues from experiencing the game, then the game is virtuous. Information ethics includes the game design, the developers, and the other informational agents in a network of distributed responsibility that is perhaps more appropriate for understanding the ethics of computer games.

28. Mythic Entertainment 2001.

29. Nintendo 1985.

30. See Floridi 2005 and Turilli 2007.

31. Afkar Media 2001.

32. See Eskelinen 2001.

33. Bad design has many faces: from poorly balanced maps in strategy games to the lack of feedback for some actions in some first-person shooters, or usability problems in the control or visual layout of the game. In essence, everything that disturbs the game experience and creates unnecessary difficulties in the gameplay is to be considered bad design.

34. Persuasive Games 2006.

5 Applying Ethics: Case Studies

1. Introversion Software 2006.

2. Irrational Games/Looking Glass Studios 1999.

3. Valve Software 1998.

4. Smith 2006 has a very complete analysis of these modalities related with player behaviors.

5. Persistent online game worlds or social environments are those that keep on existing and functioning after logout, like *World of Warcraft* or *EverQuest 2* or *Second Life*.

6. At least in two of the three game modes: in "Genocide" mode, players are rewarded for killing the most. In this analysis I will focus on the other two modalities of the game, "Default" and "Survivor," where the scoring system is ethically more interesting.

7. See IGN's review: http://pc.ign.com/articles/732/732711p1.html (accessed March 15, 2008); Gamespot's: http://www.gamespot.com/pc/strategy/DEFCON/review .html (accessed March 15, 2008), or playthisthing.com's: http://playthisthing.com/ DEFCON (accessed March 15, 2008).

8. Chris Crawford 1985.

9. It became famous in the case of a gay-friendly guild that got a warning from the developers for "infringing the harassment policy." See http://news.com.com/ 2100-1043_3-6033112.html (accessed March 15, 2008).

10. There is detailed information about classes in World of Warcraft at http://www .wow—europe.com/en/info/classes (accessed March 21, 2008).

11. For example, if a player types "/wave" in her chatbox, the avatar will perform a predetermined waving animation. There are, nevertheless, emoticons that are sound-only (like "/silly") or those that are only described in the text but not performed as an animation, like "/spit."

12. An instance is a map generated exclusively for the group of players that enters a certain area of the map. Instances, then, are areas of the geography that are created for the group of players that enters this space. These players will be alone in this area, uninterrupted by other players. Typically, instances are self-enclosed areas where the opposing bots are stronger and the rewards are higher. Also, instances are areas specifically designed to be played in groups. The name and concept of instance is derived from object-oriented programming, where it defines a member of a class loaded in the memory at a specific time.

13. Funcom 2001.

14. For a critical analysis of player-versus-player gameplay, see Rollings and Adams 2003, pp 525–530.

15. Available at http://www.wow-europe.com/en/policy (accessed March 16, 2008).

16. The current version of the honor system is explained at http://www. worldofwarcraft.com/pvp/honor-system-faq.html (accessed 16/3/2008).

17. "Ganking" is the action of attacking an enemy player so low in the level hierarchy that she has absolutely no chance of winning the combat. Players generally perceive it as an unethical action.

18. By grievous actions I refer to all those actions deemed as acts of harassment by the player community or the developers, through their public harassment policy (http://www.wow-europe.com/en/policy/harassmentp1.html—accessed March 16, 2008). One example of these behaviors is corpse camping.

6 Unethical Game Content and Effect Studies: A Critical Ethical Reading

1. Sony Computer Entertainment 2006a.

2. Raven Software 2002.

3. Exidy 1976.

4. A map of that legislation can be found at http://www.gamepolitics.com/legislation.htm (accessed March 17, 2008).

5. Along with *Postal* (Running with Scissors 1997). In fact, the *Grand Theft Auto* games are often the most referred to by the media because they are big sellers and known outside the relatively limited world of devoted gamers.

6. Grasshopper Manufacture 2005.

7. ImpactGames 2007.

8. See Bushman and Huesman 2000.

9. See Anderson and Dill 2000; Anderson and Bushman 2001; Smith, Lachlan, and Tamborini 2003; Gentile et al. 2004; Funk et al. 2004; Uhlmann and Swanson 2004; and Krahé and Möller 2004. Keep in mind that I am only addressing those studies that are concerned directly with ethical issues such as the representation of violence. Other effect studies related to the educational potential of computer games are not targeted in this chapter.

10. Essentially, effect studies use empirical correlation methods to link the use of games by specific samples of players with their violent/aggressive behavior, and other issues like school failure and media desensitization.

11. Ensemble Studios 1999.

7 The Ethics of Game Design

1. As it is a gameplay feature present in the game system, I believe it was the designers who are ethically responsible for it. Nevertheless, I am not here stating that the ethical gameplay of a game is an exclusive decision or responsibility of the game designers.

2. Bogost 2004.

3. Core Design 1996.

4. Black Isle Studios 1999.

5. Roughly, subtracting design means eliminating from the game design all those accessory elements that do not enhance a central experience. Ueda's games *Ico* and *Shadow of the Colossus* have been praised for their highly emotional immersive capacities. Ueda presented this methodology at the 2004 Game Developers Conference.

6. See Mulligan and Patrovsky 2003, pp. 152–154.

7. Discussion about these laws can be found at: http://www.atitd.net/forum/forumdisplay.php?s=297a760ef7e871648a3ba0a93a59538e&f=8 (accessed March 17, 2008).

8 Conclusions

1. In early 2006 the Japanese magazine *Famitsu* published the results of a poll conducted amongst their readers to decided the 100 most popular games. In the results there were only four non-Japanese games See http://www.next-gen.biz/index.php?option=com_content&task=view&id=2401&Itemid=2 (accessed March 17, 2008).

References—Literature

Aarseth, Espen. 1997. *Cybertext: Perspectives on Ergodic Literature*. Baltimore: John Hopkins University Press.

Aarseth, Espen. 2000. "Computer Game Studies, Year One." *Game Studies* 1, no. 1. Available at http://www.gamestudies.org/0101/editorial.html.

Aarseth, Espen. 2003. "Beyond the Frontier: Quest Computer Games as Post-Narrative Discourse." In *Narrative across Media*, ed. Marie-Laure Ryan. Lincoln: University of Nebraska Press.

Aarseth, Espen. 2005. "Doors and Perception: Fiction Vs. Simulation in Games." Paper presented at the Digital Arts and Culture Conference, IT University of Copenhagen, Denmark, November 30–December 4.

Anderson, Craig A., and Brad J. Bushman. 2001. "Effects of Violent Video Games on Aggressive Behavior, Aggressive Cognition, Aggressive Affect, Psychological Arousal, and Prosocial Behavior: A Meta-Analytic Review of the Scientific Literature." *Psychological Science*. 12, no. 5: 353–359.

Anderson, Craig A., and Karen E. Dill. 2000. "Video Games and Aggressive Thoughts, Feelings and Behavior in the Laboratory and in Life." *Journal of Personality and Social Psychology* 78, no. 4: 772–790.

Aristotle. *Metaphysics*. The Internet Classics Archive. Available at http://classics.mit.edu/Aristotle/metaphysics.html.

Aristotle. 1998. *Nicomachean Ethics*. Trans. William Kaufman. Mineola, N.Y.: Dover.

Audi, Robert, ed. 1999. *The Cambridge Dictionary of Philosophy*, 2nd ed. Cambridge: University of Cambridge Press.

Badiou, Alain. 1988. *L'être Et L'événement, L'ordre Philosophique*. Paris: Editions du Seuil.

Badiou, Alain. 2000. *Ethics: An Essay on the Understanding of Evil*. Trans. Peter Hallward. New York: Verso.

Badiou, Alain. 2003. *Infinite Thought: Truth and the Return of Philosophy*. Trans. Oliver Feltham and Justin Clemens. London: Continuum.

Bartle, Richard. 2004. "Hearts, Clubs, Diamonds, Spades: Players Who Suit Muds." *The Journal of Virtual Environments* 1, no. 1.

Bartle, Richard. 2004. *Designing Virtual Worlds*. Indianapolis: New Riders.

Becker, Barbara. 2000. "Cyborgs, Agents and 'Transhumanists': Crossing Traditional Borders of Body and Identity in the Context of New Technology." *Leonardo* 33, no. 5: 361–365.

Becker, Barbara. 2003. "Marking and Crossing Borders: Bodies, Touch and Contact in Cyberspace." *Body Space and Technology* 3, no. 2. Available online at http://people .brunel.ac.uk/bst/vol0302/barbarabecker.html.

Bogost, Ian. 2004. "Asynchronous Multiplayer: Futures for Casual Multiplayer Experience." Paper presented at the Other Players Conference, IT University of Copenhagen, Denmark, December 6–8.

Bogost, Ian. 2006. *Unit Operations: An Approach to Videogame Criticism*. Cambridge, MA: MIT Press, 2006.

Bogost, Ian. 2007. *Persuasive Games*. Cambridge, MA: MIT Press.

Brey, Philip. 2000a. "Method in Computer Ethics: Toward a Multi-Level Interdisciplinary Approach." *Ethics and Information Technology* 2, no. 3: 125–129.

Brey, Philip. 2000b. "Disclosive Computer Ethics." *Computers and Society* 30, no. 4: 10–16.

Bushman, Brad. J., and L. Rowell Huesman. 2000. "Effects of Televised Violence on Aggression." In *Handbook of Children and the Media*, eds. Dorothy G. Singer and Jerome L. Singer. Newbury Park, CA: Sage.

Byrne, Ed. 2005. *Game Level Design*. Hingham, MA: Charles River Media.

Caillois, Roger. 2001. *Man, Play and Games*. Trans. Meyer Barash. Urbana: University of Illinois Press.

Consalvo, Mia. 2005. "Rule Sets, Cheating, and Magic Circles: Studying Games and Ethics." *International Review of Information Ethics* 4: 7–12.

Crawford, Chris. 2003. *On Game Design*. Indianapolis: New Riders.

D'Agostino, Fred. 1995. "The Ethos of Games." In *Philosophic Enquiry in Sport*, eds. William J. Morgan and Klaus V. Meier, 42–49. Champaign, IL: Human Kinetics.

Dodig-Crnkovic, Gordana, and Thomas Larsson. 2005. "Game Ethics—Homo Ludens as Computer Game Designer and Consumer." *International Review of Information Ethics* 4: 19–23.

Eskelinen, Markku. 2001. "The Gaming Situation." *Game Studies* 1, no. 1. Available at http://www.gamestudies.org/0101/eskelinen/.

Feezell, Randolph. 2004. *Sport, Play, and Ethical Reflection*. Urbana: University of Illinois Press.

Fink, Eugen. 1995. "The Ontology of Play." In *Philosophic Inquiry in Sport*, eds. William J. Morgan and Klaus V. Meier, 100–109. Champaign, IL: Human Kinetics.

Floridi, Luciano. 1999. "Information Ethics: On the Philosophical Foundation of Computer Ethics." *Ethics and Information Technology* 1: 37–56.

Floridi, Luciano. 2003a. "On the Intrinsic Value of Information Objects and the Infosphere." *Ethics and Information Technology* 4, no. 4: 287–304. Available online at http://www.philosophyofinformation.net/pdf/oivioi.pdf.

Floridi, Luciano. 2003b. "Two Approaches to the Philosophy of Information." *Minds and Machines* 13: 459–469.

Floridi, Luciano. 2005. "The Ontological Interpretation of Informational Privacy." *Ethics and Information Technology* 7, no. 4: 185–200.

Floridi, Luciano, and Jeff Sanders. 1999. "Entropy as Evil in Information Ethics." *Etica & Politica* I, no. 2.

Floridi, Luciano, and Jeff Sanders. 2001. "Artificial Evil and the Foundation of Computer Ethics." *Ethics and Information Technology* 3, no. 1: 55–66.

Floridi, Luciano, and Jeff Sanders. 2004. "The Method of Abstraction." *Yearbook of the Artificial,* no. II: 177–220.

Floridi, Luciano, and Jeff Sanders. 2005. "Internet Ethics: The Constructionist Values of Homo poieticus." In *The Impact of the Internet in Our Moral Lives*, ed. Robert Cavalier. New York: SUNY. Available online at http://www.philosophyofinformation.net/pdf/iecvhp.pdf.

Foucault, Michel. 1980. *Power/Knowledge: Selected Interviews & Other Writings 1972–1977*. Ed. Colin Gordon. New York: Pantheon Books.

Foucault, Michel. 1997. *Ethics: Subjectivity and Truth: Essential Works of Foucault 1954–1984*. London: Penguin.

Foucault, Michel. 2000. *Power: Essential Works of Foucault 1954–1984*. Ed. James D. Faubion. London: Penguin.

Frahleigh, Warren. 1995. "Why the Good Foul Is Not Good." In *Philosophic Inquiry in Sport*, eds. William J. Morgan and Klaus V. Meier, 185–187. Champaign, IL.: Human Kinetics.

Frasca, Gonzalo. 2003. "Simulation Vs. Narrative: Introduction to Ludology." In *The Video Game Theory Reader*, eds. Mark J.P. Wolf and Bernard Perron, 221–236. London: Routledge.

Frasca, Gonzalo. 2004. "Videogames of the Oppressed: Critical Thinking, Education, Tolerance, and Other Trivial Issues." In *First Person: New Media as Story, Performance, and Game*, eds. Noah Wardrip-Fruin and Pat Harrigan, 85–94. Cambridge, MA: MIT Press.

Funk, Jeanne. B., Heidi Bechtoldt Baldacci, Tracie Pasold, and Jennifer Baumgardner. 2004. "Violence Exposure in Real-Life, Video Games, Television, Movies, and the Internet: Is There Desensitization?" *Journal of Adolescence* 27: 23–49.

Gadamer, Hans-Georg. 2005. *Truth and Method* 2nd ed. Trans. Joel Weinsheimer and Donald G. Marshall. London: Continuum. Originally trans. 1975, New York: Seabury Press.

Gentile, Douglas A., Paul J. Lynch, Jennifer Ruh Linder, and David A. Walsh. 2004. "The Effects of Violent Video Game Habits on Adolescent Hostility, Aggressive Behaviors, and School Performance." *Journal of Adolescence* 27: 5–22.

Heidegger, Martin. 1988. *The Basic Problems of Phenomenology*. Trans. Albert Hofstadter. Bloomington: Indiana University Press.

Honderich, Ted. 1995. *The Oxford Companion to Philosophy*. Oxford: Oxford University Press.

Huizinga, Johan. 1950. *Homo Ludens*. Boston: The Beacon Press.

Ihde, Don. 1990. *Technology and the Lifeworld: From Garden to Earth*. Bloomington: Indiana University Press.

Iser, Wolfgang. 1978. *The Act of Reading: A Theory of the Aesthetic Response*. London: The John Hopkins University Press.

Järvinen, Aki. 2003a. "Making and Breaking Games: A Typology of Rules." Paper presented at the Digital Games Research Association Level Up, Utrecht, the Netherlands, November 3–6.

Järvinen, Aki. 2003b. "The Elements of Simulation in Digital Games: System, Representation and Interface in *Grand Theft Auto: Vice City*." *Dichtung-Digital* no. 4. Available at http://www.dichtung-digital.de/2003/4-jaervinen.htm.

Johnson, Deborah G. 2004. "Computer Ethics." In *The Blackwell Guide to the Philosophy of Computing and Information*, ed. Luciano Floridi, 65–75. Oxford: Blackwell.

Juul, Jesper. 2004. "Introduction to Game Time." In *First Person: New Media as Story, Performace, and Game*, eds. Noah Wardrip-Fruin and Pat Harrigan, 131–142. Cambridge, MA: MIT Press.

Juul, Jesper. 2005. *Half-Real: Video Games between Real Rules and Fictional Worlds.* Cambridge, MA: MIT Press.

Keating, James W. 1995. "Sportsmanship as a Moral Category." In *Philosophic Inquiry in Sport,* eds. William J. and Klaus V. Meier Morgan, 144–151. Champaign, IL: Human Kinetics.

Koster, Raph. 2005. *A Theory of Fun for Game Design.* Scottsdale, AZ: Paraglyph Press.

Krahé, Barbara, and Ingrid Möller. 2004. "Playing Violent Electronic Games, Hostile Attributional Style, and Aggression Related Norms in German Adolescents." *Journal of Adolescence* 27: 53–69.

McCormick, Matt. 2001. "Is It Wrong to Play Violent Video Games?" *Ethics an Information Technology* 3: 277–287.

Morgan, William J. and Klaus V. Meier (eds.). 1995. *Philosophic Inquiry in Sport.* 2nd ed. Champaign, IL: Human Kinetics.

Mulligan, Jessica and Bridgette Patrovsky. 2003. *Developing Online Games: An Insider's Guide.* Indiana: New Riders.

Murray, Janet. 1998. *Hamlet on the Holodeck: The Future of Narrative in Cyberspace.* Cambridge, MA: MIT Press.

Norman, Donald. 2002. *The Design of Everyday Things,* Basic Books. New York. Perseus.

Provenzo, Eugene. F. 1991. *Video Kids: Making Sense of Nintendo.* Cambridge, MA: Harvard University Press.

Retaux, Xavier, and Juliette Rouchier. 2002. "Realism Vs. Surprise and Coherence: Different Aspect of Playability in Computer Game." Paper presented at the Playing with the Future: Development and Directions in Computer Gaming, Manchester University, England, April 5–7.

Reynolds, Ren. 2002. "Playing a 'Good' Game: A Philosophical Approach to Understanding the Morality of Games." Available at http://www.igda.org/articles/rreynolds_ethics.php.

Reynolds, Ren. 2007. "MMOs as Practices." Paper presented at the Digital Games Research Association Conference, Tokyo, Japan, September 24–28.

Rollings, Andrew, and Ernst Adams. 2003. *On Game Design.* Indianapolis: New Riders.

Rouse, Richard. 2000. *Game Design: Theory and Practice.* Plano, TX: Wordware Publishing.

Salen, Katie, and Eric Zimmerman (eds.). 2005. *The Game Design Reader: A Rules of Play Anthology*. Cambridge, MA: MIT Press.

Smith, Stacy L., Ken Lachlan, and Ron Tamborini. 2003. "Popular Video Games: Quantifying the Presentation of Violence and Its Context." *Journal of Broadcasting and Electronic* 47, no. 1: 58–76.

Smith, Jonas Heide. 2006. *Plans and Purposes: How Videogame Goals Shape Player Behavior*. Ph.D. Thesis. Copenhagen: IT University of Copenhagen.

Suits, Bernard. 1978. *The Grasshopper: Games, Life and Utopia*, Toronto: University of Toronto Press.

Sutton-Smith, Brian. 1997. *The Ambiguity of Play*. Cambridge, MA: Harvard University Press.

Taylor, T. L. 2006. *Playing between Worlds: Exploring Online Game Culture*. Cambridge, MA: MIT Press.

Turilli, Matteo. 2007. "Ethical Protocols Design." *Ethics and Information Technology* 9, no. 1: 49–62.

Turing, Alan. 1936. "On Computable Numbers, with an Application to the Entscheidungproblem." *Proceedings of the London Mathematical Society* 42, no. 2: 230–265.

Turing, Alan. 1950. "Computing Machinery and Intelligence." *Mind* 59: 433–60.

Turkle, Sherry. 1984. *The Second Self: Computers and the Human Spirit*. Cambridge, MA: MIT Press.

Uhlmann, Eric, and Jane Swanson. 2004. "Exposure to Violent Video Games Increases Automatic Aggressiveness." *Journal of Adolescence* 27: 41–52.

Verbeek, Peter-Paul. 2005. *What Things Do*. University Park, PA.: Pennsylvania State University Press.

Wiener, Norbert. 1965. *Cybernetics: Or Control and Communication in the Animal and the Machine*. Cambridge, MA: MIT Press.

Winner, Langdon. 1986. "Do Artifacts Have Politics?" In *The Whale and the Reactor: A Search for Limits in an Age of High Technology*, ed. Langdon Winner, 13–39. Chicago: University of Chicago Press.

References—Games

/////////fur////. 2003. *Painstation*.

2KBoston/2KAustralia. 2007. *Bioshock*. 2K Games.

Afkar Media. 2001. *Under Ash*. Dar al-Fikr.

Alexey Pazhitnov. 1985. *Tetris*.

Atari. 1972. *Pong*. Atari.

Bethesda Game Studios. 2006. *The Elder Scrolls IV: Oblivion*. Bethesda Softworks & 2K Games.

BioWare. 2003. *Knights of the Old Republic*. LucasArts.

Bizarre Creations 2003. *Project Gotham Racing 2*. Microsoft.

Black Isle Studios. 1999. *Planescape: Torment*. Interplay.

Blizzard Entertainment. 1994. *Warcraft: Orcs & Humans*. Blizzard Entertainment.

Blizzard Entertainment. 2005. *World of Warcraft*. Vivendi Universal.

Blizzard North. 2000. *Diablo II*. Blizzard Entertainment.

Braben and Bell. 1984. *Elite*. Acornsoft.

Bullfrog. 1989. *Populous*. Electronic Arts.

Bungie Studios. 2006. *Halo 3*. Microsoft.

CCP Games. 2003. *Eve Online*. CCP Games.

Chris Crawford. 1985. *Balance of Power*.

Core Design. 1996. *Tomb Raider*. Eidos Interactive.

Criterion Games. 2004. *Burnout 3: Takedown*. EA Games.

Cryptic Studios. 2004. *City of Heroes*. NCsoft.

CyberConnect2. 2002. *.hack//Infection*. Bandai.

Danny Ledone. 2005. *Super Columbine Massacre RPG!*

Digital Illusions CE. 2002. *Battlefield 1942*. EA Games.

DMA Design/RockStar North. 2001. *Grand Theft Auto III*. Take-Two Interactive.

eGenesis. 2003. *A Tale in the Desert*. eGenesis.

Ensemble Studios. 1997. *Age of Empires*. Microsoft Game Studios.

Ensemble Studios. 1999. *Age of Empires II: The Age of Kings*. Microsoft.

Exidy. 1976. *Death Race*. Exidy.

Funcom. 2001. *Anarchy Online*. Funcom.

Grasshopper Manufacture. 2005. *Killer 7*. Capcom.

Harmonix Music Systems. 2005. *Guitar Hero*. RedOctane.

id Software. 1996. *Quake*. Activision.

id Software. 1999. *Quake III*. Activision.

ImpactGames. 2007. *PeaceMaker*. ImpactGames.

Introversion Software. 2006. *DEFCON*. Introversion Software.

Ion Storm Inc. 2000. *Deus Ex*. Eidos Interactive.

Irrational Games/Looking Glass Studios. 1999. *System Shock 2*. Electronic Arts.

Jason Rohrer. 2007. *Passage*.

Konami. 2002. *Dance Dance Revolution*. Konami.

Konami. 2004a. *Pro Evolution Soccer 4*. Konami.

Konami. 2004b. *Metal Gear Solid 3: Snake Eater*. Konami.

Linden Research. 2003. *Second Life*. Linden Research.

Lionhead Studios. 2001. *Black & White*. EA Games.

Lionhead Studios. 2004. *Fable*. Microsoft Game Studios.

LucasArts. 1998. *Grim Fandango*. LucasArts.

Maxis. 1989. *Sim City*. Electronic Arts.

Maxis. 2000. *The Sims*. Electronic Arts.

Maxis. 2004. *The Sims 2*. Electronic Arts.

MicroProse. 1991. *Civilization*. MicroProse.

Mystique. 1982. *Custer's Revenge*. Mystique.

Mythic Entertainment. 2001. *Dark Age of Camelot*. Mythic Entertainment.

Namco. 2004. *Donkey Konga*. Nintendo.

NanaOn-Sha. 1999. *Vib-Ribbon*. Sony

Newsgaming. 2003. *September 12th*. Powerful Robot Games.

Nintendo. 1985. *Super Mario Bros*. Nintendo.

Nintendo. 2004. *Daigasso! Band Brothers*. Nintendo.

Origin Systems. 1997. *Ultima Online*. Electronic Arts.

Persuasive Games. 2006. *Disaffected!*

Quantic Dream. 2005. *Fahrenheit*. Atari.

Rare. 2000. *Perfect Dark*. Nintendo.

Rare. 2005. *Kameo: Elements of Power*. Microsoft.

Raven Software. 2002. *Soldier of Fortune II*. Activision.

RockStar North. 2002. *Grand Theft Auto: Vice City*. Take-Two Interactive.

RockStar North. 2003. *Manhunt*. RockStar Games.

RockStar North. 2004. *Grand Theft Auto: San Andreas*. Take-Two Interactive.

RockStar North. 2008. *Grand Theft Auto IV*. Take-Two Interactive.

Running with Scissors. 1997. *Postal*. Ripcord Games.

Sony Computer Entertainment. 2001. *Ico*. Sony Computer Entertainment.

Sony Computer Entertainment 2006a. *24: The Game*. 2K Games.

Sony Computer Entertainment. 2006b. *Shadow of the Colossus*. Sony Computer Entertainment.

Sony Online Entertainment. 1999. *EverQuest*. Sony Online Entertainment.

Sony Online Entertainment. 2004. *EverQuest 2*. Sony Online Entertainment.

Stainless Games. 1997. *Carmageddon*. Sci/Interplay.

Taito. 1978. *Space Invaders*. Midway.

U.S. Army. 2002. *America's Army*. U.S. Army.

Ubisoft. 2003. *XIII*. Ubisoft.

United Game Artists. 2001. *Rez*. SEGA.

Valve Corporation. 2004a. *Counter-Strike: Source*. Valve Corporation.

Valve Corporation. 2004b. *Half-Life 2*. Valve Corporation.

Valve Software. 1998. *Half-Life*. Sierra Studios.

Index